To Ellie,
(or whoever if +
a gift)

Hope you enjoy.

FROM THE
JAWS OF
VICTORY

Compiled and Edited by
Adam Bushby & Rob MacDonald

HALCYON
PUBLISHING

PRAISE FOR
'FROM THE JAWS OF VICTORY'

"A series of beautifully crafted love stories about teams to make the heart soar and suffer with them. The meaning of those nearly moments, an inevitable part of the football experience, come to life in these pages."

Amy Lawrence, The Athletic

"A hugely entertaining look at the many reasons — and many teams — that show football is about much more than trophies, from a great team of writers."

Miguel Delaney, The Independent

"The best stories in any book are the colourful anecdotes ... and this book is filled with them. Great tales, beautifully told and with a real passion for the game — even in defeat."

John Cross, Daily Mirror

"As every Scot knows, there is only one thing to do when you have snatched defeat from the jaws of victory: wallow in it. This delightful collection of curated suffering will speak to any fan who, with their team, has loved — and lost."

Jonathan Northcroft, The Sunday Times

"They say that history is written by the victors, so who writes the devastating stories of glorious failure? This collection of phenomenal writers do. And they are truly brilliant."

Sarah Winterburn, Football365

"Football's not just about what you do, it's about the way you do it. Or, as this book shows in glorious variety and detail, the way you don't manage to do it."

Tim Vickery, BBC

"Intelligently curated, written with knowledge and insight and most importantly passion, *From The Jaws Of Victory* merely confirms what most football fans have always secretly known: sometimes, failure really can be more beautiful than success."

Jonathan Liew, The Guardian

"Looking at all these excellent stories, it struck me how often the killjoys who spoiled the party happened to be German. So, on behalf of our national team — sorry."

Uli Hesse, author of Tor! The Story of German Football

"A fine line cuts between sporting glory and grief, delight and disaster. Scars of defeat can persist and run far deeper than the laughter lines of success. Evidence? Look no further than these pages."

Keir Radnedge, World Soccer

Published by Halcyon Publishing
a trading name of Monument Creative & Publishing Ltd

First published 2020

ISBN: 978-1-5272-7479-2

Front cover designed by Steve Leard
Layout & design by Michael Kinlan

Printed & bound by:
Bell & Bain Ltd
303 Burnfield Road
Thornliebank
Glasgow
G46 7UQ

"It is better to fail aiming high than to succeed aiming low. And we ... have set our sights very high, so high in fact that even failure will have in it an echo of glory."

Bill Nicholson

CONTENTS

FOREWORD
BARNEY RONAY

If you've already got this far — the first sentence of a foreword to a collection of eclectic football writing — I probably don't have to lure you in any further.

You've already glanced at the chapter list, a genuinely delicious confection of writers and subject matter. You want this product. I don't have to sell it. Marcela Mora y Araujo on Lionel Messi? Patrick Barclay on Dundee? Yeah, we can hook you up.

There is more to this collection, though, than simply fine writing, the fruits of an agreeably contagious passion on the part of the editors.

For one thing, it's a book, which is a gamble in itself right now. The urge to put words between hard covers has always been about lending a sense of permanence to something that might otherwise be simply passing thoughts or, worse, journalism.

That binding says: this isn't just some scribbled words on a sheet of paper. No. It's some scribbled words on several sheets of paper enclosed in cardboard. Look on our eternal works and tremble.

The obvious paradox is that these days even the most trifling daily publication, the most abject five things we learnt from José's latest meltdown, lives on forever in the digital dump of the internet.

Whereas books such as this one are destined to exist only for as long as the stitching lasts, and for as long as our fondness for arch, intelligent, football writing can survive the triumph of visual media and arguing in small text boxes on the internet.

Happily, given the richness of the writing here, that date seems a long way off. Adam Bushby and Rob MacDonald have gathered a brilliant selection of writing here, but also something that seems to reflect a moment.

Football writing lives in interesting times right now. The industry has never seemed so threatened, so wracked by change, so obviously hostage to declining revenues. And yet the audience has never been so diverse, the talent pool so rich, the quality of writing so thrillingly varied, the fruits of which are evident in these pages.

That richness is present just in the contents list. *From the Jaws of Victory* brings you episodes as diverse as Wales at the 1958 World Cup, brilliantly told by Andi Thomas, to the doomed Liverpool title challenge of 2013-14, taking in along the way the almost-glory of Romania in 1994 and the beautiful strangeness of Don Revie's Leeds.

This is also a collection of stories that keeps on contradicting itself, in the best possible sense. The premise of this book may be sporting almost-greatness, moments of falling just short. But the writing also tells another kind of story.

It is one of sport's great lessons that victory and defeat are often a kind of chimera, that the real glory comes from something else, and this is a constant theme of the collection.

What links Hungary 1954, Dundee 1963, Ghana 2010 and the grand operetta of Brazil's 1982 World Cup team? Fascination, affection and, above all, the feeling of what might have been; that a glimpse of near-perfection is more illuminating than a standard winner-takes-all model of sporting glory.

Also striking is the range of writers on view in these chapters. A generous estimate would put the age range at around 40 years. The stories told cover three continents (plus Scotland) and 60 years of football and societal history. Present within these pages are all-time sporting luminaries and bit-part players framed by their presence at a moment of shared semi-greatness.

Best of all, a book like this reminds us that football isn't simply a matter of unceasing triumphalism, but is often its best self in those moments where it deviates from the standard plot-lines of triumphs and trophies won, and looks instead into the spaces between.

INTRODUCTION
....
ADAM BUSHBY & ROB MACDONALD

Around the time we publish this book, in November 2020, we'll be (hopefully) enjoying a night's drinking in the Guy Fawkes pub in York. Why is this significant? Certainly not for the night spent drinking, but because Guy, later Guido, Fawkes, born in 1570 in what is now the pub that bears his name in the shadow of York Minster, is the British figure of folklore perhaps most — and forever — associated with the highest of stakes and the most dramatic, spectacular and infamous of failures.

It was in this atmospheric pub, situated on a tall, Georgian terrace, that we conceived of this book. It was pre-lockdown. Just. A simpler time indeed.

> *"Remember, remember, the fifth of November,*
> *gunpowder treason and plot."*

When Fawkes was discovered in a cellar deep in the bowels of Parliament, surrounded by kegs of gunpowder, planning to blow the House of Lords and with it King James I to kingdom come, little did he know of the impact he would have on British culture — and vice versa. Remembered less now as a terrorist and plotter and more as a folk and/or anti-fascist hero, the legend of Fawkes could not be further from the likely contemporary response were a man to be discovered, in hiding, with enough explosives to decimate the whole of Westminster and the monarchy in one go. Effectively immortalised in mask form in the film *V for Vendetta* and then various anti-capitalist movements, he has become a pervasive populist figure.

> *"We see no reason, why gunpowder treason,*
> *should ever be forgot."*

History has been kind, then. Thanks to the films, the songs and the masks, but also to the bonfires and the fireworks, it has dramatically reconfigured Fawkes in popular culture. And almost 400 years after he jumped to his death on the scaffold from which he would have been hung, he was named the 30th-greatest Briton in a BBC poll, somewhat incongruously finishing one place below David Bowie, six below Queen Elizabeth II and three above David Beckham.

We certainly love an underdog, us Brits. We hold a special type of regard for those who come implausibly close to achieving their goals — and the later they are thwarted, the better. The higher the stakes, the sharper the intensity, the greater the resonance.

Fawkes is, undoubtedly, an extreme and extravagant example. Plenty of villains with less dastardly aims are not remembered anywhere near as fondly, if they are remembered at all — but we are specialists at canonising someone coming a complete and utter cropper at the final hurdle.

All of which is relative, of course, particularly as we return to this anthology. Painful defeat, inflicted when victory appears not only possible, but so palpable you can almost touch it, is not only a recurring theme in football, but arguably a far more regular companion to all fans than whatever period of sustained success your club or country can muster.

Why else would Italia '90 and Gazza's tears, Euro '96 and a slumped Gareth Southgate, be viewed not just as results in sporting contests, but fundamental cultural markers by the English? Why does Archie Gemmill's goal against the Dutch in 1978 hold such a place in Scottish hearts, when all it did was presage their second consecutive group-stage exit on goal difference? It's the heady mix of hope and expectation balanced on a knife-edge, completely out of our control, threatening to become joyously, improbably real one minute, shatteringly non-existent the next.

All of these moments and more are captured here, brought together because although it's often said that history is the preserve of the victors — after all, to them the spoils — sometimes it is the losers that tell the greatest stories. The teams remembered in these chapters created fireworks of their own and this anthology celebrates those nearly men. The ones who missed out on silverware, but won hearts and fired imaginations. The ones who are truly deserving of a fond reconfiguration, duly afforded them by our excellent contributors.

Six years on from our first book, our glasses are no less rose-tinted. We are not here to castigate or lampoon. Rather than failure being a melancholy subject, we're celebrating the joys of coming so close. How success can be within reach, but not quite grasped — and that's ok. Like with *Falling for Football*, we asked our contributors to consider the wider context. We love the idea and the experience of putting football at the centre of a universe that includes everything from the mundane to the profound; maybe that's just part of the addiction. But we very much hope you will be as thrilled by these stories as we were when we first read them. We are all basically fans of football, and fans of quality football writing.

It was Samuel Beckett who wrote: "Try again. Fail again. Fail better" in his 1983 novella *Worstward Ho*. As far as we are aware, he wasn't describing the Welsh World Cup quarter-finalists of '58, the Scottish also-rans of the '60s or the Dutch masters of 1974. Or, for that matter, the eponymous anti-hero of the York pub where our idea took root, who wouldn't get the chance to try again, never mind fail better. Remember, it isn't all about the winners. Sometimes immortality requires the harsh reality of defeat. This book celebrates the despair and lauds the hope in equal measure. Some of us football fans face more despair than others, but it is the hope that unites us.

BOLTON WANDERERS 1953

SCOTT MURRAY

That it had come to this for the great Stanley Matthews. At 4.10pm on Saturday May 2 1953, during the early second-half exchanges of what was increasingly looking like a one-sided FA Cup final blowout, Bolton Wanderers winger Eric Bell rose above Blackpool captain Eddie Shimwell and guided a header into the net. The goal put the Trotters 3-1 up, and their star striker Nat Lofthouse, the newly-crowned footballer of the year, allowed himself to start dreaming. "The cup's in our hands!" he told himself. Matthews, 38 years of age, several pints necked at the last-chance saloon, tired and emotional with the bell long rung and the landlord getting increasingly impatient, contemplated his journey into the long, dark night: the greatest English player ever to pull on boots appeared destined to end an otherwise storied career without tangible reward. All that talent, yet no medal for the Maestro.

That Matthews found himself in such legacy-tarnishing peril was little short of ludicrous. His unique brand of wing wizardry (copyright all contemporary sportswriters) had dished up a smorgasbord of delicious chances in both the 1948 and 1951 finals, but his Blackpool teammates proved unable to take advantage of his dazzling man-of-the-match displays; Manchester United and Newcastle heel-clicked off with the spoils in turn. Even more preposterously, his hopes of winning the first league championship after the war went down the swanny in circumstances that would have the internet whirling off into a fourth dimension were they to unfold today.

Matthews sashayed onto the scene back in 1932 as a precocious 17-year-old right-winger for Stoke City. He quickly took the place of Bobby Liddle, a detail that would be wholly unremarkable had Liddle not been good friends with manager Bob McGrory, a dour authoritarian from the old Caledonian school; a man whose taciturn manner would make your average fire-and-brimstone minister sound like Harry Lauder. McGrory had little choice but to play Matthews, such was the public clamour to see this talent in action, but never quite forgave the kid for taking the number seven shirt off his old pal. Neither did he have much truck with young Stanley's increasing celebrity, nor his consistent demands for coin commensurate with his pulling power.

The pair bickered publicly throughout the '30s in a thoroughly modern fashion: candid interviews, sly press briefings, hot-faced transfer requests, the lot. At one point, Matthews' desire to leave was so great he was prepared to accept a cheeky offer from Manchester United, at the time a second-tier music-hall joke. McGrory, often just to be awkward and annoy, dug his heels in. Matthews continued to kick out. The six years set aside to boot Hitler up the hole did little to re-establish perspective or reduce the temperature in the Potteries, and so the two men continued to lock horns during the 1946-47 season, despite Stoke being midway through a serious tilt at the title. Matthews found himself in and out of the side as McGrory made a season-long performative act of showing who was boss ... before eventually going one step too far. With his team on a seven-game winning run, within touching distance of glory with three games to go, McGrory inexplicably sold his star player to Blackpool.

Now, it's true that Matthews was going to miss two of Stoke's last three games anyway while on England duty. It's also the case that he'd missed the first four of the aforementioned seven-game tear-up thanks to the increasingly tedious back-and-forth with McGrory; Stoke were not a one-man team. Yet unquestionably the decision to get rid of Matthews cost Stoke a maiden league title. The best player in England would have been available for the final match at Sheffield United, where a win would guarantee Stoke the championship. His creativity was sorely missed as the Potters slipped to a limp 2-1 defeat.

Stoke didn't even get the consolation prize of runners-up, somehow contriving to finish a tight three-horse race with Liverpool and Wolverhampton Wanderers in fourth. Without Matthews, the team went into a slow tailspin; by 1953, three days before their old winger rocked up at Wembley for his and Blackpool's third FA Cup final appearance in six years, Stoke were relegated. Oh, Bob! Did it really have to end up like this?!

The cup final was still the most important game of the season, no question, and 1953's showdown would be the biggest yet by far. Sales and rentals of new-fangled television sets had just gone through the roof ahead of the new Queen's upcoming Coronation — just exactly one month to go, girls and boys — and the BBC Television Service was showing everything live. Cup final as well as Coronation. No pressure to deliver, chaps, but a groundbreaking audience of millions expects.

Neither team could lay claim to being the best in the land. Blackpool had finished the league campaign in seventh, while Bolton ended up a thoroughly nondescript 14th. Still, Matthews and Lofthouse brought more than enough star power to the show. The year before, Lofthouse had found fame as the Lion of Vienna, scoring for England despite half the Austria team either hacking away at or hanging off him. He continued to notch goals for club and country at a scoreboard-smouldering rate: six in a challenge match between the English and Irish leagues, 22 in the league to earn that Player of the Year bauble, plus one in every round of the cup as Bolton made it all the way to Wembley.

Lofthouse's supporting cast of Willie Moir, Harold Hassall and Bobby Langton were all internationals, while 37-year-old keeper Stan Hanson, like Matthews, was searching for that elusive first medal in the late autumn of his career. Matthews, meanwhile, would be well served by Ernie Taylor, the diminutive force of nature whose artful bustle helped Newcastle see off Blackpool in 1951, and Stan Mortensen, matching Lofthouse goal for goal on the international stage.

Given the medical standards of the day, Mortensen's participation in the final was bordering on a miracle. In early January, he'd damaged his knee after slipping on icy ground at, of all places, Bolton, and required a cartilage operation. Twelve weeks later, he was running out at Wembley. That injury, suffered early in the game, condemned Blackpool to a 4-0 defeat, substitutes still a dozen years away. Was the result any sort of harbinger ahead of the big match? Perhaps, especially as Bolton achieved it without the great Lofthouse. On the other hand, Blackpool had won their corresponding home fixture earlier in the campaign 3-0. The outcome of the final was almost impossible to predict.

You could at least be fairly certain that, if the semi-finals were anything to go by, there would be goals. Bolton had a fairly easy ride to the last four, beating Fulham, Notts County, Luton Town and Gateshead; Everton, at this point in history a second-division shambles, hardly looked equipped to stop them from reaching Wembley. Indeed by half-time at Maine Road, Lofthouse had scored two, while winger Doug Holden and Moir added a couple more. But the Toffees, who missed a penalty in the first half, launched an onslaught in the second, pulling the score back to 4-3. Bolton were left hanging on towards the end as, according to the *Manchester Guardian*, the match "passed beyond the frontier of the normal into the realm of pure delirium". A whole month before Aldous Huxley first started knocking back the mescaline in California, the turnstiles of perception were spinning around in Moss Side.

In the other semi at Villa Park, Blackpool — who'd had a much tougher run to the last four, seeing off Sheffield Wednesday, Huddersfield Town, Southampton and champions-elect Arsenal — faced down Tottenham Hotspur. Matthews set up speedy striker Bill Perry for an early opener, but Tottenham took charge, pushing the ball around in the easy style that had won them the championship two years previously. Eddie Baily hit the bar, Len Duquemin equalised, and Blackpool keeper George Farm was forced into a series of spectacular saves to keep his team in it, building up plenty of moral credit he'd one day have to cash. A Spurs winner seemed inevitable, until studious full back Alf Ramsey attempted a backpass to his keeper Ted Ditchburn, only to allow the ball to clank off his thigh. Jackie Mudie nipped in to score. Did they think it was all over? It was now. Ramsey walked off close to tears, contemplating the sort of cataclysmic error that could end up defining, perhaps even destroying, a man. Could his career ever recover? A story for another day.

But if you really insisted on finding some sort of pre-match advantage, Bolton probably edged it, by dint of being able to name their first-choice XI of ten Lancastrians plus Aberdonian captain Willie Moir. Blackpool by contrast were in the wars. Allan 'Bomber' Brown broke his leg while forcing home the winner against Arsenal in the quarters, while left-half Hughie Kelly chipped his ankle the previous weekend against Liverpool. Meanwhile, left-back Tommy Garrett was fit to play, but would be facing the no-nonsense Lofthouse with a freshly-broken nose.

Also, if you look good, you feel good, and Bolton certainly had the fancier duds. That's not to say Blackpool's famous tangerine shirts didn't shine sweetly in the early-summer sun. But they were nothing on Bolton's shimmering silky outfit, bespoke tailored for the big day by a Macclesfield dandy. Not that everyone appreciated such a glam look. As Prince Philip was introduced to both sets of players before kick-off, he berated Bolton's knights in white satin. "You're like a lot of chorus girls! Pansies!". Up in the stand, the new Queen looked on from the royal box, thankfully oblivious to her husband's pig-ignorant club-comic styling.

Soon after, referee Sandy Griffiths (Abertillery) made his presence felt for the first, but not last, time that afternoon. Peep! It was on! Mortensen tapped to Taylor, who sped away on an intricate dribble down the centre of the park. The ball broke to Mortensen, who fed Matthews down the right. A 100,000-strong Wembley rumble gathered momentum. Matthews crossed. Eric Bell headed behind. The first corner of the game after 22 seconds, and a dream start for Matthews and Blackpool was already a distinct possibility! The main man himself prepared to take.

Major spoiler alert: the 1953 FA Cup final has gone down in folklore as the Matthews Final. Read into that what you will, pop kids. But one step at a time — for vast swathes of this game, Stanley Matthews wasn't that good. The delivery of that first corner did indeed lead to a dream start, but not for Blackpool. A poor effort was easily cleared and worked out to Holden on the Bolton right. After sitting down Garrett in a manner Matthews himself would have appreciated, then interchanging with Hassall, Holden teed up Lofthouse for an early rangefinder. Lofthouse completed a sweeping move by creaming a first-time diagonal shot into the bottom left corner from 25 yards, though Farm should never have let it pass. Just 75 seconds gone, and Bolton led, Lofthouse completing his set of a goal in every round in short order.

But Bolton were brought crashing down from their early high with a double whammy just before the 20-minute mark. Left-half Eric Bell suddenly pulled up in great distress. On came trainer Bert Sproston with a large white towel — sports science still very much in its infancy. Bell shook his head sadly as he limped off, his hamstring gone. Thoughts immediately turned to the previous year's final, when Arsenal's Walley Barnes damaged knee ligaments as he turned sharply on Wembley's lush turf. Ten-man Arsenal were eventually defeated by Newcastle. And if Bolton weren't already acutely aware that the footballing gods may be beginning to conspire against them, the ten men hit the post immediately after the restart, Moir releasing Lofthouse down the middle, the striker caroming a shot off the base of the left-hand post. Bobby Langton tried to force home the rebound from a tight angle, but Farm and Ewan Fenton managed to somehow turn the ball round the post, with Moir sniffing around for a tap-in.

Bell bravely returned, though it became apparent soon enough that he was only back as a nuisance, to clutter up the place. Lurching for a loose ball, he staggered like a dipsomaniac in downhill pursuit of a wind-assisted hat. He gave up the chase after four painful steps. "I think we can write him off," sensitive BBC Television Service commentator Kenneth Wolstenholme told the nation. Blackpool, sensing opportunity knocking, finally stepped it up. Mortensen attempted a curler into the bottom right; just wide. Taylor snatched at a chance 12 yards out. Perry dragged an even better chance wide right from the edge of the six-yard box. Then, on 35 minutes, Mortensen powered down the left channel, drifting past Malcolm Barrass and John Ball, and aimed a forensic strike towards the bottom right. It was heading in ... but Hassall, filling in for the injured Bell at the back, deflected the effort into the bottom left, deceiving the wrong-footed Hanson.

Just about everything that could go wrong for Bolton was doing so. Their response to all the ill-fortune, then, should go down as one of the great FA Cup final performances. Two minutes after conceding the equaliser, Lofthouse fizzed a shot wide left when through on goal. Another minute, and the same player barged down the left to fashion another half-chance. Then on 39 minutes, Holden swung one in from the right towards the far post. Moir rose above the flapping Farm, racing out to claim in futile style, and flicked the ball home with the tip of his quiff. Bolton had restored their lead in double-quick time, and nearly made it 3-1 before the break when the increasingly ludicrous Farm, giving Scotland international keepers one hell of a reputation, misjudged a looping Holden cross, the ball arcing over his bemused head and nearly finding the top-left corner. It grazed the crossbar instead.

Dignity went further AWOL during the opening exchanges of the second half. Lofthouse teed up Bell with a cute diagonal chip, 12 yards out, but the wounded soldier couldn't sort his feet out, and a glorious chance went begging. A ballboy gathered a loose ball and sent it arcing towards Farm, who was looking the other way as it clanked with perfect Warner Bros. timing off the top of his startled noggin. Lofthouse took delivery of a hoofed clearance in his special area; Sproston could finally put his big towel into action, drying the striker down after the application of a soothing wet sponge. Eddie Shimwell then rugby-tackled Lofthouse by the ankles as Bolton's superstar threatened to tear clear down the left. Just a talking-to, the past being a different country with its own set of laws.

A third Bolton goal seemed inevitable, and it came on 55 minutes, 4.10pm, in storybook fashion. Holden dropped a shoulder out on the right and curled into the centre. Rising highest, the stricken Bell somehow beat big Shimwell to the ball and planted it past Farm. A herculean leap under any circumstances, never mind these absurd ones: how he was able to win the header is almost beyond comprehension, given he was subsequently barely able to jog back to his own half for the restart, despite the bonus shot of adrenaline that comes free with every cup-final goal at Wembley. Bell's worst nightmare was metamorphosing into the headiest dream. Lofthouse rewarded him with a big sloppy kiss. Bolton, a team consisting of ten and a half men, had one hand and at least two, maybe three, fingers on the cup. That it had come to this for the great Stanley Matthews, who was now staring into the long, dark night.

A reminder of that major spoiler: the 1953 FA Cup final has gone down in folklore as the Matthews Final. An hour in, though, and despite a few electric, but ultimately inconsequential runs down the right, he hadn't really turned up yet, not by his own ludicrously high standards, anyway. And Blackpool's immediate response to going 3-1 down was ... well, not much really. Demoralised to a man, they ghosted around Wembley for ten minutes following Bell's goal, utterly devoid of purpose or direction. On 67 minutes, a melancholic, borderline eerie, hush enveloped the stadium. With only a quarter of the game remaining, Bolton looked home and hosed. Blackpool's jig looked up.

A minute later, Matthews finally snapped out of his sleepwalk and moved through the gears, belatedly realising it was now or never. He knocked the ball past Ralph Banks and jetted away from the helpless left-back at cartoon pace, sending a ball towards the far post while travelling at top speed. The swerving cross caught Hanson in two minds, the resulting fumble bundled into the bottom left amid a close-range melee by Mortensen. Wembley stayed silent for a couple of beats, the 100,000 remaining as dazed and unsure as Hanson. On the BBC, Wolstenholme required eight seconds of dead air to work out what had happened. Goal. Volume up. Out of nothing, production of the Matthews Final, previously suspended, was back on.

Injuries continued to bedevil Bolton. Lofthouse, already having had his fruit bowl rearranged, took a whack to the ribs, then to the head, the latter causing his legs to momentarily buckle in a very alarming fashion. He kept on keeping on, as brave Viennese lions are wont to do, but was a diminished force for the remainder of the

FROM THE JAWS OF VICTORY   23

match. Barrass planted his face in the grass while clutching a leg. Poor Banks, twisted this way and that by Matthews, went down with a thigh problem. Bolton trainer Sproston is mainly remembered these days for his part in England's 6-3 win over Nazi Germany in 1938, plus the geopolitical analysis he famously offered team-mate Matthews in a Berlin coffee shop while on tour: "I know nowt about politics and the like. All I know is football. But the way I see it, that Hitler fellow is an evil little twat." Succinct and perfect, though history should also record his sterling work in this final, having clocked up the best part of a half-marathon sprinting back and forth from bench to pitch clutching various absorbent materials in lieu of medical supplies.

Blackpool pressed desperately. It was only a matter of time before the incessant pressure brought an equaliser. But when it came, with two minutes left on the clock ... well, it really wasn't Bolton's day, was it. Mudie, to the left of the Bolton D, prepared to sashay his way into the box. Holden tapped him on the back. Mudie took the opportunity to go over. Peep! Free kick! Referee Sandy Griffiths (Abertillery) made a decision that seems about right by modern standards ... but judged by the mores of 1953, looks awfully harsh. Bolton's defence stood around, hands on satin-clad hips, barely able to process a very generous gift for Blackpool.

None of which should diminish what happened next. Mortensen was on a hat-trick and in the mood. He grabbed the ball off Taylor and teed it up with great purpose and extreme prejudice. "Stan, there's no way you can fucking well do that," spluttered Taylor. "You bloody well watch me," responded Mortensen, who whistled a right-footed screamer into the top left. Hanson hardly had time to turn his head to watch the net billow.

Years later, Mortensen described his free kick as "a thousand-to-one chance" and "a miracle". Add it to the injuries, the deflection, the contentious award of the free kick, the first hat-trick in a final for 62 years and the very first at Wembley. But if Bolton hadn't already twigged that it just wasn't meant to be, confirmation was in the post. In the first minute of injury time, Langton dribbled down the left, only to be clipped by Fenton. It should have been a free kick, allowing a reeling Bolton to clear their heads and see out the clock, before resetting for extra time. But Langton sportingly tried to stay on his feet, and Sandy Griffiths (Abertillery) kept the pea in his whistle stock still. Langton tried to find Lofthouse upfield, but the ball sailed through to Farm. Time for Blackpool to roll the dice one last time.

On the halfway line, Taylor sent Matthews off down the right with a delightful first-time diagonal pass. Matthews drove into the box. He dropped a shoulder to see off the limping Banks, headed towards the byline, and while falling backwards cut back for Perry, who leathered an unstoppable drive into the bottom left. Matthews was quickly lost in a tangerine wave of backslaps, pats, kisses and cuddles. At 38, after all the arguments of the '30s, the years lost to war, and the near misses of 1947, 1948 and 1951, it was finally about to happen for the greatest player ever to pull on boots. A medal for the Maestro!

There was just enough time left for the Wembley scoreboard to display BLACKPOOL 4, BOLTON 4, which only added insult to injury for the soon-to-be vanquished Trotters. Bolton's tally was quickly revised downwards, the whistle went, and before Matthews disappeared under another rolling maul of well-wishers, he was congratulated by the heartbroken Hassall and Barrass. Stan Mortensen had scored a hat-trick, Ernie Taylor conducted in the middle, but there was only ever going to be one man of the match, even if he only really got going in the last quarter of the game. Like the spoiler said, this was Stanley Matthews' final.

As for poor Bolton? They traipsed back to the dressing room and sunk into an extremely damp pit of despair. "We were sat in the bath looking at each other, tears rolling down our faces," said the captain Moir. "It wasn't so much the fact of losing. I think we were all jiggered." Ralph Banks admitted: "I cried. When we went into the dressing room, they came round with the champagne, but I said I don't want any. I just couldn't face it." Lofthouse later reflected on the aftermath with a wry smile. "It went a bit quiet, but you get over it," he recalled. "I'd like to go to Wembley every year for the cup final even if we lost. Still be nice."

Truth be told, in the pantheon of beautiful losers, Bolton '53 aren't the most iconic. Lofthouse was the only truly top-drawer act in the team, and along with the excellent Holden, made it back to lift the cup in 1958 anyway. No Hungary '54 or Holland '74-style everlasting yearning here. But they were arguably the most unfortunate side to ever come up short, having shown up and performed to their full potential, only to find the barm repeatedly landing butter-side down. In that sense, there are no regrets and, in any case, everyone was happy for old Stan. Anyway, somewhere in a parallel dimension, the final played out with every little thing going Bolton's way. Another major spoiler alert: in the multiverse, the match has gone down in folklore as the Lofthouse-Moir-Bell-Holden Final. Bolton won 4-3, like you needed to be told.

HUNGARY 1954

JOHN ASHDOWN

The Wankdorf Stadium in Bern was getting a soaking, but the sun was shining on Hungary's brightest generation. Gusztáv Sebes's side had not lost since May 1950 — an undefeated international streak that would not be surpassed until 1993 — and here they were, with 63,800 increasingly sodden souls watching on from the open terraces, cruising to victory in the 1954 World Cup final.

Their four matches en route had brought a faintly ludicrous 25 goals: South Korea hammered 9-0 and West Germany taken apart 8-3 in the group stage, Brazil swept aside 4-2 in a brutal quarter-final and Uruguay, the holders, edged out by the same score after extra time in a semi-final for the ages.

West Germany, the tournament's surprise package, were lined up to go under the steamroller again in the final and their fear seemed palpable in the opening ten minutes. Werner Liebrich played the ball straight to József Bozsik 40 yards from his own goal. Bozsik fed Sándor Kocsis, whose shot deflected off a defender and fell to Ferenc Puskás, who crashed the ball home. Two minutes later, Werner Kohlmeyer and goalkeeper Toni Turek appeared overwhelmed by panic as Kocsis pressed, allowing Zoltán Czibor to scoot in from the right and prod the ball into the empty net. 2-0, eight minutes gone.

No team before or since has held a two-goal advantage in a World Cup final and failed to lift the trophy. No team before or since has entered a World Cup final on the back of a 30-game unbeaten streak. No team before or since has ever faced, in a World Cup final, a team they had already battered 8-3 in the group stage. But then no team before or since was ever quite like Hungary's *Aranycsapat*, the Golden Squad, the Magical Magyars.

Hungary's appearance in the 1954 final was no bolt from the blue. Like their neighbours to the east, Austria, Hungary had been a pre-war European powerhouse. The *Wunderteam* of the early 1930s had knocked Hungary out of the 1934 World Cup at the quarter-final stage before losing to Italy in the semis; Hungary, though, went one better than their central European rivals four years later, reaching the final of the 1938 tournament before Italy, again, proved a bridge too far.

Both nations would see their footballing fortunes fall prey to authoritarian regimes, Austria prior to the second world war, Hungary in the aftermath. After the horrors of the conflict — close to a million Hungarians lost their lives — it took four years for the Soviet Union to fully bring the country into the communist bloc, but by the middle of 1949, when communist parties won 97% of the vote in elections, the job was done. Mátyás Rákosi's Stalinist regime brought secret police, show trials, murder and the end of free speech; it also helped create the conditions for one of the greatest teams in football history to prosper.

It would thrive in the hands of Gusztáv Sebes. Sebes, the son of a cobbler, had enjoyed an unspectacular playing and coaching career before and during the war but, crucially, was a stalwart trade unionist and a longstanding communist. That and the odd usefully powerful old buddy — he and János Kádár, a former Communist Party leader and member of the Hungarian politburo, had played youth football together — meant that by the middle of 1948 he was second-in-command at the Ministry of Sport, chair of the Olympic committee and the head of a three-man coaching committee that ran the Hungarian national football team.

As authoritarian states so often are, the new regime was well aware of the power of sport and began a drive for national sporting excellence. No player from the top two tiers would be permitted to move abroad to play. The interests of the national side would take complete precedence over the club game. Sebes set about making it happen.

There's a hint of Ocean's 11 get-the-gang-together montage in the way the side formed. Goalkeeper Gyula Grosics was banned after attempting to defect, but was brought back into the fold. Gyula Lóránt was in a labour camp having — spot the theme — attempted to form a team to get out of the country. Jenő Buzánszky was plucked from the tiny northern town of Dorog. The drive for youth meant key roles for wide-eyed teenagers Zoltán Czibor, Sándor Kocsis and László Budai.

But Sebes's plan did not solely rest on bringing the best of Hungary's talent together for the national side. He had seen the success of Vittorio Pozzo and Hugo Meisl, with Italy and Austria respectively, when selecting national squads from just a couple of teams — Juventus and Torino for Pozzo, Rapid and Austria Vienna for Meisl. Sebes was determined to have the same set-up.

As luck would have it, the various tentacles of the communist regime were quick to take an interest in the sporting sphere and by the end of 1949 the army were keen to have their own club. Ferencváros was the biggest in the country but was historically right-wing so, in the end, the small team of Kispest was chosen. Handily enough, Puskás and Bozsik were already there and would be joined by many of their international teammates at the club now renamed Honvéd.

Honvéd's status as the army club made the unseemly business of transfers unnecessary. Conscription was the only tool required. Players were given the choice of playing football or grabbing their rifles and heading to the border. Initially, players were given uniforms, ranks (hence Puskás's Galloping Major sobriquet) and were housed in army barracks, but the pretence was soon dropped. With the secret police then taking over MTK in Budapest, providing Sebes with the second of his two domestic hothouses, everything was in place.

Everything apart from a winning team. Sebes's first game in sole charge was a 5-2 defeat to Czechoslovakia in Prague, Hungary's own

Wembley moment four years before they destroyed England's sense of superiority in north-west London.

"After that game, the issue could no longer be avoided," Puskás wrote in his autobiography. "Hungary had to evolve an entirely new method of play if we were to make any headway in international football."

What emerged was one of the earliest iterations of Total Football. "Players ... constantly changed position according to a prearranged plan," wrote Puskás. "The result was that our opponents could not guess our plans and found themselves in difficulties which would not have been experienced had we followed the usual English method of play." The outdated W-M formation that featured five forwards became something much closer to a 4-2-4, with first Péter Palotás and, from 1952, Nándor Hidegkuti, wearing number nine, but playing in a much deeper free role behind the front four. It was a system designed, said Hidegkuti, to cause "maximum confusion".

And it worked. They won six (exacting revenge for that defeat in Prague with a 5-0 win over the Czechs in Budapest) and drew two of their next eight. A 5-3 defeat against Austria in May 1950 (a loss that persuaded Sebes to get Grosics to Honvéd and back into the team) ended that run, but it would be the last game they would lose for more than four years.

By the time the Helsinki Olympic Games arrived in the summer of 1952, Sebes had his first XI nailed down: Grosics in goal; a back three of Buzánszky, Lóránt and Mihály Lantos; József Zakariás patrolling in front of them with his midfield partner Bozsik given more licence to attack; Budai on the right wing, Czibor on the left; and Hidegkuti playing as a deep attacker behind the inside forwards Puskás and Kocsis. Six played at Honvéd, three at MTK (Czibor would be called up to Honvéd in 1953, though Buzánszky remained at little Dorogi throughout his career). Five, maybe six, of the side could claim to be among the very best in the world in their positions.

The side swept all before them in Finland, battering Sweden 6-0 in the semi-final before a 2-0 win over Yugoslavia secured gold. The train home — shared with the rest of the Hungarian Olympic squad and the various swimmers, fencers and wrestlers who had also won gold (Hungary came third in the medals table behind the US and Soviet Union) — was stopped at stations by crowds as it neared Budapest and in the capital, 400,000 people lined the streets to welcome home their sporting superstars.

But the gold medal wasn't the most important thing the Hungary team brought back from Helsinki — they also returned with the promise of a date with destiny.

The FA president Stanley Rous had watched the semi-final rout of Sweden (a performance reckoned by some to have been the apotheosis of the Golden Squad) alongside his Hungarian counterpart Sándor Barcs and, suitably impressed, had invited Barcs to bring his team over for a friendly in London. Arrangements for a clash between nations on opposite sides of the Iron Curtain were not straightforward (the top brass of the Hungarian government were keen to know whether Sebes could guarantee them victory), but on the afternoon of 25 November 1953, Puskás led his side out at Wembley.

The 90 minutes that followed on that dreary late autumn day remain among the most significant in English football history as Walter Winterbottom's side and the 100,000 watching in the stands were given a lesson in football's future, "firemen heading to the wrong fire" and all that. Hidegkuti thundered home an effort from distance inside the first minute and by the half-hour mark it was 4-1. It finished 6-3.

The third goal, scored by Puskás, perhaps best encapsulates the brilliance of Sebes's side. Four neat, short passes in midfield helped smuggle the ball out to right winger Budai who was dropping deep close to halfway. He clipped the ball down the line to Czibor, the left winger, who had drifted across to enjoy the acres of space between England's baffled defenders. His low pass into the box from the right found Puskás six yards out. A quite ludicrous drag back befuddled Billy Wright, who lunged in and past, disappearing as if on a water slide. Puskás crashed the ball home, beating Gil Merrick at the near post.

"Football from another planet," reckoned the England defender Syd Owen. "Carthorses against racehorses," said Tom Finney. While England's lions licked their wounds and embarked on a bout of self-reflection that would eventually lead to glory at the 1966 World Cup, Hungary marched on.

A warm-weather training camp in Egypt provided number 24 in the undefeated streak, a narrow win over Austria made it 25 and England's visit to Budapest for Hungary's final World Cup warm-up resulted in a 7-1 home win, an even more emphatic performance than at Wembley. Hungary were ready to take on the world. And the world expected to lose.

Hungary, then, travelled to Switzerland as tournament favourites on the back of a 26-game unbeaten streak. The draw pitted Puskás and co against West Germany (a team that had existed for four years and had not particularly impressed in bettering Norway and Saarland in their qualifying group), Turkey (who, in typically well-thought-out FIFA style, had reached the tournament after the 14-year-old son of a stadium worker in Rome had drawn their name out of hat following a draw in their play-off against Spain) and the debuting South Korea.

In further time-honoured FIFA fashion, what should have been a simple group stage was needlessly complicated. The two seeded teams — Hungary and Turkey (the seedings having been based on world rankings prior to their play-off and formulated with Spain in mind) — would not face each other, but take on only the two unseeded teams, with the top two in the group qualifying for the quarter-finals. If second and third ended level on points, a play-off would be used in preference to any more sensible decider.

Sepp Herberger, though, saw a clear path through the mess. The West Germany manager saw no point in trying to beat the Hungarians and considered a Turkish victory over the Koreans as a certainty. His team, then, would need to beat Turkey in their opening game and then again in a play-off to make it out of the group.

It worked a treat. Turkey were dispatched 4-1 in the opener while Puskás was helping himself to a hat-trick against South Korea in a 9-0 win. Three days later, Turkey also had little problem in swatting aside the Koreans 7-0 in Geneva, while at St Jakob Stadium in Basel, Hungary and West Germany were embroiled in one of the more intriguing and controversial group games in World Cup history. Hungary thrashed a German side featuring only four of those who had played against Turkey, Kocsis scoring four in an 8-3 win. Of greater significance than the score, though, was the fate of Puskás.

The Hungarian captain had been in top form: "I could feel the ball as a violinist feels his instrument." Jupp Posipal was run ragged so switched positions with Liebrich. It made no difference. And as the scoreline grew, so did German frustration. English referee William Ling (more of him later) turned a blind eye to the various clatterings dished out by West Germany's defenders — three blatant penalty shouts were almost comically ignored — and eventually the inevitable happened. Puskás looked to spin away from Liebrich on halfway; Liebrich hoofed his opponent into the Basel air. A cynic might argue West Germany had achieved the perfect result despite the score: Sebes had a strong hand but had revealed it; Herberger had kept his best cards close to his chest; and Puskás's tournament appeared to be over.

While Puskás put a brave face on his ankle injury — "I kept saying to myself: 'All over! Finished! Forever!' … What had I done to deserve such punishment?" — the rest of the squad prepared for a quarter-final against Brazil. In another baffling organisational decision in a tournament of baffling organisational decisions, the teams who finished top of their groups went into one half of the knockout draw, with the runners-up in the other. Thus, Hungary would face Group One winners Brazil in the quarters, and then whoever came out on top between Group Three winners Uruguay and Group Four winners England in the semis.

Brazil had been runners up on home soil (and not particularly happy about it) last time around and would go on to win the tournament in 1958, 1962 and 1970. The only answer they had for Hungary in 1954, though, was one of violence. Bozsik and Nílton Santos were sent off for fisticuffs and Humberto Tozzi saw red for putting the boots to Lóránt. Sebes described it as a "brutal, savage" match. But the real action in the Battle of Bern came after the final whistle, Hungary having seen off a spirited Brazilian fightback to prevail 4-2.

Swiss police had struggled to contain a few pitch invaders as things got a little rowdy but Puskás, who had hobbled down from the stands, paints a scene of almost bucolic post-match innocence in the Hungary changing rooms — "an ecstasy of happiness and comradeship" — into which the brutal Brazilians rushed. The truth is presumably a little more nuanced but either way, an almighty stramash broke out in the tunnel, with players, fans and officials involved. Broken bottles and boots were wielded as weapons. There were "blood and fists everywhere", said Czibor. Sebes caught a bottle in the face and needed stitches. Brazil's Pinheiro suffered a similar fate — Puskás was reckoned to be the guilty party.

After the briefest of investigations FIFA, in trademark style, shrugged and decided both sides were equally to blame, leaving it up to the respective FAs to dish out punishments. It was a decision that suited everyone and allowed both FAs to follow FIFA's lead, wash their hands of the whole sorry affair and do absolutely nothing.

Uruguay, the holders, awaited in the semis. In a story that would become horribly familiar, Hungary were 2-0 up and cruising only to throw away the lead. To their credit, however, Sebes's side rallied and two Kocsis headers ensured a 4-2 win and Hungary's second final in three World Cups.

And then came the Miracle of Bern. Hungary were 2-0 up after eight minutes but with a thud of his left boot, Helmut Rahn made it 3-2 with six minutes to go, completing the greatest comeback — and arguably the biggest shock — ever seen in a World Cup final.

There were plenty of reasons for the unlikely result. While Hungary had battled (literally) past Brazil and Uruguay, the finalists of 1950, West Germany had a far more serene passage against Yugoslavia and Austria (who they beat 6-1 in the semi-finals). The rain and stodgy pitch sapped what energy was left from Hungarian legs. The Swiss national battle-of-the-brass-bands was held in the town of Solothurn, where Hungary were based, the night before the final and the players struggled to sleep. In the morning, reckoned Puskás: "We were not at all refreshed, but nearer a state of nervous exhaustion."

The referee, one William Ling, made a series of questionable decisions. Puskás even scored a late equaliser to make it 3-3 only to see the linesman rule it out for offside (it's not by any means clear from the footage, but he looks more on than off). Puskás may (or may not) have been fit enough to play, but he clearly wasn't at 100%. Hidegkuti hit the post. Kocsis hit the bar. Turek made save after save. They relaxed too much at 2-0, they were always vulnerable at the back, West Germany had worked them out, West Germany were on steroids ... the how and why of the 1954 final remains one of football's great mysteries (needles were found after the final; the German team doctor Franz Loogen insists they were simply vitamin supplements). Nevertheless, the unbeaten run was over. West Germany had not won the World Cup though, ran the thought in Budapest. Hungary had lost it.

The reaction back home forwent most of the five stages of grief and focused simply on the anger. The team was not permitted to return to Budapest but instead redirected to a training camp in Tata for their own safety. Theories swirled of the squad throwing the game for a Mercedes each. The outpouring of rage on the streets would prove a trial run for the uprising two years later.

Sebes, whose son was beaten up at school, and Puskás took much of the blame — "People looked at me as if I had some kind of disease," said the captain — but despite the furious reaction to the final, the team soon returned to winning ways with another 18-game unbeaten streak (West Germany, on the other hand, had rather gallingly lost to England, France and Belgium by the end of the year). That meant that between May 1950 and February 1956, Hungary only lost one of the 49 games they played — the one that really mattered.

Behind the successes, the team was crumbling. Grosics was arrested on suspicion of spying, Czibor was left out after rowing with Puskás,

Zakariás and Lóránt were ditched for younger players. Defeat in Turkey in early 1956 was followed by a home loss to the Czechs — their first ever defeat in the Népstadion — a 5-4 reverse in Belgium and a 2-2 draw with Portugal in Lisbon. Sebes was shown the door.

The final nail came as the country exploded in revolution in October of 1956. As the uprising ignited in Budapest, Honvéd left the country to travel to Bilbao for a European Cup tie, while MTK headed to Austria for some hastily arranged friendlies. Soviet tanks rolled into the country while both squads were away and, with neither particularly keen to head home, each embarked on mini-European tours to keep the money rolling in. Honvéd even headed to Brazil on tour and by the time the players regrouped in Vienna, the revolution had been crushed. The Soviet Union was brutally restoring its authority.

Despite obvious fears of defections (48 of the 60-strong Hungarian Olympic squad had refused to come home after the Melbourne Games in 1956 and the entire Under-21 football squad, who had been playing in Belgium at the time of the uprising, had followed suit) the Hungarian FA felt the best way to woo the stay-away players home was with a stick rather than a carrot. Lengthy bans were promised on their return.

So some chose not to. Kocsis instead went to Barcelona and was joined by Czibor (whose move to Roma had been blocked by the Italian FA). Puskás trained with Internazionale before accepting an offer to join Real Madrid (he would play for Spain in the 1962 World Cup). It was over. The Golden Squad was no more.

It's sometimes difficult to get a grasp on just how good the teams of earlier eras were — the game Puskás and co were playing was a very different beast to the modern version, and the grainy, jerky black-and-white footage only makes it more so. But, nearly 70 years on, there is still something *other* about the *Aranycsapat* — a sense of movement, space and swagger, of opponents scrambling at full pelt just to keep up. Eventually they did, and then went past them, the same political system that provided the fertile soil in which this special team grew proving deeply inhospitable when things started going wrong. The consolation, if one is needed, is the fact the Golden Squad are always in the conversation when talking about not just the greatest teams not to win the World Cup, but the greatest teams full stop.

WALES 1958

ANDI THOMAS

The 1958 World Cup was held in Sweden — wait, no, hang on. Hang on just a second.

Released in 2002, the Swedish documentary *Konspiration 58* (*Conspiracy 58*) investigates the theory, once marginal but apparently growing in support, that the 1958 World Cup was not held in Sweden. Or anywhere else. That the competition was in fact staged somewhere on the west coast of the USA, as a joint effort between American Intelligence, FIFA and various international television networks.

Their motivation: the Cold War. Their goal: to demonstrate that televised propaganda could fool the world. Their success: well, you're the proof of that.

You want evidence? The film follows an investigator called Bror Jacques de Wærn, who has dedicated his life to analysing the myriad flaws in the conventional narrative. Buildings in the backgrounds of games that cannot be found anywhere in Gothenburg. Shadows that are too long, too dark, for Swedish latitudes, but just right for Los Angeles. The curious case of West Germany's goalkeeper, clearly smiling — laughing, even — as he concedes to Sweden in the semi-final. And the Brazilian team's boots? They simply didn't exist.

Wikipedia and IMDB will tell you that this film is a 'mockumentary'. That the director and producer were trying to satirise conspiracy theorists, to make a point about historical revisionism and the importance of good sourcing. But then, that's exactly what they would say, isn't it?

As one of the interviewees is forced to concede:

"I saw Wales-Hungary in Sandviken Jernvallen … [Bror Jacques de Wærn] might be right there."

Even a man dedicated to maintaining this fiction cannot seriously claim, with a straight face, that he saw Wales play at a World Cup.

The 1958 World Cup was — apparently, allegedly — held in Sweden, across 12 cities over three weeks. Just Fontaine scored 13 goals, while England went out in the group stages. Brazil won, and Wales didn't.

Looking back at World Cups, you see 'Brazil won' quite a lot. You don't see 'Wales didn't' all that often, even though Wales have failed to win many more World Cups than Brazil have won: 21 and counting. A 100% 0% record. The dragon prances under starless skies.

Twenty of those tournaments came and went with Wales gone in qualifying, a melancholy litany of inadequacy, injustice and penalties sent over the bar into nothingness. All smaller footballing nations have their own version of this story, of course; there are Paul Bodins of Syria, of Finland and Venezuela. But not all of them have a 1958.

For there are two ways not to win a World Cup. There is the usual way, achieved by most, which is to not win and to never look, at any point, as though winning was even a possibility. And then there is the other. The defeat that could have been victory. Hell, why not: the defeat that *should* have been victory. Here, the win exists alongside the not-win, but only as an imagined thing, a counterfactual. Curse and consolation.

Perhaps fittingly for a team that's always struggled with conventional qualification, Wales' path to Sweden '58 was a tangled mess of bureaucratic improvisation. Europe had 27 teams competing for nine places, so: nine groups of three, winners go to Sweden. Simple enough. Wales were drawn with Czechoslovakia and East Germany and won their first game against the Czechs in Cardiff, despite going in as underdogs.

But next came the two away games, and Wales lost them both. A tiny squad — 13 players, almost outnumbered by ten national team selectors — managed only a limp, 2-1 defeat to East Germany in Leipzig and then, with injuries necessitating emergency call-ups from back home, lost 2-0 in Prague. That meant that Wales needed their two opponents to exchange wins, but Czechoslovakia strolled to victory home and away, leaving Wales out with a game to play. They beat East Germany 4-1 to round off the campaign, but there was no prize for second place.

Except this time, there was. Israel had emerged as the victors of the Africa & Asia qualifying section, but they'd done so without playing a single match, as one by one their opponents defaulted the games. Turkey did so in protest at being included in the Asian section of qualifying; Indonesia after their request to play on neutral ground was refused; and Egypt and Sudan in light of the recent Suez crisis and the ongoing Arab League boycott of Israel. FIFA's rules specifically required all qualifying teams to have played at least one game on the way to the finals — the competition might look a little silly otherwise — so Europe's runners-up were all thrown into a hat. Out came the name: Belgium! But they decided they were too embarrassed to accept such charity. So out came another name: Wales! No such embarrassment.

Following the draw, Wales manager Jimmy Murphy told the press: "Wales has got a second chance of qualifying for the World Cup and you can take it from me, the lads are going to grasp the opportunity with both hands." And he was right: Wales dispatched Israel's young semi-professionals handily, scoring four unanswered goals over two legs. And the play-off also amounted to another, much bleaker stroke of luck for Murphy, whose day job was assistant to Matt Busby at Manchester United. It was the day after the second leg, when he returned to Old Trafford, that he received news that United's plane had crashed that morning after refuelling in Munich. His replacement for the trip, Bert Whalley, was numbered among the dead.

Mario Risoli, author of the definitive *When Pelé Broke Our Hearts: Wales and the 1958 World Cup*, believes the impact of the disaster on Murphy's role as Wales manager "remains debatable" but notes that the man himself was powerfully affected. It is well-documented that

Murphy essentially ran the club while Busby recovered, and Risoli notes that he frequently did so without sleep. It is almost impossible to imagine that there was no impact, even just in terms of Murphy's state of mind. But if Wales' summer preparation was affected, then at least they had a talented squad to call upon as they headed to Sweden as the World Cup's first African representatives.

Three of the squad — Mel Hopkins, Terry Medwin, and the great Cliff Jones — would go on to win the Double under Bill Nicholson at Tottenham. They were joined in Sweden by Jack Kelsey, title-winning Arsenal goalkeeper, and the elegant Ivor Allchurch, named by Bobby Moore as "one of the best inside-forwards he'd played against". And alongside his brother Mel, who would likely have been the best player in any other family, was John Charles, the Gentle Giant: beloved in Leeds, adored in Turin, and unquestionably one of the finest footballers ever to play the game. More on him later.

Wales' draw could have been a lot worse: they dodged West Germany and France from the Western European pot, and Brazil from the Americas. But they, along with Mexico, were expected to finish behind Hungary and Sweden. Certainly, Wales' selection committee felt that their adventure would be a short one: they were booked on flights back to London immediately after the last round of group games. But Wales proved themselves the equal of their competitors in highly literal fashion, drawing every game. They could have beaten Hungary, they should have beaten Mexico, and they were perhaps a little fortunate that Sweden were resting players for the last round of games. Three points left them level with Hungary, but behind on goal average.

Once again, the bureaucratic shenanigans fell in Wales' favour. FIFA, all-knowing and all-powerful, announced that goal average would replace the tried and tested play-off, a decision that would have sent Wales home. However, FIFA, moving in mysterious ways, made this announcement *after* the first round of group games had been completed. The Swedish Football Association complained that changing the rules mid-tournament wasn't fair on anybody; it has also been suggested that their motives weren't entirely Corinthian, and that they quite fancied the extra revenue that would come with a couple more games. But either way, FIFA conceded the point, reinstated the play-offs, and Wales' lousy goal average mattered nothing: they were still in. The Welsh selectors, not a group of men to let a ticket go to waste, flew to London and then immediately back to Sweden.

It's at this point that we need to pause and talk about John Charles. Comparing players across eras is always a futile exercise in personal preference and prejudice. *My favourite is better than your favourite because I like them more. About this I cannot possibly be wrong: this is not a statement of fact but of taste. You might think me tasteless. You might even be right about that. But I can't really be wrong, because it's nobody else's business but my own which footballer I find the tastiest.*

Players can be compared within context, however, and within his game, at his time, Charles wasn't just one of the finest players in the world. He was two: Nat Lofthouse named him the best central defender he'd ever faced, while Bobby Moore named him the best attacker. Unfortunately, the laws of football and metaphysics meant that Wales couldn't pick him twice.

Charles had played Wales' first qualifier in defence, but he started the World Cup as a striker and scored the equaliser in Wales' first game against Hungary. This was not the great Hungary side of the early 1950s, the magical side that humiliated England home and away, and reached the World Cup final in 1954. Most of that team had gone into exile after the Hungarian uprising of 1956, and the few that left were the wrong side of 30. Murphy made sure his charges wouldn't be overawed, describing the opponents as "an ordinary side living on reputation". But even the most ordinary of sides knows how to put the boot in: as Brian Glanville later recalled, Charles was "chopped down three times in the first 16 minutes". In the interests of even-handedness we should note that Hungary weren't the only team solving the problem of greatness in the opposition ranks with a little applied violence. According to Risoli, Dave Bowen kicked Nandor Hidegkuti "from the first to the last whistle", rendering the former great "virtually anonymous".

But when the play-off came around, the Hungarians, who took an early lead, redoubled their efforts. Glanville recalled that "at corners, Charles found his arms pinioned by one opponent while another crashed into him from behind". Eventually, he limped off with an injury and then, since substitutes were not permitted at the time, limped back on. His movement limited, he didn't score, but he did play the pass that set up Ivor Allchurch for the equaliser, a luscious, dipping half-volley that almost certainly stands as the most beautiful goal Wales have scored in a World Cup, even if the competition is slim. Terry Medwin pinched the winner after a defensive mix-up, and Wales were through to the quarter-finals. But — and here the dramatic music swells — at what cost?

This is the point where we part company with reality. In reality — boring reality, miserable reality, enemy of romance and beauty — Wales held Brazil 0-0 for just over an hour, before some skinny teenager called Pelé scuffed a deflected shot past Kelsey for the only goal of the game. Wales lost and went home, and are so far yet to trouble the World Cup again. Brazil dispatched France in the semi-finals, then Sweden in the final, and lifted their first World Cup of five.

This, incidentally, is one of the reasons this particular *what if* is so much fun: it's not just because 'Wales' and 'World Cup winners' look strangely good together. Brazil's win in '58 is widely credited with laying to rest the ghost of the *Maracanazo*, that nation-scarring defeat in 1950. They won again in 1962, and 1970, in the process becoming Brazil as we understand them today: carnival, sex, Pelé. The Brazil that Nike pay through the nose to be allowed to sell back to us. Presumably Pelé, Garrincha, Vavá, and the rest would have gone on to have pretty decent careers regardless, but international football would look at least a little different, and possibly a lot.

The crucial point is this: John Charles didn't play. His rough treatment at the hands and feet of the Hungarians had knackered him beyond even the grit-your-teeth standards of the 1950s, and so Colin Webster played in his stead. Webster, though a perfectly competent footballer, wasn't really a line-leading striker. And he certainly wasn't John Charles, because nobody else has ever been John Charles.

And oh, how Wales needed a John Charles. Terry Medwin and Cliff Jones found early space down the wings, and sent cross after cross into the Brazilian box: into that vast empty space where Charles should have been, where he conspicuously wasn't. On the bench, after Webster came close, but not close enough to one Welsh cross, Charles turned to Murphy and said "I would have scored that". And you don't have to take my word for it, or Charles', biased as he might have been. Here's Glanville again, from John Charles' obituary:

"Had he not been viciously treated and injured by the Hungarian team in a sulphurous group play-off, who knows whether Brazil would have reached the semi-finals, let alone have won that tournament?"

And here's Glanville again, in his role as the eulogiser of British football, returning to the theme in the obituary of John's brother Mel:

"There were those who believed that had John been able to play in Gothenburg, Wales might even have won, since they put over more high, searching crosses that day than in any previous game, and John was formidable with his head."

There is a terrible sadness in this second image. As if in denial, as if hazy with grief, Wales played a near-perfect game for a side with John Charles up front and so, accordingly, they lost. But that probably wouldn't be fair: as he had done with the Hungarians, Murphy pulled his "this lot? Rubbish" trick again, and Wales were in decent heart throughout the game.

There's another important absence, too: the absence of a Brazilian rout. The eventual champions played six games at the tournament. Four of them were comfortable to handsome wins: 3-0 against Austria, 2-0 against the Soviet Union, 5-2 against France in the semi-final and the same score again against Sweden in the final. But they couldn't score against England in the group stage, and they couldn't break down the Welsh for more than an hour. Mel Charles kept Altafini quiet; Mel Hopkins did the same with the great Garrincha. Stuart Williams marked Mário Zagallo completely out of the game. Behind them, Kelsey was getting his sticky hands on everything. Eventually, it took a deflection, almost a fluke, that Pelé later called the most important goal of his career. But then, Pelé said a lot of things.

So there's the evidence, as thin or as rich as you like. Unlike any other team in the tournament bar England, Wales were capable of keeping Brazil quiet at one end. At the same time, they were capable of creating chances at the other; sadly, the player to take those chances was sat on the sidelines with a grimace on his face. Therefore, Wales could have won, should have won, would have won the game — and, by the rules of conkers, the tournament — had things only gone a little differently. Had the Hungarians not sharpened their studs, the bastards.

This is, of course, completely absurd.

Most footballing *what ifs* have the decency to stop at one fork in the road: a penalty not given here, a post cracked there. This one requires a cascade of abstractions and suppositions, a whole tube train of sliding doors. *If* Charles J. had played and *if* Wales had found him and *if* he'd scored and *if* Pelé hadn't and *if* all the other brilliant Brazilians hadn't as well and *if* the Welsh defence had kept Fontaine quiet and *if, if, if, if, if* … you can nod in agreement, or laugh in dissent — you can call me and Glanville's anonymous friends rude words if you really want to — but that changes nothing. It's inarguable in a literal sense: there isn't enough sense in it to hang an argument on.

It is notable that Glanville approaches this through rhetorical questions and anonymous whispers. He was writing obituaries, and obituaries are serious things, and this is, at heart, a deeply unserious exercise in making things up. But that's the strength of it. This isn't a coulda-woulda-shoulda to get energised about. There is no injustice; it's too vague for that. This is a daydream, several layers deep; something to drift in and play with. Almost entirely untethered from, and so largely untroubled by, reality. It doesn't have to have happened. It doesn't even have to have nearly happened. It just has to have not happened in such a way as to not quite totally destroy the possibility of it having happened. Which, luckily for everybody, it did. Or didn't. One of the two. Possibly both.

As Sweden striker Agne Simonsson says in *Konspiration 58*: "Of course, some details might have been wrong throughout. But that all fades away as time passes."

When Mel Charles returned to Wales, there was no crowd waiting to greet the team. No seething horde of autograph hunters behind panicked security guards. And when he made it back to Swansea train station, he was greeted by the conductor: "Have we been on holiday again?" Wales, you see, hadn't won the World Cup. Again.

DUNDEE 1961–63

PATRICK BARCLAY

This is written with arthritic fingers. Oh yes — I suffered for such iotas of art as sprinkled across a career of four decades covering football for a succession of national newspapers. And now it's your turn to suffer for the pleasure football gave me, and keeps on giving, through a love of Dundee and the dark blue. Writing about the game professionally was never much fun. Of course there was gratitude that it paid the bills and afforded the privilege of a nose pressed against the window of glamour: trips to places such as Barcelona, Madrid, Milan and Munich, fantasy-inducing strolls down tunnels trod by Maradona and Messi and a presence at the history etched during a couple of dozen Champions League climaxes, nine World Cups and ten European Championships with a couple of Africa Cups of Nations adding Mali and Senegal to a long list of countries visited. When you factor in the camaraderie and memorable meals, I suppose even an old curmudgeon must embrace his luck with warmth. But I do promise you that, at every final whistle, as the crowds streamed for the exits, I envied the purity of their experience whether it had led to joy or despair. At least none of them had to shape what they had seen into a thousand purportedly definitive words against a deadline that I, for one, always found distressingly unfeasible. When football is your job, it's a very different game indeed: sometimes, quite literally, a headache.

And then one day the recurrent wish came true. To the indecisive, a decision foisted is a decision made. Suddenly there was no more work. I was a football fan again. I bought season tickets for Dundee's Dens Park and Craven Cottage, home of my favourite local club, Fulham. It was like instant time-travel back to where the love affair began, to an age of hope and innocence that happened to be the greatest in the history of a club formed in 1893. And, as if by a miracle, this was the love of old that gave and gave and made no demands. Not that it will ever again give as it did between 1961 and 1963.

Dundee had enjoyed great days before. I'd learned about them at the knee of a grandfather who often mentioned the Scottish Cup triumph over Clyde. The winning goal was scored by John 'Sailor' Hunter. This was in 1910, two years before the Titanic went down and four before the outbreak of the First World War. My grandfather would have been about ten when the team rode gloriously home to the city of jute — in which industry he was to make his living — and jam and journalism and I was roughly the same age when he agreed to take me to a match at Dens in the mid-1950s. He wasn't too bothered about seeing it himself, having lost interest in football despite Dundee's consecutive Scottish League Cup successes in the early part of the decade, so he just drove me to Dens one midweek evening, gave me a shilling for admission to the main stand and collected me as the 15,000 crowd dispersed in the afterglow of victory over Hibernian; people had yet to become obsessed by risk to children.

My obsession from then was with those navy shirts, their intense hue beautifully offset by deep white collar and cuffs, and the heroes who wore them, inevitably led by the principal goalscorer, George Merchant, whose persona I daily borrowed, without his permission, for playground games. This was a generally mid-table team managed by Willie Thornton and it was destined to be refashioned by his successor, Bob Shankly, who was engaged just before the Dundee board received a letter of application from his brother Bill (then managing Huddersfield Town but shortly to move to Liverpool).

Thornton had left a lot of talent and Shankly blended his young men brilliantly with the experience of wing-halves Bobby Seith and Bobby Wishart, who had been national champions with Burnley and Aberdeen respectively, and the great Gordon Smith, a title winner with both Hearts and Hibs whose consistently classy displays were to belie his age; he was 36 when he joined the club on a free transfer. Even so, if I were to tell you we could sense this was to become Dundee's best team ever, one worthy of comparison with the Lisbon Lions of Celtic who were to follow them deep into Europe, I'd be telling you next that I'd never heard of a club called Dundee United.

Ah, the elephant in the room. I was wondering when you'd mention the tangerine leviathan that for much of the past half century has felt able to claim bragging rights in Tannadice Street, which contains the grounds of both Dundee clubs. But before 1960, the neighbours were considered less a threat than a source of amusement: when the mighty Rangers were drawn away to United in the Scottish Cup, the facilities within their main stand, a little wooden thing, were deemed so inadequate that the renowned internationals from Glasgow chose to change at Dens and walk the hundred yards or so to the match venue. In 1960, United, then wearing white with black hoops, were promoted to the top division under the pipe-smoking Jerry Kerr, and even finished ninth, a point above us, in their first season up. But I don't remember noticing this. My pals and I had a new hero, for the shirt once worn by George Merchant now clothed the lean and elegant Alan Gilzean, a 22-year-old from the small semi-rural town of Coupar Angus who had been the last Dundee player to complete his National Service after the Second World War.

Gilzean had become the regular centre-forward towards the end of the previous season and, despite a deceptively languid style that we later came to recognise as cerebral, made an explosive impact with seven goals in five matches including a home win over Celtic. Now his first full season brought 32 in 42. Schoolboys gathered to watch stars such as Gillie and Alex Hamilton — the wisecracking frontman of the team pop group, Hammy and The Hamsters, but a full-back whose talent was to be rewarded with 24 caps — disport themselves under the H. Samuel clock in the city centre. If pretty girls walked past, the players seemed to glance through us. I noticed the lightweight brown shoes favoured by Gillie's soft feet. Some 60 years on, they are known as desert shoes and I always have at least one pair of them. That's hero-worship, I suppose: impervious to fashion.

Gillie was partnered up front by Alan Cousin, a leggy dynamo noted for beating opponents with the 'double shuffle'. Cousin was never to become a full-time professional, for he combined being Dundee's leading scorer for the three years before Gilzean's establishment with studies in Greek and Latin at St Andrews University and thereafter became a languages teacher in his home town of Alloa, yet he kept fit enough to perform with enough energy and skill to merit more than under-23 selection for Scotland. Cousin's link play was outstanding. He was to Gilzean what Gilzean later became to Jimmy Greaves and then Martin Chivers at Tottenham: a creator who also scored plenty of goals.

The influence of Thornton's signings was also there in Ian Ure, the main defensive bulwark, who was to graduate to the full Scotland side along with Hamilton and (for one cap only) the left-winger Hugh Robertson. One who certainly deserved a cap was Bobby Cox. A Dundee boy, born a few hundred yards from Dens, he was the captain and fierce heart of the team, his sliding tackle as much a personal hallmark as Cousin's shuffle. It was, then, a team with a trick or two, as well as a blend of pace and guile and a measure of tactical consciousness unusual at the time, one with such constructive intent running all the way through — even Ure had begun his career in midfield — that Bob Crampsey, a noted historian of the Scottish game, was to hail "the best pure footballing team produced in Scotland since the war".

The evidence began to emerge in the 1961-62 season. A crucial factor was that Shankly had prepared them with a summer tour of Iceland that completed the formation of a true bond. Ability apart, they were a bunch of lads who liked a laugh — and big Ure never minded being the butt. In Reykjavik they stole away to a nightclub for a few beers and were into their third or fourth when a rumour started that Shankly had arrived looking angry. In the half-light, Cox slipped something small, round and hard into Ure's hand, explaining that it was a boiled sweet guaranteed to take away any smell of alcohol. Ure had been desperately sucking it for several minutes before the dam of mirth burst; Cox had made sure everyone else saw him lift a pebble from an ornamental fountain. Another time Gilzean, straight-faced, suggested a tactical innovation which involved the ball being knocked long into space for Smith, now in his 38th year. Shankly wasn't sure how to react and settled for: "Christ Gillie! Don't complicate things!". Shankly could, like many managers, be a formidable figure. But the players loved him and soon as the league campaign began, it became clear he had built something special.

The first home fixture saw the newly promoted Dundee United fall 4-1 and, when Celtic came to Dens, they were beaten too. But a more stringent test awaited at Ibrox in November. Rangers were the champions. They had the exquisite Jim Baxter. And they were taken apart, Gilzean scoring four of five goals to Rangers' one. In only one respect were Dundee lucky; although fog prevented our goalkeeper, Pat Liney, from seeing some of the goals, the blanket never quite descended with the intensity required for the referee to call a postponement. A week later Dens saw the match of the season. Dundee trailed Raith Rovers 4-2 with less than half an hour left and yet won 5-4, Smith completing a task of recovery begun by long-range stunners from Seith and Wishart. It was the spirit this exuded that convinced Shankly and his players that the title could be claimed and they duly built up an ominous rhythm. Towards the end of January 1962, they had won 18 of their 21 League matches and drawn two of the other three. Then came another useful result. It did not seem so, for Dundee were knocked out of the Scottish Cup at St Mirren. Nor did it appear to have concentrated their minds, for they took a mere point from the next five matches. But a scoreless match at home to Rangers, watched by 35,000 in a ground that now holds fewer than 12,000, settled Shankly's men and they resumed their victorious habit to stay in what had become a thrilling two-horse race.

The most exciting stage was the penultimate. In a time of two points for a win, each side had 50 with two matches to play and Dundee's assignments, though ostensibly less demanding, were against teams fighting relegation. On the evening of Wednesday April 25, the visitors to Dens were St Mirren, who struck a post before Cousin infused the 20,000 crowd with optimism by putting Dundee ahead late in the first half. Then it filtered through that Rangers were a goal down at Aberdeen! The title was in our grasp. But with 12 minutes left, the veteran Smith was judged to have handled. Penalty to St Mirren. They needed that point as much as we did and skipper Jim Clunie's kick was true enough to beat many a goalkeeper — but not the agile Liney, who was mobbed by youngsters on the final whistle. There had been just enough time for Andy Penman, a highly gifted 19-year-old midfielder, to make it 2-0. The score we wanted to know, however, was that from Pittodrie and the stadium announcer knew no one would leave until we heard it. He was part of the Dens experience, this fellow, with his robotic delivery and minimalist approach to information: "Attention please. Here is today's line-up. Dundee. Liney, Hamilton, Cox …". That was about it most days. But tonight, he was to achieve immortality without saying anything of substance. The public-address system crackled into life and the announcer, his voice breaking with obvious joy and relief, could hardly get out his "Attention please". The rest was lost in a great roar.

Rangers, having been unable to equalise at Pittodrie, trailed Dundee by two points. If they won their final match at home to Kilmarnock on the Saturday, they could remain champions by virtue of a superior goal average. But that relied on Dundee losing at St Johnstone and the likelihood was eloquently indicated by an attendance of little more than 10,000 at Ibrox. St Johnstone, by contrast, almost set a new record at Muirton Park (their ground until 1989) with some 20,000 of the 26,500 present making the short journey from Dundee to Perth on a day warm and sunlit enough to make the strawberry fields of the Tay Valley seem to beckon like the Garden of Eden.

An attempt at temptation was duly made. A draw would have clinched the title for Dundee and kept up a St Johnstone featuring the 20-year-old attacker Alex Ferguson and, because this was almost the habit of the time, a bribe was offered (the intermediary was a former Dundee player now associated with St Johnstone). Ian Ure, though still only 21, took leadership. Just in case a couple of his teammates were even thinking about taking a sum that would almost treble their weekly wage, he threatened to report the offer to Shankly and that was the end of it.

Any last drop of sympathy Dundee might have felt for the home team was wiped away by a couple of heavy tackles on Gordon Smith, who recovered and provided the cross from which Gilzean headed us into the lead. Gilzean's 27th goal of a 35-match season further eased any tension and a fulminating drive from young Penman allowed the celebrations to begin. I was among the thousands who invaded the pitch. Four months short of my 15th birthday, I'd been a wee bit naughty in taking one of the buses to Perth in the knowledge that it wouldn't get back along the crowded road to Dundee in time for work. I delivered newspapers and on Saturday evenings most of them were the Sporting Post, which contained the football scores and reports. I arrived at the paper shop nearly two hours late and expected hell, only to be given just a full satchel and an almost kindly shake of the head. Nor was there a single complaint from the customers on my round, even though some must have been supporters of Dundee United or the big Glasgow clubs or no one at all. It was, after all, the first time the championship of Scotland had ever come to our city. And these were different times. All in all, it was like being in Heaven.

Could this be a permanent state? Of course not. We knew the title came with obligations, chief among which was representing Scotland in the tournament now known as the Champions League, and the draw brought Cologne, champions of West Germany and among the competition favourites, to Dens for the first leg. Along with a couple of pals, I used to stand behind the goal at the Provost Road end — Dundee's version of the Kop — and it was into that net, before our disbelieving eyes, that Dundee put the ball five times before half-time. While rolling up our home-made banner in preparation for the match, we'd reflected on poor domestic form since the resumption and agreed that a draw with Cologne would be acceptable before the inevitable exit by the Rhine. Now Gilzean was leading a performance worthy of Real Madrid. We ended up winning 8-1.

There is a detail that should be added in that the German goalkeeper, Fritz Ewert, had been concussed in an early accident with Cousin. I know what you're thinking, but of all the footballers I've seen in my life, the last I would believe capable of deliberately incapacitating an opponent would be Alan Cousin. At any rate Ewert was replaced by an outfield player in the second half, for there were no substitutions at the time, and Dundee travelled for the second leg aware they would be facing not only Karl-Heinz Schnellinger and other stars, but a very strong sense of grievance.

Cologne did not disappoint them. At the start of the season Liney, despite his role in the march to the title, had lost his place to Bert Slater, signed by Shankly from his brother's Liverpool and nicknamed 'Punchy' because, being stocky and with a nose that looked as if it had taken much punishment, resembled a boxer. Now it was Slater's turn to step up to what could only be described in retrospect as the plate. Dark pre-match hints appeared to be borne out after 27 minutes in the Müngersdorf Stadium when, with Dundee already a goal down, Slater suffered a cut behind an ear in saving at the feet of Christian Mueller and was replaced in goal by Penman. By half-time Cologne had scored twice more. If they were to keep going like this without reply, a 9-8 aggregate victory was likely. Slater, his head heavily bandaged, bravely returned, initially to the right wing but then, after Penman had conceded again, between the posts, where his defiance was rewarded with a second-half clean sheet. Dundee had prevailed by 8-5 on a night that tested their courage.

Their prize was a more technical, again difficult, assignment against Sporting in Lisbon, where Gilzean felt Dundee were lucky to lose only 1-0. At Dens they scored four times, Gilzean's hat-trick owing much to an inspired performance from Smith on the wing, and the Portuguese could contrive only a late consolation. Now it was off to Brussels to meet Anderlecht, where Paul van Himst led an array of some of the best footballers ever to represent the Belgian club. Desperate to follow my favourites' fortunes, but aware there would be no coverage on the BBC, I tuned my tinny radio until it picked up a Belgian station. The language was Flemish but it was obvious we were doing well because just about every time the commentator used words such as 'Gilzean', 'Cousin' or 'Smith' a groan followed. Next morning The Courier and Advertiser confirmed we had won 4-1 with a classic counter-attacking display.

A 2-1 victory at Dens followed, watched by 40,000; I was quite a big lad but still needed my tiptoes to see Smith complete the task with the style he seemed always to ooze. We were in the semi-finals. Among British clubs entering Europe's top competition, only Hibs (in the first season), Rangers, Tottenham and Manchester United had done that. And not one — not even the Busby Babes — had reached the final. And, as if that were not an exciting enough prospect, the final that year was to be at Wembley, a ground arguably revered even more by Scots than the English; many years later Gilzean was to tell me the main reason he left Dundee for Tottenham was for the opportunity to perform under the Twin Towers. Which gives you a clue to how this story ends.

While Benfica, Eusébio and all, took on Feyenoord, Shankly's men were handed Milan, initially at San Siro, where after 45 minutes all seemed to be going well despite the quality of the opposition: Maldini Snr, Trappatoni, Sani, Altafini, above all Rivera. The Italians led, but Cousin headed Dundee level. We were, however, lacking the leadership of the injured Cox. Moreover, the most trusted deputy down the left side of defence, Craig Brown (later to become Scotland manager), was also missing. And in the second half we paid for it as the wingers Bruno Mora and Paolo Barison scored twice each.

Excuses were advanced on Dundee's behalf: photographers' flashbulbs had kept distracting Slater; one assist was clearly delivered from off the field, while another was converted from an offside position; the ref was bent and in possession of lavish pre-match gifts from the hosts. But 5-1 was the score and the players knew the principal reason for its severity, Milan's class apart, was their captain's injury.

Dens bulged once more for the second leg, but although Gilzean put Dundee ahead on the night, there were no further goals and our great striker's frustration was demonstrated when, tiring of Victor Benitez's often cynical attentions, he lashed out and was sent off.

Milan beat Benfica 2-1 at Wembley.

What if we had not endured that nightmare second half at San Siro? Would we have been there, recipients of all Britain's support on and maybe even, with this advantage, winners, immortal inhabitants of the positions in history now held by Jock Stein's Celtic and the last great side built by Matt Busby at Old Trafford? Would we then have had the resources, and the will, to prevent Gilzean from leaving for Spurs, or Ian Ure for Arsenal? Would we have built on the wider consciousness of our club so that even now, all these decades on, mention of Dundee Football Club would induce in my London friends something more than a sympathetic grin? It's all fantasy.

Reality is that Rangers had regained the Scottish title as we finished ninth, two places below Dundee United. We did enjoy a more than respectable return to Europe with a new team in 1967-68, reaching a semi-final against Leeds United. Our midfield featured Jim McLean, who retired a couple of years later and was 18 months into a coaching career at Dens when he became as significant a loss as any, accepting an offer to move along Tannadice Street and succeed Jerry Kerr. The skill with which McLean built there compared only with Alex Ferguson's achievements at Aberdeen and eventually Dundee United became the second club in our city to reach a European Cup semi-final. Not bad for a single street, we had to admit, through gritted teeth.

They say you should never meet your heroes, but in 2012, to mark the 50th anniversary of the title win, a celebration packed out Dundee's Caird Hall. Because I was contributing the first of an ascending order of speeches after dinner, I found myself next to Alan Gilzean. He had time for everyone and, when a young man from Coupar Angus shyly approached, asked after many of the older townsfolk by name. At one stage he picked up a bottle of red wine and asked if he could fill my glass. Nervous on more than one level, I said I didn't dare until my speech was done. When I sat down, he smiled and poured. I'm still pinching myself. We kept in touch and once, when I was with a Premier League party being entertained at a Spurs match, he briefly broke off from his hospitality duties at White Hart Lane to say hello. As he made his way to our table, it was noticeable that, although well into his seventies, he retained a light gait of balletic grace. Gillie died in 2018, by which time only Liney, Seith, Ure and Wishart were left along with the irrepressible Craig Brown.

Dundee supporters of a certain age will expire proud of every one of these exceptional people, who were so happy together. Only for the purposes of this anthology could they be called nearly men. To our dwindled ranks, it's like saying Tenzing Norgay and Edmund Hillary climbed to a height of nearly 30,000 feet. Bob Shankly's men took us to a football Everest.

SCOTLAND 1964-68

ROB MACDONALD

Wembley's cramped and crowded away dressing room was shaking. The shouts of encouragement reverberated out into the corridor, but Jim Baxter was quiet. As others clattered around the room he was, unusually, a study in concentration. He tapped the studs on the heel of his right boot idly, and exhaled slowly. The volume of the shouts, the barks, the back-slapping increased. In the far corner, Denis Law was so flushed with intent it looked like he might explode. "Jim," a voice said, cutting through the noise. "Jim," it said again. "You should warm up. It is England after all."

Baxter lowered the pages of his *Racing Post* and stretched his left leg out in front of him. He stretched his right leg, languid and disinterested. Lowering the *Racing Post* appeared the most strenuous exercise. He raised his eyes.

"That's me warmed up."

Outside, nearly 100,000 expectant pairs of eyes waited. This wasn't any old international duty for Baxter and his Scotland teammates, but a Home International. Doubling as a qualifier for the Euros. Against the reigning World Champions. Away. As big-game preparation goes, it was unconventional.

Back in April 1967, though, it inspired Scotland to bring England's unbeaten run of nigh-on two years to an abrupt end. It inspired Baxter too, who more or less strolled around Wembley like he owned the place for 90 minutes, famously finding time to play keepy-uppy while wandering down the left wing, bringing the ball down only to take three England players completely out of the game with a scooped pass to Law. "A performance," said Sir Alex Ferguson, "that could have been set to music".

On a spring Saturday afternoon in London, Scotland led from the 28th minute. Law bundled the ball in from a few yards and, in contrast to Baxter's detached grace, tore into England throughout. Not that anyone was surprised, even among the opposition — Law's Manchester United team-mate Nobby Stiles later reflected: "I knew the Scots were taking it very seriously when Denis came on to the pitch wearing shinpads. I had never seen him wear them before."

It was a cathartic 3-2 victory for Scotland's 'Anglos' — the five starters based in England, of which Law was one — after nearly a year of dressing room taunts. Equally, it was a tough end to England's 19-game 'invincible' run, forced as they were to field Jack Charlton up front from half-time onwards, the big centre-back injuring himself tackling Bobby Lennox just 15 minutes in. Both were still on the field over an hour later, Lennox's shot scattering daisies in its wake to make it 2-0 in the 78th minute. Charlton, by contrast, was labouring and by then had been joined in England's proverbial on-pitch treatment room by Jimmy Greaves and Ray Wilson.

Minor mayhem ensued in the closing stages — Scotland captain John Greig headed off the line moments after Lennox's goal, before Gordon Banks made an astonishing save from Law's delicate chip as the ball looked certain to drop over his head and in. A sensational backheel from Jimmy Greaves sent Alan Ball haring towards the Scotland six-yard box; his swerve away from 36-year-old debutant goalkeeper Ronnie Simpson put the ball in Jack Charlton's path, who became an unlikely scorer with six minutes to go. Up the other end, almost immediately, a quick one-two with Lennox saw another debutant, 21-year-old Jim McCalliog, smash the ball past Banks at his near post to restore Scotland's two-goal cushion. Geoff Hurst then headed home from a Bobby Charlton cross on 88 minutes, before Scotland recovered to see out the remainder of the game. Perhaps the mayhem wasn't that minor after all.

Not that it mattered. Back home, the win was rapturously received, and apparently never in doubt. "Scots always had it buttoned up," wrote Jack Harkness in *The Sunday Post*. "The truth is, Greig, [Ronnie] McKinnon, and Baxter had the whole English attack in their pockets right from the beginning, and the other Scots players took it from there."

England's injuries were clearly a factor, but it was a notable and unexpected defeat — their line-up was virtually the same as the previous summer's World Cup campaign and though a fine side, with players in Law and Baxter that would become legends, Scotland were clear underdogs. "On the surface at least, we had no reason to feel confident," Greig said afterwards, even if for much of the decade, the playing field had been fairly level. They did have additional motivation though and Greig hinted at why Law had packed his shinpads: "We had considered ourselves unfortunate not to qualify for the 1966 finals and we were desperate to make a point."

Victory at Wembley clinched the 1966-67 Home International Championship, but though Scotland made their point, it was a flash of domestic success along the more well-trodden path to major tournament disappointment.

The qualifying group for the European Championships of 1968 combined the results of the Home Internationals in 66-67 and 67-68, with the winners facing a two-legged 'quarter-final' play-off against Spain for a place at the four-team finals in Italy. Scotland had the initiative with three matches to play, but a desperately poor 1-0 defeat in Northern Ireland and a stalemate with England at Hampden in early 1968 meant they ultimately finished second. The group winners, who duly dispatched the Spanish and headed to Florence? England, of course, by a single point.

'Considered ourselves unfortunate.' A phrase so often uttered in post-mortems of the national team that it should probably just be put on the badge.

It was the story of the decade. The 1960s was an auspicious time for Scottish football as its teams gained a foothold, then trophies, in Europe. By extension, the national team contained some of the finest players ever to wear the dark blue and it's remarkable that they were unable to qualify for any international tournament in that time. A disastrous 9-3 defeat at Wembley in 1961 aside, they even had the better of meetings with England, who, by virtue of winning a World Cup, made for a handy benchmark.

But, 1961 was a tough year, mostly because it also included the curtailment of Scotland's interest in a World Cup that wasn't even starting until 1962. And it happened in a manner that would warrant an entry in this book all of its own — within seven minutes of qualification, a bitterly disputed Czechoslovakia equaliser took their play-off in Brussels to extra time, during which the eventual World Cup finalists scored twice more to win 4-2, whipping the wheels off quicker than you could say: "I hope this doesn't become a habit."

Noble victory and ignominious defeat were rarely far apart. Next exhibit: a celebrated 2-1 win at Wembley in 1963, Baxter scoring twice and none other than Bobby Moore opining that the '63 vintage was the best Scotland had ever produced. Right on cue, it was followed up with one of the worst defeats in their history, a catastrophic 4-1 loss to Norway, a team of amateurs. Scotland rarely did things by halves.

But they had the Auld Enemy's number — victory in '63 was just the start. Victory, too in '64, albeit a fairly stultifying 1-0 win. A 2-2 draw in 1965, the scorers (Law, Greaves, Charlton, St John) a veritable who's who of international class and/or late-'80s TV personalities, depending on your perspective. A narrow 4-3 defeat in 1966 and the 'Unofficial World Championship' victory in '67. Scotland had the upper hand in the very period England got their hands on the Jules Rimet trophy — but they would just miss out on the chance to make the biggest statement of all.

The draw for the 1966 World Cup qualifiers took place in Zurich in January 1964. After the pain of missing out on the 1962 tournament in Chile, a new campaign, with the finals in England, would surely see the stars align.

No such luck. As tradition was already dictating, Ian McColl's men were somewhat unfortunate to find themselves in a group with Italy, Poland and Finland, with only one team qualifying for the finals. It was difficult to think of a sterner test.

Nor were the early signs particularly promising. A shock 3-2 defeat to Wales in a Home International in Cardiff, with two goals in the final three minutes from the improbably-named Ken Leek, was an embarrassing start to the autumn's international fixtures. Second-half weakness was becoming a slight cause for concern. Nevertheless, a gentle start to the qualifiers was at least assured with Finland, a team comprised almost entirely of part-timers, the visitors to Hampden in October.

Law opened the scoring after two minutes with a header, then goals from Stevie Chalmers and Dave Gibson gave Scotland a 3-0 lead before half-time. That was about as good as it got — true to form, a dreadful second half ensued and the Finns actually pulled a goal back in the only action of note, the Scots roundly jeered from the Hampden turf by a 55,000 crowd feeling robbed of half a game's entertainment. About the best that could be said for the performance was done so by McColl, who testily remarked: "A win's a win. That's all that matters."

The next qualifier was seven months away, but things would get worse before they got better. Baxter broke his leg that December playing for Rangers against Rapid Vienna, robbing Scotland of a talisman and robbing the man himself of the limited structure keeping football ahead of the Glasgow nightlife on his priority list. Already "an awful trainer and a legendary drinker," as John Litster puts it, it was a long road back to fitness and he would miss out on international duty for nearly a year.

The small matter of the 1965 Home Internationals rolled around and the England fixture, at Wembley, finished as a credible enough 2-2 draw. On the face of it, anyway — Scotland took some absolute pelters for not securing victory against ten men, Ray Wilson succumbing to injury at half-time with the home side 2-1 up, but no subs allowed. Scotland managed to pull themselves level, but were unable to find a breakthrough, fading away in the second half again, now not only a worrying habit but a darkly portentous one.

A tumultuous month followed, with a friendly against Spain next up at Hampden in early May. It finished 0-0, to yet more fierce criticism (suffice it to say Spain were not the side they are now). And, in somewhat cloak and dagger circumstances, it cost McColl his job — the SFA, through Secretary Willie Allan, issued a statement saying McColl had resigned, though it also later issued a report to its members containing reflections on a "slavish adherence to an unproductive style of play". Ronnie McDevitt reports in *Scotland in the Sixties* that, following a meeting with Allan on May 12, McColl maintained that he hadn't jumped, which would have made little sense, but was pushed — "five years of work … for no purpose," as he put it.

Nevertheless, his replacement was waiting in the wings. And although his Celtic tenure was still in its infancy, no one in the national team — even the selectors — were left in any doubt that big Jock Stein was now in charge. He assumed near-total control; squad selection was his, the starting XI was his and the decisions were final. Together they travelled to Poland for the next qualifier, two of Stein's former players at Hibs, Neil Martin and Willie Hamilton, added to the squad.

Conditions in Poland, after a 12-hour journey, were challenging on and off the pitch. A communist regime held sway over almost every aspect of daily life, including the turning on and off of the lights. In a stormy Chorzow, Scotland drew 1-1, Law cancelling out a Roman Lendtner opener. Perhaps not a major power, but certainly no mugs, the Poles boasted Włodzimierz Lubański up front — the country's all-time leading goal-scorer until Robert Lewandowski overtook him in 2017. Nevertheless, the opening game of Stein's first era was met with a positive reaction, the *Daily Record*'s spirits undimmed by the horrendous conditions as they hailed "Stein's sizzlers".

An arduous trip was only half over. A lengthy journey to Helsinki followed for the qualifier with Finland. It was a nervy encounter — Scotland were already 1-0 down when Law hit the post with a penalty, though minutes later he would set up Davie Wilson for the equaliser. It stayed that way until half-time, but a spectacular 30-yarder from Greig finally put the Scots in front after 50 minutes, where they would stay despite adding no further goals.

Emotions among the Scottish press had cooled to somewhere around 'lukewarm' as they assessed the performance in Helsinki. And although it perhaps underwhelmed, there surely can't be many eras where a win and a draw in two qualifiers could be viewed as indicative of a side failing to perform, even if one game was away against a team of relative international novices*.

*Not until 2020 anyway, when the entire Czech Republic squad and management would have to go into quarantine as a deadly virus circled the globe, and Scotland would then get panned for recording a 2-1 win over the team of relative international novices replacing them. Compelling evidence that even at the end of human civilisation, supporting Scotland will still be a bewildering and stressful ordeal.

The close-season saw Stein rather ominously confirmed as manager of the national team, writes McDevitt, "so long as it had an interest in the 1966 World Cup". A 3-2 defeat in Ireland in October 1965, notable for Baxter's long-awaited return, was hardly the best preparation for the crucial return fixture with Poland — a match Scotland had to win to ensure an advantage over the Italians, who were their opponents for the two final group games. While Poland were by no means amateurs, Italy really were one of the best teams in Europe, and not exactly given to missing out on World Cups. Defeat wasn't unthinkable, but it wasn't exactly pleasant to think about either.

Remarkably, or perhaps not given they were without Lubański, Poland had suffered a humiliating defeat of their own a few weeks earlier, losing 2-0 in Finland and putting their own qualification hopes almost out of sight. And despite Stein leaving out Baxter and Dave Mackay, also struggling to return to fitness, Scottish hopes were high — defeat to Ireland was their first for a year and, many hoped, an aberration that would be rectified by the deadly serious business of qualification.

Hampden was packed, 107,000 crammed in. Scotland took the lead after 14 minutes, a Billy McNeill strike from a corner scant reward for their early dominance. A litany of missed chances (Law and Willie Henderson particularly culpable), penalty claims ignored (with indirect free-kicks inexplicably awarded instead), and various goalmouth and goal-line scrambles (in particular an Alan Gilzean backheel cleared just off the line) followed. One final chance to make their dominance count just before the break saw Law, Billy Bremner and Gilzean all trying to force the ball in, but to no avail; the goal that could have changed it all never materialised.

They led at half-time though; "a first half of pace, interest and enthusiasm," said *The Herald*. But Poland reasserted themselves at the start of the second, spurning a couple of chances of their own as Scotland failed to regain their rhythm. With their full-backs in particular struggling against Poland's wingers, they were under the cosh, Law dropping deeper in an attempt to get on the ball, though he mostly found himself "plugging leaks," as *The Scotsman* put it.

They led at the hour-mark, but it was getting tough – "hanging onto their lead as uneasily as a mountaineer clinging to a ledge," said *The Herald*. But Hampden found its voice. Law was again denied, this time by Polish defender Zygmund Anczok. Goalkeeper Konrad Kornek made a flying save from Gilzean. Scotland hauled themselves towards the line.

They led at 80 minutes, but now it was torture.

They led on 81 minutes, 82 minutes.

The 83rd minute passed; the moment at which World Cup dreams had faded four years earlier against Czechoslovakia, passed. But Scotland's slump was deepening, cover now disappearing in wide areas, Henderson hampered by injury, Bremner overwhelmed, Greig out on his feet. The ball went left and as it was lofted in, Eddie McCreadie, craning his neck to get something, anything on it, got caught underneath the flight of the cross, recovering only in time to see Jan Liberda lifting the ball over Brown and into the far corner.

The air was sucked out of Hampden. The vacuum starved Scottish legs of energy — heads bowed, fighting fatigue and errors on the pitch as much as they were expectations from the stands. But the Poles were liberated. A second goal followed on 86 minutes, scored by Sadek, architect of the first. Even the match reports sounded exhausted — he cut straight through "a weary, dispirited Scottish defence" (*Herald*) and shot, at no great pace, straight through Brown as Scotland "disintegrated" (*Scotsman*). The game was up, hearts broken all over again by an improbable first World Cup defeat at Hampden in 11 years. McDevitt catches it right in *Scotland in the Sixties*, and it's fitting to repeat here — they had "snatched defeat from the jaws of victory".

Mathematically — that domain of football fans who need to escape what's actually happening — qualification was not completely lost. Scotland were level with Italy at the top of the group, having played a game more and with two matches to go. All eyes turned to Rome, especially Stein's, who travelled in person to the *Azzurri*'s game with Poland in early November. It was more in hope than expectation. Those hopes were duly dashed, Italy running out 6-1 winners and needing only one win from their two games with Scotland to qualify ahead of them.

The first showdown at Hampden took place five days later, with Stein making six changes. Baxter returned as captain, his talismanic qualities undimmed as Neil Martin told *The Scotsman* nearly 40 years later: "He was so arrogant — the Italians were frightened of Baxter."

With the game underway though, the captain couldn't quite unlock them at will: "Italian football was renowned the world over for its defensive nature," said Martin. "AC Milan and Inter were the top club sides of the day and their players found it second nature to defend for 90 minutes … I played alongside Alan Gilzean and the Italians were so quick and skilful we didn't get many chances. I remember thinking, because of the ability they had, Italy didn't need to play that way. They could easily have been more attack-minded …"

Having been in Scotland for days, in the middle of a month left deliberately free of league fixtures, there was no doubt the Italians were taking things very seriously. So seriously, in fact, they appeared to have come only to play for a draw, staying narrow, sitting off Scotland and generally squeezing the life out of the game while looking to threaten on the break. But, bucking their usual second-half trend, Scotland stuck at it, Bill Brown hampered by a thigh injury but making important saves from Giovanni Lodetti in particular, McKinnon acrobatically getting to one rebound to clear and Greig diverting another goal-bound effort off the line.

Time ticked on and the Italian wall stood firm, *catenaccio* thriving in the wintry Glasgow night, where it's often best to bed in and wait for the storm to pass. But Scotland's moment was coming. Later than the Czechs, later even than the Poles, as late as the 88th minute. And it's simple and it's glorious to watch, even in grainy black and white.

Baxter (who else?) receives the ball from Brown and checks his run, the slightest feint to hit it long. An Italian flinches and the ball is flicked past him to Bremner in midfield, who finds Greig going forward from full-back on the right. Greig finds Baxter — who has somehow materialised, despite going at no more than a canter, 70 metres from where he was a couple of seconds before — in exactly the right place, as if placed there by some unseen power. Baxter's first-time, *outside of the foot* return is nonchalant and perfect and Greig is in, so simply, as if actually Jim Baxter can unlock these at will, thank you very much. Just four passes have taken Scotland from one penalty area to the other, the great defensive shield unable to repel any of it.

Greig hits the ball on the run, left-footed, inside the near post — and Hampden roars. The players pile on, the photographers dance on the touchline, the stands shake. Those heading to Mount Florida for the trains back to town curse, then cheer. There is no time for the Italians to react. Scotland are somehow alive again, still fighting, joint top with a game to play.

Greig continued his scoring habit in the Home International with Wales a couple of weeks later, the fourth goal in a 4-1 win. Scotland wore their away kit in preparation for the Italy fixture in Naples, Stein wanting the players accustomed to every detail, leaving nothing to chance. Confidence remained high.

Unfortunately, the build-up was hampered by much more traditional means. Injuries were rife in the squad after the win over Italy, Brown having already withdrawn from the squad to face Wales. Law was missing again, as questions were asked — only semi-seriously, one assumes — about his international future, having sat out the Italy win. During the Wales match, Baxter seemed to pick up an ankle injury too, but that didn't stop him being named in the provisional squad to make the trip to Italy, along with the recalled Law.

While the Italians had allowed their national team priority and cancelled domestic fixtures prior to their qualifiers, Scotland were hampered by the fact that not all the players plied their trade in the domestic league. Negotiations to release the Anglos continued almost up until the squad left for Naples, by which time Law had been injured playing for Manchester United against West Ham and Baxter, who had returned to Sunderland, was deemed unfit, joining McNeill and Gilzean on the injured list. Having made it to Naples, Scotland also lost Henderson on the day of the game.

Only six of the side responsible for the famous win at Hampden took to the field in Italy. Nevertheless, Stein was bullish, believing all the pressure to be on the Italians. He set Scotland up to frustrate the home side, new addition to the squad Ron Yeats announced as the wearer of the number nine jersey, despite being a centre-half. It was a ruse to the last, Yeats even beginning the game on the centre-circle at kickoff, before taking his place in defence as Scotland aimed to out-Italy the Italians. It was bold, for sure, and despite the first half-hour descending into an almost attack-versus-defence spectacle, Scotland approached half-time grimly hanging on.

They didn't quite make it. After 39 minutes, McCreadie reprised his unfortunate role against Poland, missing a cross and allowing Ezio Pascutti to score from six yards. A killer blow, though it was followed by a rousing start to the second half in which McDevitt recalls Bobby Murdoch and John Hughes coming close to pulling Scotland level and the Italians looking "rattled ... trying to preserve the 1-0 scoreline". But a sucker-punch — another sucker-punch in a campaign full of them — came in the form of a breakaway goal on 72 minutes, with a third following just before the 90th.

It was an anti-climactic end, certainly relative to the qualifiers that preceded it. With the anti-climax came acrimony, international football exercising its common habit of being fine one minute, and laying bare fundamental structural and ideological issues the next. Stein was disconsolate, having clearly been able to rally the players on occasion, but with limited ability to change a system and a set-up in the space of 14 months.

Looking back, it's natural to wonder what might have been, with only nine months separating the World Cup in England from Scotland's victory in '67. Had it been Scotland qualifying from Group 8 instead of Italy, it's less natural, but still tempting, to think that particularly galling English defeat could have come in a World Cup semi-final.

To get to that fanciful point, we have to stretch the logic a little. Italy, qualifying comfortably enough in the end, would go on to famously crash out of the 1966 finals at the hands of Pak Doo-Ik and North Korea, the penultimate game of a group in which all the matches were staged at either Roker Park or Ayresome Park. While the Italians wilted in a ferocious atmosphere, it's hard to imagine it favouring the Koreans quite so much if the Tartan Army had pitched up in the north-east of England. A full stadium's-worth would almost certainly have mobilised with the game so near the border, especially given that some 40,000 were at Wembley the following year, their expectations significantly lower.

Italy gone, North Korea went on to lose remarkably to Portugal in the quarters, collapsing from being 3-0 up inside 25 minutes to lose 5-3. Eusébio and company had played a pre-tournament friendly at Hampden and were 1-0 victors, as Scotland, despite being in indifferent form with little to play for, also drew 1-1 with Brazil. The match would at least have been competitive. Portugal, of course, went on to lose to England in the semis and the rest, as they say, has been the founding principle of completely unreasonable expectations for nearly 55 years. Scotland's hypothetical success is fanciful, yes, but not implausible.

It's tempting, too, to try and find a moment, a 'what if' or a sliding door via which the destination of Scotland's decade might have changed, particularly as their fiercest rivals flourished. But really, we can look back on a whole decade of them. What if they'd qualified in '62, for starters? What if Poland hadn't scored their 86th-minute winner at Hampden? What if Baxter had been fully fit that entire campaign? What if he'd orchestrated England's embarrassment on their own turf in a World Cup semi-final, rather than an annual Home Nations Championship?

What if, indeed. It's a question that has led the way in Scottish football for some time, certainly as long as I can remember, and shows little sign of abating. But it does mean that when Scotland do give us those moments — those flashes — they seem to mean so much more as a result. Greig and Italy, Jordan and Czechoslovakia, Johnston and France, McFadden and Holland, McFadden and France, McFadden and anyone really, even Leigh Griffiths' two free-kicks against England … you never see 'delirium in the stands' quite like Hampden in full meltdown. Those moments, whether in a winning cause or a losing one, are the ones that remain, long after the fixtures, results and tables are forgotten. And that's why this team — all these Scotland teams in fact — should be celebrated. We owe them a lot.

LEEDS UNITED 1967–70

DANIEL CHAPMAN

How did Leeds United lose the FA Cup semi-final to Chelsea in 1967? Nobody could understand it.

"If it had happened to me I would have been very sick," said the victorious Chelsea manager Tommy Docherty.

The Leeds manager, Don Revie, said: "For about half an hour after the final whistle, I felt completely numb." If only he could have stayed that way. At least numbness doesn't hurt. He went on: "The remorse really began to hit me when I met my son, Duncan, outside the ground. He was sobbing — and I felt like sitting down and crying with him."

Chelsea had taken the lead just before half-time, when Tony Hateley headed in Charlie Cooke's cross. Leeds had thrown everything they had at the second half, and thought Terry Cooper had equalised with a powerful volley. Referee Ken Burns disallowed it for offside.

There were seconds left and Chelsea were resorting to fouls, giving Leeds a free-kick 25 yards out, and a chance. Peter Lorimer was still only 20, his cannon boot just becoming known, and John Giles kept him out of the frame as he directed the set-piece. When the time was right, Giles flicked the ball sideways, and when Lorimer hammered it, Peter Bonetti had no chance of keeping a sensational equaliser out of his top corner. And Leeds had nowhere to turn when referee Burns refused to let the goal stand.

He said Chelsea's wall had not been ten yards back. The Leeds players crowded him and jostled him and lost their minds. Eventually, they took the kick again as if trapped in a nightmare, and as soon as the ball was cleared, they were sunk into reality by the referee's final whistle. They fell to the grass, Don Revie felt numb, Tommy Docherty would have been very sick if it happened to him. But it didn't happen to him. It happened to Leeds United.

The Peacocks had just got through to the semi-finals of the Inter-Cities Fairs Cup, the stage they'd been beaten in a replay the previous May. But due to the oddness of that competition, the final, if they got there, wasn't until September.

In the league, they were on a run of six wins and two draws, and in the aftermath of the cup, they beat Liverpool. But within a week, a 2-2 draw at Chelsea — them again — meant they could no longer catch Matt Busby's Manchester United, who won the First Division for the second time in three seasons.

Leeds had finished second to them on goal average in 1964-65, then lost the FA Cup final in extra time to Liverpool, narrowly missing an incredible double in their first season after promotion from Division Two. In 1965-66, they were second again, six points behind Liverpool. Now they ended 1966-67 in fourth, five points from the top. They did reach that Fairs Cup Final in the end, but then they lost that too.

A statistic that should have been a point of pride for Don Revie was fast becoming his albatross. In three seasons since arriving in the top flight in 1964, Leeds had won 71 First Division matches, more than Manchester United's 68, more than any other team. Leeds had also won nothing. Manchester United had won the league twice. Liverpool could only boast 62 wins in that time, but they'd won the league and the FA Cup.

The brutality of the FA Cup defeat by Chelsea, their chance of a trip to Wembley stolen by a capricious referee, hit Leeds particularly hard. They felt they'd let themselves down in the 1965 final and wanted to put that right. The prestige of the FA Cup would surely win them the respect that their peers, so far, were refusing to show to the Real Madrid impersonators from industrial Leeds.

But more than respect, they needed trophies. They needed silverware to prove that the reason they won more games than anyone else was that they were a better team than anyone else. To prove it to the world and to prove it to themselves. The question after the Chelsea match was how much more losing England's best team could take.

The end of the 1966-67 season was the end of Don Revie's sixth full season in charge of Leeds, and life ought to have been high at Elland Road. His first task, in 1961, had been to prevent years of slow, careless erosion from causing a landslide into Division Three, and a win on the last day of his first full season was all that kept them up. It wasn't just that the team wasn't good enough. In the 1950s, manager Raich Carter had done what Major Frank Buckley couldn't and taken Leeds into Division One, but his lack of interest in training and youth development meant all Buckley's foundations were lost. While clubs around them modernised, Leeds let their scouting system disintegrate, wilfully ignored modern coaching ideas, and only altered their 1920s stadium when they had to; the Main Stand — dating from 1906 — had burned down. The players hardly seemed to care and, if there had been any fans watching them, they might not have been bothered by any of it either.

But a few did care, and Revie's transformational effort was not a solo act. The director who put him forward for the job, Harry Reynolds, was a kindred spirit who became chairman, and there were forward thinkers on the backroom staff. Coach Syd Owen had been centre-half when Hungary's Ferenc Puskás and Nándor Hidegkuti out-thought England 7-1, and he didn't forget the lesson; Revie had copied Hungary's tactics for his own innovative role as a deep-lying forward for Manchester City. Trainer Les Cocker and scout Maurice Lindley were keen students of the FA's coaching courses and they had all absorbed the television coverage of Real Madrid beating Eintracht Frankfurt 7-3 in 1960, the first European Cup final shown live on TV. Madrid's influence went further than the change to an all-white strip.

Jack Charlton was watching too, the team's best player. He'd been so bored by the atmosphere at Leeds that, in between angling for a transfer, he'd become a qualified coach by the age of 23; by 1961, he was also the team's angriest player, frustrated by the lack of ingenuity around him. His teammate Billy Bremner, his junior by seven years, hadn't done anything in the game yet, but had an instinctive grasp that standards at Elland Road were not high enough. In 1962, Revie bought Bobby Collins, Everton's former Scottish international midfielder, and he knew damn well that standards were not high enough. Aged 31 and furious at being let go from Goodison Park and dropping a division, he would fight and argue until Leeds was a proper club that could take him back where he belonged. The £25,000 cheque for Collins probably did more to modernise Leeds United than any other investment in their history.

Leeds had been late to soccer at every turn — United weren't founded until 1919, while their predecessors City only formed in 1904 — and no Leeds club had ever won a thing in association football. It was a rugby city, and proudly so; the oval ball game had been so tightly wound around social and religious life in the 19th-century city that to many, the round ball 'sockerists' still had a foul air of delinquent inadequacy. Leeds United's poor playing record was a disappointment to the city, which while happy to get behind them when times were good, saw Revie's attempts to build a world-class club as gauche and rather quixotic.

But now one of his team, Charlton, had a World Cup winner's medal; Norman Hunter was also in the squad in 1966; Cocker was the trainer. The 1966-67 season might have been the season for United to win their own city over to their side, as well as the nation, and 45,000 came to watch a 3-1 win over Manchester United at the start of the campaign. But the visit of Sheffield Wednesday to finish the season, after Leeds had lost everything again, only attracted 23,000. Carter used to complain that the menfolk of Leeds must go to bed on Saturday afternoons, so rarely were they seen at Elland Road, and now Revie was sharing his despair. In three First Division seasons, Leeds had only lost seven out of 63 home games; they'd won 45. What more did people want? The answer was always the same: a team that doesn't just win games, but wins things.

Well, they might never have that. 36,252 were optimistic enough to attend 1967-68's opener, a 1-1 draw at home to Sunderland.

But the reports of two away defeats without scoring sounded too much like the same old Leeds, and only 25,760 turned out for the next home game. That happened to be a 2-0 win over Fulham, but what good was that? Every team has their day and Leeds had had theirs. The good players would want transfers to clubs where they could win trophies. Johnny Giles would soon be 27, and he couldn't play forever; Charlton was already 32. There had been talk of a transfer for Peter Lorimer, and the other good young players would surely follow. Revie had done a lot in six years, but maybe it was time for someone else to try. Yes, he'd built a great team, but where were the big signings? He claimed his players were better than anybody's, but he didn't have anything to show for it.

Revie's team of the mid-1960s was a great one, as those 71 First Division wins demonstrated. They caught the eye in Europe, too; after their first away match in the Fairs Cup, in 1964, the Italian press wrote: "This team said a word about British soccer which for years has not been heard and which convinced the crowd. The whole team seemed to be spurred by fire." But Revie's first XI in those years contained players whose faces don't look familiar now. It's true that Charlton looked the same managing the Republic of Ireland in 1996 as he did playing for Leeds in '66 or even '56, but his young defensive partner, Hunter, still had the shy smile of the slim teenager Revie was trying to beef up with sherry and eggs. Giles, famous later for his midfield partnership with Bremner, was on the wing, and only moved inside when, in that first European trip to Torino, Collins' thigh was snapped by a terrible tackle. Gary Sprake had hardly been out of goal since taking over as a 17-year-old, but players like him and Lorimer, or the Pauls Madeley and Reaney, were just boys when Leeds won promotion. Eddie Gray was only 16 when Leeds started life in the First Division with a 2-1 win over Aston Villa, the goals scored by Charlton and winger Albert Johanneson.

Johanneson was the player people wanted to see, out of curiosity about a rare black player in English football, and from Johannesburg, too, but after curiosity came thrills. He'd been joint top scorer in the promotion year and added nine in his first top-flight season and, even as injuries started to affect him, he scored seven in 22 games in

1966-67. Confidence had affected him too, after a frozen performance in front of 100,000 in 1965 as the first black player in an FA Cup final, but at his best, he had the beating of any First Division defender and the tricks to make them look incompetent.

The other measure in which Leeds led the division was the meanness of their defence, letting in only 132 in three seasons compared to Manchester United's 143. Young Hunter and Reaney never looked out of their depth, but they were helped by Charlton and experienced left-back Willie Bell, who played his way to international honours with Scotland the same as Charlton did for England.

In front of the back four were a cast of unsung but formidable players. Alan Peacock had been signed to lead the line for promotion and scored on his last of six England appearances in 1965, but the aftermath of a serious knee injury meant he couldn't stay fit enough to play regularly. The work in attack was taken on by Jim Storrie, bought from Airdrie in 1962, who was the top scorer in the season before promotion, 1962-63, then in the First Division in 1964-65 and jointly with Lorimer in 1965-66, when he too began to struggle with injuries. Youngster Jimmy Greenhoff moved from midfield to take his place and Revie hoped winger Mike O'Grady, bought from Huddersfield Town, would supply the crosses for him to finish, but in 1966-67, Greenhoff only scored seven. Lorimer didn't do much better, scoring nine, and Giles was top scorer with 12. In fact, going back to 1961-62, the only player to score more than 13 in a season was Jim Storrie, twice.

Leeds United were a great team, but they didn't have a great striker, and without one, they hadn't developed a great attacking urge. On the three-season rolling tally, Manchester United had 257 goals and Leeds just 224. A single Greenhoff goal in the opening three games of 1967-68 spurred Revie into his least favoured arena — the transfer market — but he returned from Sheffield United with a striker he'd researched well: Mick Jones. He was not instantly prolific: he injured his ankle and only scored eight that season. But he was a player the team could aim at with the idea that they might score. He only managed half of his third league match before going off injured, at home against Chelsea, but there was a change: six different Leeds scorers and an own goal in a 7-0 win crowned by Bremner's acrobatic overhead kick. It was United's biggest league victory since 1961 and soon there were back-to-back 5-0 wins, over Fulham and Southampton, and at the end of the season, a League Cup won against Arsenal at Wembley, before a Jones goal was the difference in a 1-0 aggregate victory over Ferencváros in August that won the Fairs Cup.

As important as Jones' arrival was the promotion of Terry Cooper in place of Willie Bell. A left-winger converted to left-back, he was soon regarded as the best attacking full-back in the world, combining with the emerging teenage brilliance of winger Eddie Gray, who took over from Johanneson. But in the league, they had only finished fourth again, and the emphasis in the rest of the First Division was now on defending, not scoring: Leeds only conceded 41, but Liverpool and Everton both bettered that by letting in just 40 each.

Revie doubled down on their strengths in 1968-69 by selling Jimmy Greenhoff to Birmingham City and letting Jones attack on his own, with service from Gray and O'Grady; Lorimer was restricted to a bit part, and Madeley brought a defensive mind to midfield. It worked. Leeds were unbeatable at home, winning 18 and drawing three, scoring 41 and conceding just nine. There were only two defeats on the road, but it was fitting that the title was secured at Anfield by a 0-0 draw, to follow one six days before at Goodison Park. Those were United's fifth and sixth scoreless away draws from a total of ten; the other four were 1-1. Liverpool's defence was actually two goals meaner, but Leeds outscored them by three, and only Everton and Chelsea scored more. Leeds, as the Liverpool Kop sang to them, were not only worthy champions, but the best there had ever been: more points, more wins and fewer defeats than any previous First Division winners.

The contradiction that drove Leeds United forward, something that seemed to be imposed by the character of the city, was that it not enough merely to win. Many a Leeds schoolkid knew the feeling of bringing their glowing report home, and being asked, what did they think that made them? Special or something? Leeds had won their first silverware, the League Cup, but after another semi-final defeat in 1968, the prestigious FA Cup still eluded them. And they'd won the First Division, but that ought to have been theirs in any of the previous five seasons. It was about time, that was all. Their record compared to Manchester United now stood at 120 wins to 107, 39 defeats to 47. Manchester United led in goals scored by 42, but Leeds had the better defence by 52. One title was the least they should have won. Manchester United had two, and could argue that the true mark of greatness was winning it again. And they had also won the European Cup, the trophy that defined the club Revie modelled his team upon, Real Madrid.

The sense of urgency had not gone away, nor the sense of doubt with which the city of Leeds imperiled its soccer team. Revie wanted to write Leeds United's name in history and test the limits of what the city would actually deem good enough. And while Gray might only have been approaching 22, Charlton was 34 and still ferociously ambitious, raging against the wasted years he'd spent in Division Two. He had come of age in the 1950s, the era of the Cold War, the atomic bomb, the four-minute warning; he was haunted by the senseless loss of his brother Bobby's Manchester United teammates in the Munich air disaster in 1958. Those players had been Jack's friends, too; they had everything still to win, and it was all taken away in one night. You couldn't hang around. Giles was about to turn 29 and even Bremner was fast approaching 27. Revie had taken charge of Leeds in March 1961, and it felt like they'd waited all of the 1960s for their chance of success. Now all their chances were coming at once, just when time was running out, and who knew when Leeds would have this chance again?

Revie's mind was clear. Leeds began 1969-70 by winning the Charity Shield, beating Manchester City 2-1 at Elland Road. That was one trophy. They would win the First Division again, like Manchester United. Many teams had won the title, but few had retained it. They would win the FA Cup, like all the best teams had to. They would win the European Cup to emulate the great Real Madrid. And then they would do something no team had done before. There was talk that FIFA were talking control of the increasingly violent Intercontinental

Cup matches between the winners of the European Cup and the Copa Libertadores, and would be expanding them into a 'club world cup' tournament including the champions of every continent. If Leeds won the European Cup, they would enter, and make themselves the first FIFA champions of the world.

Leeds made a declaration of intent by strengthening their attack with Allan Clarke, bought from Leicester for a British record £165,000, a year after he'd joined them from Fulham for a British record £150,000. The pundit Jimmy Hill wasn't happy: under the transfer regulations, Clarke had the right to £13,800 from the two moves, and given both Fulham and Leicester were relegated with Clarke in their team, Hill thought he was being overpaid already. He also saw trouble ahead for Clarke at Leeds. "Thank goodness, success demands more than just talent," he wrote, in the *News of the World*. "Matches are won by blending unselfishly the skills and energies of 11 human beings to one end. That is a lesson Clarke has yet to learn." Hill wasn't finished there. "To Allan Clarke, I can only say: 'Football is a team game. You won't half be worth some money if you ever get that into your noddle box.'"

Revie was a manager with a perceptive eye for the contents of noddle boxes, and that insight settled a preoccupying selection dilemma of previous seasons; he threw his lot in with Lorimer for the right wing and recouped £80,000 by selling Mike O'Grady to Wolves. Among the deciding factors were that O'Grady had been bought from Huddersfield aged 23, whereas Lorimer had grown up at Leeds from a boy of 15; there was no steady girlfriend for O'Grady, either, which Revie felt could prevent a player from concentrating on his football. Third, he complained too much when he was out of the team. O'Grady had helped win the league with 38 games and eight goals the previous season, and his sale was perhaps a sign to the likes of Clarke that nobody would be too big for a team in which every first team player was an international. To underline the point to his new signing, he was made to room with Bremner, author of the club's 'side before self, every time' philosophy, and Clarke's ego was soon buried beneath the weight of an immediate and lasting friendship.

Revie's new team was complete: Gary Sprake in goal, Paul Reaney and Terry Cooper the full-backs, Jack Charlton and Norman Hunter in defence, Billy Bremner and John Giles in midfield, Peter Lorimer and Eddie Gray on the wings, Allan Clarke and Mick Jones up front. Usually Paul Madeley would be wearing the shirt of one of them. The only drawback was age — Clarke was 27, the same as Bremner — and, therefore, their only enemy was time.

They attacked their foe time as if they meant to live forever. Their European Cup campaign started against Lyn Oslo, who were beaten 10-0 at home and 6-0 away. Ferencváros were beaten next, 3-0 and 3-0, then Standard Liège, 1-0 and 1-0. Leeds were in the semi-finals, facing Celtic, without conceding a goal.

It took a little longer to gel in the First Division. The season was being compressed due to the World Cup in Mexico; domestic football was to be over by mid-April to give Alf Ramsey's England time to prepare the defence of their trophy. That meant seven games in August, and Leeds only won two, drawing four and losing 3-2 away to Everton. But they only lost one more game between August and March 28, winning 18 of 29 matches, gaining a one-point lead over Everton at the top with seven games to go. They'd reached the semi-final of the FA Cup, too. Revie had told the players he wanted the league, FA Cup and European Cup treble, and such was his influence, they not only believed they could do it, but that they were about to make it happen.

The FA Cup semi-final was, again, where their plans started to come unstuck. This time, Leeds won, beating Manchester United. But the original match, on March 14, finished 0-0, and so did the replay on March 23, after extra time. The second replay, on the 26th, was settled by a Billy Bremner goal, but it came at a cost of injuries and tiredness at Bolton's muddy Burden Park. Two days later, at home to Southampton, Leeds were without Reaney, Bremner, Hunter, Giles, Cooper and Jones; they led through a Lorimer goal with 20 minutes left, but collapsed to lose 3-1. Everton now had a five-point lead in the First Division, and Revie had to make a decision to save United's season. The next league game was in two days, and there were four to come after that, plus the FA Cup final and the two-legged European Cup semi-final, all in less than three weeks. The FA and Football League refused to move any fixtures, and Revie claimed a doctor's report made his mind up for him: citing medical advice that his players were close to exhaustion, he sent 11 reserves to play Brian Clough's Derby County, where they lost 4-1. The fight for the league title was over; the only fight left was with the authorities, who fined Leeds £5,000.

Matters quickly got worse. A league game at West Ham had to be played the day after the first leg of the European Cup semi-final against Celtic at Elland Road. Bowing to the league's opinion that his doctors' opinions didn't matter, Revie took a number of first picks from Glasgow to Upton Park: nine of the starters had played the night before, and Paul Reaney, with horrifying predictability, broke his leg, ruling him out of the rest of the season, and England's World Cup squad. Almost without mercy, the FA caused another fight by choosing Paul Madeley to replace him. Madeley turned his country down, claiming he was already too tired from the season he was having to contemplate Mexico at the end of it. He was on course for 59 games for Leeds that season.

By letting the league go, Revie had hoped to focus on the FA Cup that had eluded Leeds so far, and the European Cup that was his dream. To win the first, they only had to beat Chelsea at Wembley, between the two legs of the semi-finals of the second, against Celtic, that would decide who played Feyenoord or Legia Warsaw in the final. Leeds would have preferred the draw to give them Celtic in the final, not only because of the number of Scots at Elland Road who would relish the match, many of them Celtic fans, but because their own scouting reports estimated Celtic were the best team Leeds had ever played in Europe.

The first leg proved that report. "Whoever it was in the Leeds United jerseys that Celtic beat 1-0 at Elland Road," wrote the *Yorkshire Evening Post*'s reporter, "it was not Leeds United". Celtic had scored after a minute, and Leeds were confused all night by their winger, Jimmy Johnstone. Bremner was confused on the hour mark when he banged his head on Elland Road's hard ground; in his concussion, it took ten minutes to get him to leave the field, and after the match he went wandering, still dazed, into Celtic's dressing room, looking for his taxi home.

Revie hoped that going to Hampden Park as FA Cup winners would give them a second leg advantage, but despite a superb performance by Eddie Gray, tormenting Chelsea right-back David Webb on what little grass Wembley had to offer after hosting the Horse of the Year show, Jack Charlton's header was cancelled out before half-time when Sprake let Peter Houseman's soft shot under his body. Jones' late goal in a second half Leeds dominated wasn't enough either, as Charlton let Ian Hutchinson get ahead of him to head a free-kick past Sprake with just minutes left. Extra time couldn't separate them, and four days later Leeds went to Glasgow not elated, but knackered.

For a moment, Billy Bremner silenced all but the 4,500 from Leeds in the 136,505 crowd at Hampden Park, when his shot hit the top corner to equalise the aggregate score. But that was as close as Leeds got. Johnstone was again unplayable and even unkickable; Sprake was injured and had to go off; Celtic had a 3-1 aggregate lead before the hour. A frantic last 30 minutes couldn't produce a goal for Leeds.

Leeds United were in a daze. They finally had a break of sorts — two weeks until the FA Cup final replay at Old Trafford — but there were still two league matches to get through in that time, and no respite. In the last home match of the season, Revie played Bremner, Lorimer, Clarke, Gray, Cooper and Bates; and new signing John Faulkner, earmarked as a replacement for Charlton, who suffered a fractured kneecap. Leeds lost 3-1, and the local press were not generous. Revie was on record saying it was up to home teams to entertain: "United should have pulled themselves together and put on a show," wrote the *Yorkshire Evening Post*'s reporter, "I suggest they practice what they preach." There had, in any case, only been 22,932 there to entertain, a far cry from the 46,000 who had watched them beat Everton in December.

The players sounded sick of everything. Revie had all but replaced training with rest, putting his good relationship with the players' wives to use by calling on them to 'coddle' his men as much as possible. Even so, Charlton made the news when he spent an hour chasing his family's runaway puppy, Corrie, around the streets near his home in Halton. In his newspaper column, he said he was so sick and tired of soccer he didn't even want to get two straws and a ping-pong ball to play 'blow football' with his children. But he and Bremner were still determined to get if not their due, then at least something from the season. "If we fail to beat them this time, we will feel cheated," said Charlton. "We simply can't miss out on some silver this season," said Bremner. "We've worked too hard to fail now."

The story of the FA Cup final replay is well known, but mostly thanks to its retelling by Chelsea's Ron 'Chopper' Harris. His boast that he stopped Gray from repeating his Wembley brilliance with a foul in the first five minutes is overblown: Harris tried, but it was nearly half-time before he could catch Gray, hitting him high behind the knee with a scything tackle calculated to injure. Gray played on, stepping inside to let Cooper carry the attacks down the wing from left-back.

By that time, Leeds were a goal up, Mick Jones scoring a brilliant effort after 35 minutes, swerving out of midfield with the ball, beating two and shooting past Bonetti into the top corner. But with referee Eric Jennings happy to let the players sort things out for themselves, that sorting out became increasingly violent, and not just towards Gray. Peter Osgood headed an equaliser with 12 minutes left, then Bremner was denied two penalties — one for a flying kick to his head by Eddie McCreadie — and that meant extra time.

"I thought we were going to win right up to when Chelsea equalised," said Bremner later. "As soon as they scored, I knew we weren't." The player Gray had run rings around at Wembley, David Webb, scored the winner, heading in from a long throw, and although the FA had set a date for another replay, an equaliser was beyond Leeds. They had come closer to an incredible feat than any other team before them, setting out for a treble nobody else would have contemplated, let alone tried for. Sixty-three games later, they were second in the league, semi-finalists in the European Cup, second in the FA Cup final. "But not one piece of silver to show for it," said Bremner. "And that's what counts."

Charlton had never been hurt more by a defeat and went straight to the changing rooms, blaming himself for mistakes in the two games. Other Leeds players swapped shirts with Chelsea's, and that meant one final twisted laugh at Leeds' expense amid the confusion of Old Trafford's trophy presentation. When Chelsea went to collect the cup in the losers' white shirts, at first, the dignitaries thought they were Leeds, and refused to hand it over.

Dignitaries showed little patience with Revie and his players. The Lord Mayor of Leeds had arranged a civic reception for the team, win lose or draw, but the exhausting manner of defeat brought only apologies from Revie. Four players and Les Cocker had already gone to meet up with England, two others were on holiday, Reaney's leg was in plaster, the rest were too miserable to toast their defeat in public: as politely as he could, Revie withdrew. Lord Mayor John Rafferty was livid.

The front page of the *Yorkshire Evening Post* didn't carry a tribute to the team's achievements, but a broadside from the Mayor. "Their decision is not only rude, but chickenhearted," he said. "They promised to come, win or lose, and they have let everybody down ... they have failed themselves and their proud record by behaving in a way that savours of a petulant boy taking his bat home." Aside from the snub, the main complaint was the large order of sandwiches and pork pies that now had to be cancelled, the arrangements for all the civic plate and cutlery to be brought out that had to be reversed. Public opinion took the Mayor's side: Revie made another public apology, but letters to the paper said his choice was "an insult" to the city and "a shocking display of bad sportsmanship".

Of those 63 league and cup games, Leeds lost only ten, and four of those involved the weakened 'shadow' teams that played at the end of the league season; one was in the League Cup, the only cup Leeds hadn't been anxious to win; they lost in the third round, inevitably to Chelsea, inevitably only after a replay. Thirty-three games were won. In a normal season, not compressed into an April finish to help the England team, Leeds just might have turned that First Division lead, the FA Cup final and a European Cup semi-final into an unmatchable treble, surely the greatest single-season achievement of any club side. That's how it had looked in the middle of March. Six weeks later, they were back to being Leeds United again. The losers.

NETHERLANDS 1974

ADAM BUSHBY

The Westfalenstadion, Dortmund. July 3 1974. The Netherlands vs Brazil. A World Cup semi-final in all but name, given the new format had rendered such a thing obsolete. At least until 1982 that is, as knockout games were replaced with a second round of two four-team groups, the winners progressing to the final. No matter. It was a glorious goal apiece from Johans Neeskens and Cruyff in this de facto 'winner-stays-in' semi-final that got me hooked on the Netherlands side that travelled to West Germany, nine years before I was born.

Speaking of obsolescence, it was a grainy VHS box set bought from a sprawling car boot sale at Rufforth near York that would capture the imagination of my nine-year-old self. I'd become well-versed at sifting through the piles of rubbish to find the treasure. There was beauty to be found amid the junk. And so it was that *The Best of the World Cup 1954-1974* took pride of place on my bookshelf next to my copies of *The Boys from Brazil*, *101 Classic Goals of the World Cup* and *Danny Baker's Own Goals and Gaffs* — granted, not every purchase could be a gem. Pre-internet, my VHS player was my time machine.

In 1974, reigning champions Brazil had replaced beauty with brutality; Jairzinho and Rivelino were all that remained of a side that, just four years earlier, could also boast Pelé, Gerson, Tostão, Clodoaldo and Carlos Alberto. Beauty was a word synonymous with their opponents though. For one fabled summer, there was pure, unadulterated beauty.

By the time the game rolled around, the gulf in class between the two sides was notable. Desperate to reduce the obvious disparity between incumbent and challenger, the game became a war of attrition. After the Thriller in Manila and the Rumble in the Jungle, it's perhaps fortuitous that nothing rhymes with Dortmund. There were two-footed tackles. Off-the-ball smitings. Rugby tackles. Punches were exchanged. Indeed, Neeskens was knocked out cold by the elbow of Marinho Peres, who would become his teammate at Barcelona after the tournament.

But amid the cynicism, there was also splendour. Neeskens beautifully floated Cruyff's perfect centre over Émerson Leão shortly after half-time then Cruyff's controlled flying volley made it 2-0 and Brazil's fate was sealed. Luis Pereira saw red in the dying minutes for a vicious hack on Neeskens, but by this point, the jig had long been up.

After defeating Brazil, the air of invincibility that had been growing since a 2-0 win over Uruguay engulfed the entire squad. They had comprehensively beaten the reigning champions. The late, great Hugh McIlvanney ends his preview of the final for *The Observer* by describing a crown that belongs to the Netherlands as a matter of right. All that stood between the Dutch and the World Cup was the hosts. An irrelevance after beating the Brazilians, surely …

The Olympiastadion, Munich. The Netherlands vs West Germany. July 7 1974. A coronation in all but name. Considering we are talking about a World Cup final, it is perhaps the most astonishing first minute of a game ever. From Cruyff nudging the ball to Wim van Hanegem from the kick-off, to Wim Rijsbergen feeding it to Cruyff, who sets off at first languidly and then darts off towards the German box, there are 16 passes. Sixteen passes before Uli Hoeness upends Cruyff on the edge of the box … nonetheless, Jack Taylor points to the spot. Neeskens steps up and casually makes it 1-0. After 80 seconds, the first German to touch the ball is Sepp Maier, the goalkeeper. And when Cruyff picks up the ball before wheeling away from Bertie Vogts, remarkably he is the man nearest to Dutch goalkeeper Jan Jongbloed.

Vogts, who is man-marking Cruyff in an echo of a youth team game featuring the two, is then shown a yellow card in the fourth minute. This is going to be embarrassing for the Germans. Very embarrassing indeed … except, it isn't, is it. Because this is the Netherlands. And we have the beauty of hindsight on our side. We know that the Netherlands will go on to lose this final. And another four years later. And a third in 2010. Three World Cup finals, three defeats. The Olympiastadion. July 7 1974; in a way, everything subsequent was a repetition of it.

In stark contrast to the proud footballing nation we see today, the early experiences of the Netherlands on the international stage weren't just underwhelming, they were almost non-existent. They hadn't done anything on the world stage until 1974, failing to qualify for every World Cup since 1938 and not reaching the European Championships in Belgium in 1972 either. But their pedigree was improving. Extraordinarily, the European Cup didn't leave the Netherlands between 1970 and 1973, with a Feyenoord win over Celtic in '70 succeeded by three Ajax wins on the trot.

One could argue that Ajax sticking five past Bill Shankly's first great Liverpool side in 1966 sounded an early warning that the Dutch were starting to stir. By 1974, however, this had been largely forgotten. Sticking four past Bayern Munich in 1973 hadn't though. In fact, this result is far more instructive to what would follow in West Germany in the summer of '74, bearing in mind that six players from both sides that night would play in the final.

Not so well known to a contemporary audience is the door-sliding moment in Amsterdam in November 1973, whereby the Netherlands didn't qualify for the '74 World Cup. Belgian striker Jan Verheyen had a perfectly good goal ruled out for offside in the dying seconds of the crucial final qualifying match. If the flag stays down, Belgium win 1-0 and take the Netherlands' place at the finals. No Total Football. No Cruyff turn. No hipster chic. But the door remained shut. The game finished 0-0 the Dutch qualified on goal difference and breathed a collective sigh of relief, echoing all the way to

Antwerp, where they had been held the first time by the Belgians in November 1972.

Rinus Michels had taken the reins of the Dutch national side just three months before the '74 World Cup began. Although Michels would depart Ajax for Barcelona in 1971 after the first of three successive European Cup wins, it was essentially his Ajax side that won the next two and formed the basis of the national team he took to West Germany.

For a country where space is at such a premium, it is perhaps little surprise that reconfiguring it became central to Michels' philosophy. Positions became interchangeable, while pressing and a liberal use of the offside trap were the side's key weapons.

Arie Haan perfectly encapsulates the essence of Total Football: "People talk of Total Football as if it is a system, something to replace 4-2-4 or 4-3-3. It is not a system. As it is at any moment, so you play." That is not to say that Cruyff was not the central figure, the lodestar around which everything turns. More than this, it was the intelligence of the football that struck the opposition dumb.

Haan was a midfielder by trade, but playing to type wasn't something that concerned Michels. The titan of a centre-back, Ajax's Barry Hulshoff, was ruled out of the tournament with a serious knee injury. Schooled in the ways of Ajax and at 27 years of age, Hulshoff would have been a sure starter in West Germany. The Dutch wouldn't miss him until the final. Hulshoff's club teammate Haan would be turned into a libero alongside Feyenoord's Wim Rijsbergen as the first generation of Dutch ball-playing centre-backs had their heyday, flanked by Ruud Krol and Wim Suurbier.

The use of the word 'intensity' to describe pressing football may be second nature to a modern sensibility. However, in this regard, the Dutch were streets ahead. Speaking to McIlvanney after Argentina's 4-0 group match defeat to the Netherlands, the veteran Argentine defender Roberto Perfumo remarked: "I received the ball from a short free-kick, I looked up and there were seven Dutch players running at me. It was unnerving."

At the centre of the maelstrom was Cruyff. He was a player who "represented an almost pathological case of self-confidence," Jorge Valdano recollected. "Never in my life have I seen a player rule games like him. He was the owner of the show. He was a player, coach and referee at the same time." The iconoclastic Cruyff would both decorate games and dominate them. Like the very best players, he appeared to be playing a different sport to everyone else.

The esteemed Brian Glanville recalled with relish a press reception at the Dutch training base in the summer of '74 where Cruyff "dealt effortlessly" with a posse of reporters, conversing in Dutch, English, German, Spanish and Italian. McIlvanney, meanwhile, remembered a journalist from Rio de Janeiro stating: "In culture, [the Dutch] are 100 years ahead of our players," before dismissing most Brazilian players as "barely literate". It was all part of the broader appeal. A team comprising numerous polyglots, looking like rock stars and playing like higher beings. Who wouldn't be seduced? The footballing world was enchanted.

The moment that best encapsulates what is at once so beautiful and so flawed about the Dutch side of '74 is the most famous of moves, showcased on the global stage against Sweden by the side's talisman. As Scott Murray wrote for *The Guardian*: "The Cruyff turn didn't actually lead to anything. At all. Certainly nothing so crass as a goal." It was, as Murray so deftly puts it, "art for art's sake".

The Cruyff turn would become the enduring symbol of Total Football. A player with a ballet dancer's poise doing something otherworldly. Jan Olsson, the unfortunate full-back to whom Cruyff sold the mother of all dummies, represents every side that the Netherlands came up against that summer — totally and utterly bamboozled. Every opponent bar one, that is; the one that mattered.

Apart from the goalless draw with Sweden, which the Dutch had dominated and showcased the Cruyff turn to a global audience, Michels' side had scored at least two in every game in Germany. A 2-0 win against Uruguay and a 4-1 trouncing of Bulgaria bookended the stalemate.

They then won their three second group stage games by a ridiculous aggregate of 8-0 and it was at this stage that this Dutch team came into their own. They played some delicious football in the 4-0 rout of Argentina, fretting and pressing and producing delightful phases of attacking play. When Krol lashed home the second goal in the 25th minute, David Coleman, commentating for the BBC, corrected himself when remarking the ball had fallen to a defender: "I'm not sure that you can particularise on this Dutch side. They're all defenders and attackers at the right moment."

In the iconic 2-0 defeat of Brazil, the Dutch showed a different side. In a game that more often than not resembled a street fight, the Dutch proved they could hold their own. This was a team that could forgo the scalpel for a sledgehammer when necessary. The world readied itself for a new order.

Nearly 600 minutes had passed before the Dutch went behind in a game at the '74 World Cup. It just so happened to be in the final and just like that, the deeply ingrained feelings of invincibility vanished, wiped away like chalk from a blackboard. "Who breaks a butterfly upon a wheel?" pondered Alexander Pope. Turns out we only had to wait 240 years to find out.

To that point, the Netherlands had played with a verve that made them the most thrilling national side on the planet. In the words of McIlvanney, they had "an attacking style at once so spirited and so cuttingly precise that the effect is of a cavalry charge of surgeons". The day before the final, he wrote: "The normal flutter of nerves is likely to be tranquilised by a deep conviction that they have the talent, the courage and the collective maturity to lay emphatic hold on the championship."

McIlvanney, however, foresaw the danger. "For some of us, those echoes of events that took place so many seasons ago tend to form ice cubes in the blood." He was referencing the fate of the mighty Magyars, who fell at the end of German boots some 20 years previously in the so-called Miracle of Bern. History may well be "bent on callous repetition," he cautioned, with the clarity of a prophet.

The opening minute of the match reinforced all of the Netherlands' feelings of superiority. They would go on to lose the final, however, because after Neeskens' penalty, they thought they had already won it. The Germans are so adept at deriving pleasure from another's misfortune, they created a word for it. "Harmjoy" doesn't quite have the same ring to it, does it?

Keeping Cruyff quiet was central to the German's plan for the final. Vogts had established a reputation as a world-class man marker. As celebrated German football writer Uli Hesse explained to me: "Vogts' rather ill-fated coaching career has made many people forget how popular he was as a player. When I was a kid, there was a saying that 'people respect Beckenbauer, but they love Vogts."

Barring the first minute of the game, Vogts' job on Cruyff is all the more impressive given the disastrous final training session where Günter Netzer was tasked with copying Cruyff and Vogts couldn't contain him. Quite why the Germans didn't call on the considerable services of a player who closely resembled Cruyff for the final remains a story in and of itself.

Legend has it that after going a goal up, the Netherlands spend the next 20 minutes toying with the Germans like a kitten with a ball of yarn; thumbing their collective noses to the hosts, minus Cruyff, who couldn't find his way out of Vogts' pocket. For *World Soccer*, Glanville wrote: "It should have been the beginning of a profusion of goals, but instead the Dutch seemed content to roll the ball about in pretty patterns." It was discomfiting. And it would prove fatal.

To expect their gossamer grip on the lead to last for 89 minutes simply by playing keep-ball was fanciful. This was a West Germany side of Franz Beckenbauer, Wolfgang Overath, Maier and Paul Breitner, after all. And in Gerd Müller, it also included the most dangerous striker in the box at the World Cup — or indeed at any World Cup.

Their reticence to land the killer blow is unfathomable. Glanville would write: "the Dutch were tempted to relax, moved to play cat-and-mouse with an opponent which, for historical reasons, they longed to humiliate." For Beckenbauer: "Going a goal down was good for us. The Dutch eased off and we were able to get into the match. And once you've relaxed your grip, it's hard to recover the initiative."

Chekhov's dramatic principle of the gun rests on the premise that anything of no relevance to the story is removed. There is no avoiding the fact that the Netherlands' fingerprints were all over the gun — they entered the final with the clarity and the swagger of winners. German winger Bernd Hölzenbein would later recollect that "in the tunnel, we planned to look them in the eye, to show we were as big as they were. They had the feeling they were invincible – you could see it in their eyes. Their attitude to us was: 'How many goals do you want to lose by today, boys?' While we waited to go on to the pitch, I tried to look them in the eye, but I couldn't do it. They made us feel small."

But drama loves a fatal flaw. There's an almost casual familiarity with the way in which the Dutch calmly knock it about in the opening stages. As if being one-nil up in a World Cup final is the natural state of things. As far as bedfellows go, self-indulgence and success are rarely compatible.

Having been introduced to proceedings, it was only a matter of time before the gun went off. Awoken from their initial stupor, the Germans drew level through a Breitner penalty after Hölzenbein dives over/is brought down by (delete as applicable) Wim Jansen's leg. Bang. Müller's winner is either a scuffed excuse for a finish or a masterful example of balance and poaching, depending on your sensibilities. Bang.

The Germans survived the Dutch onslaught on their goal in the second half. Johnny Rep could, nay should, have bagged a brace. By the closing minutes, with the score still 2-1 to Germany, incredibly, the Dutch have become like all the rest, lumping it aimlessly into the box. Chasing a football match — the eternal leveller. With every hoof, we see the dying embers of Total Football, floating away on the breeze. As the orange sun sets, Cruyff stands in stunned isolation, lonely as the cloud that obscures it.

There is a pervading train of thought that the Dutch's late, impotent rage in the final was due to a collective sense of injustice at crimes committed 30 years prior. The Germans were still hated in large swathes of Dutch society in 1974. Post-match, Wim van Hanegem famously sniped: "I hate them. They murdered my family. My father, my brother and several family members." Though by far the most vocal of the Dutch travelling party on the subject, Van Hanegem was not alone. "We wanted to make fun of the Germans," Johnny Rep recalled. "We may have not consciously thought about it, but we did it. We kept passing the ball around, passing the ball around. We forgot to score the second goal."

A World Cup final is probably a less than ideal place to attempt to settle historical scores, much less avenge brutal occupation during a world war. However, for many Dutch people, World War II was still alive, and the final felt like the perfect means to exact revenge; "Crazy, but understandable," states renowned Dutch football writer Frits Barend.

There was something of the resistance in how the Dutch dealt with contemporary Germany. As Barend puts it: "If a German asked you the way to the Ajax stadium, you sent him to the Olympic Stadium, at the other side of Amsterdam." The siren song of humiliating the Germans proved to be too alluring a proposition to resist. The weight of history would become the Netherlands' albatross.

Time can only do so much healing, however. Thirty years after the final, at a panel meeting in Rotterdam in 2004 moderated by Simon Kuper, Rep and Hölzenbein are grilled about that day in Munich. Rep says "They should give us our bikes back", referring to the greatest bike theft in history during the Second World War.

Cruyff's biographer Jaap de Groot likened the 'Lost Final' to the assassination of JFK: "Everybody knows what they were doing and where they were when the final whistle blew." For any unexpected event of any magnitude, there comes an inevitable post-mortem. The autopsy of the Lost Final would be a noisy ritual, siring a raft of origin myths. Conspiracies feed the narrative and, ultimately, the legend. And like any good conspiracy, the infamous swimming pool story that appeared in a German tabloid the day before the final divides opinion still. But every great story involves a few question marks. Every conspiracy needs its grassy knoll.

Michels treated the players like adults at a time when others, namely the Brazilians, were locked away in camp, infantalised. "In general, Michels was not as hands-on as at Ajax before: some players have told me they were surprised that the famously 'harsh' Michels was so easy-going," Dutch author Auke Kok asserts.

If only there had been a happy medium. Writing for *Football Paradise*, Srijandeep Das explains in his prelude to interviewing acclaimed author of *Brilliant Orange* David Winner that while "some called it exaggeration, others in the team called it lies. No one's account is consistent, and no one by their own admission was a participant. It must have been someone else". Rep and Krol deny the accusations flat out. Rene van de Kerkhof has called it a "good party", with a twinkle in his eye.

"They were living like rock stars," Winner then exclaims, "there were girls, there was drinking, and Michels even popped over to Spain for the Spanish Cup final during the tournament". To a contemporary audience, this seems absurd. Barend, however, dismissed the swimming pool story to me as a "*Bild* affair, directed and organised by the paper".

In his myth-busting book, ironically titled *1974: We Were The Best*, Kok paints a different picture, one that shattered the myth that the Dutch had been victims of an elaborate sting. "After the 2-0 victory over East Germany, Holland was sure they had reached the last four, which was a huge success already," Kok explained to me. "So a big party was thrown, with a famous pop group flown in at Hiltrup (The Cats), lots of German champagne flowed. Late in the evening, Cruyff was angry at the son of the hotel owner, who had taken a picture of him with a few German women. Cruyff, of course, feared the anger of his wife and wanted the picture to be destroyed, which happened.

"About four in the morning, they all went to the pool in the basement, including a few German girl friends of the owner's son. They swam naked, some flirting, but nothing serious happened. A German undercover journalist was also there in the pool and he sold his story to *Bild* for 400 Deutsche marks.

"I spoke with many people who participated, among them the hotel owner's son and the German journalist," states Kok. "The *Bild* story was correct, but Michels and Cruyff changed it into a German *hetze* [hustle] to demoralise the Dutch, in case they would meet the Germans in the final."

Hesse explains that "even in Germany, there is this myth that the *Bild* tabloid essentially set a trap for the Dutch players".

"However," he adds "it was a writer for a newspaper from Stuttgart who broke the story. True, he was staying at the Dutch team's hotel without telling anyone he was a journalist, but for all we know he crashed that swimming pool party by pure accident. Bild then did little more than publish an interview with him. It was only because the tabloid had a much bigger circulation that the Stuttgart paper that everybody thinks this was a *Bild* story."

"In any case, after the story broke, the Dutch went on to dismantle Brazil, so they can't have been too shaken," Hesse adds. We only talk of the pool party now because the Netherlands didn't win the final. It adds an extra layer of intrigue to an already irresistible story. In truth, Dutch discipline had gone. We all know that pride comes before a fall. And when we are talking about an Olympic pool size amount of pride, well, that's a fall that will make waves.

There are some football rivalries that transcend the 90 minutes on the pitch and instead become knitted into the fabric of the societies they inhabit. After the Lost Final in 1974, a myth perpetuated that the Germans had 'tricked' the Dutch, "like the making up of the swimming incident and the diving of Hölzenbein," says Kok. It was "as if the unbeatable Dutch team would never have lost under normal circumstances". It is a version of events designed to make the defeat more palatable. Why admit to arrogance or complacency when you can blame the Germans?

There had been no tricks. Kok declares that it was "easy for me to show my patriots that Germany was denied both a clear goal (by Müller) and a second penalty (Jansen hacked down Hölzenbein) in the second half. So no one could say that Germany was not the rightful winner of the final".

The passage of time and the advent of YouTube has meant that the final is ripe for revisionism. Although just a boy at the time, Hesse remembers watching the game at his grandparents' flat. "That, however, is all that I can recall. What I do know, though, is that almost everybody greatly admired the Dutch."

I put it to Hesse that there was a prominent opinion for many years, at least here in England and certainly in the Netherlands, that the Dutch were cheated and were unlucky to lose after peppering the German goal; however, when you revisit the match, it didn't play out like that. He concurs: "It's funny that you say that, because I had the same impression when I re-watched the final many years later. As a German football fan, I had grown up with the knowledge that the Dutch were the best team at the tournament and were very unlucky to lose the final."

"A prominent exception was Paul Breiter," Hesse tells me, "who said that the best team at the tournament were Poland". He adds: "The more I look at the footage, the more it seems that Hoeness brought down Cruyff just outside the box, while Jansen *did* make contact with Hölzenbein's foot."

It's perhaps easy to give credence to the false dichotomy that West Germany and the Netherlands were footballing opposites – the Germans were not merely the antithesis of the Dutch. But, although West Germany deservedly got their hands on the new version of the World Cup trophy, the Netherlands seized a prize arguably far more precious, touching down at Schiphol Airport as heroes after winning the hearts of purists everywhere.

There's something terribly *passé* about being the best team in the tournament and winning at a canter, anyway. Much too obvious. This

Netherlands side took accepted wisdom of what a football team could be up until that point and pulverised it. And in the bargain, they forgot the old adage that the perfect shouldn't be the enemy of the good.

As Barry Davies told me, with the Dutch, there was always the feeling that "they had to beat themselves before they beat the opposition". This may have become a mindset that was nourished and blossomed in later tournaments, twice more beaten finalists and twice stumbling at the semi-final stage, but it took root in West Germany. Despite being head and shoulders above the rest in '74, they couldn't get out of their own way.

Over the space of four weeks, the Netherlands brought a frenzied energy to West Germany. The narrative belonged to the Dutch: a goalkeeper wearing number eight; Cruyff's shirt missing a third stripe on his shirt due to his refusal to wear the shirt supplied by Adidas — he had an exclusive deal with Puma; Total Football; Cruyff's turn; the pool party. The spectacle of seeing this Dutch side, in almost irreverent orange, locks flowing and hunting voraciously in packs was magnetic. They looked like a bunch of hipsters who had just casually strode out of a hashish bar in Amsterdam and onto the pitch, while their opponents were the ones looking stoned.

Olsson, he who was sent to the wrong postcode so publicly by Cruyff's audacious skill in the first group stage, never felt shame at being diddled. For him, living on as part of a footballing fossil, preserved for posterity in the reserve of the sport's, any sport's, moments of magnificence, was a privilege. "I played 18 years in top football and 17 times for Sweden but that moment against Cruyff was the proudest moment of my career." Olsson *got* it.

In six of their seven matches in the summer of 1974, the Dutch were spellbinding. "In those six matches in Germany, my country showed the most exciting football ever in Dutch history," Kok proudly states. The Dutch journalist Sjoerd Mossou expands on this point: "The 70s became a new era of freedom, art and self-confidence, personified by Cruyff and all the others. That football team, wearing their hippy haircuts and fashionable beards, was the perfect symbol of that new Dutch era." It doesn't really matter that the Netherlands fell short. It wasn't about what they did, anyway. It was the *way* they did it.

This alternate timeline — the one where the Netherlands beat West Germany and win the World Cup — doesn't work. On the surface, it might sound like an interesting counterfactual. But hand on heart, I prefer the version where the Netherlands are runners up. It's heart-rending that such a great side should fall agonisingly short, of course, but ultimately, I think we all recognise it had to play out this way. If only for the sake of the stories, like this one, that are still told today.

Cruyff was very much of the mindset that a race run well can never be lost. Beautiful. Brilliant. Original. And ultimately tragic. Why have it any other way? As the great man put it himself: "There is no medal better than being acclaimed for your style." Amen.

BRAZIL 1982

ROB LANGHAM

In the wake of Brazil's devastating 3-2 defeat against Italy in Barcelona on July 5 1982, having retreated to the dressing room amid the early evening shadows, manager Telê Santana gathered his speechless players together and told them that "the whole world has been enchanted by you. Be aware of that." A little later, he was treated to a standing ovation by a 300-strong press pack while the reception provided on arrival back in Brazil was one usually afforded to conquering heroes, a far cry from the eggs and vegetable peel that greeted them on returning from the World Cup in West Germany eight years before. Yet Brazil had lost, not even managing to reach the semi-finals. Why the adulation? Why the reverence that lives on to this day?

The Brazil of 1982 are often held up as one of the three best teams never to win a World Cup, with the Hungarians of 1954 and the Dutch of 1974 put forward as their main rivals for the accolade. In addition, the team is perhaps outstripped only by the peerless 1970 side and the 1958 vintage, complete with an emergent 17-year old Pelé, as the best the nation has had to offer. Defender Luizinho himself described subsequent sides, triumphant though they were, as having destroyed the beautiful game — o jogo bonito — with the fateful second-round match against Italy perceived as a Year Zero in the development of soccer in Brazilian terms.

Stuart Horsfield, author of *Brazil 1982: The Glorious Failure*, has remarked in a podcast from *These Football Times* that this was the greatest team ever to play the game, while Barney Ronay has stated that it is as if the players stepped out of the 1970s themselves into the bright sunlight and gorgeous colour of 1982, hailing from a time when football was about entertainment and joy, before the front-end business of winning at all costs started to choke the game. Indeed, Brazil in 1982 might be considered as the ultimate manifestation of the last major tournament of the previous decade.

It's often said that South American teams of the era were all the more beguiling because they were so unfamiliar. The Brazil squad contained only three Europe-based players in Edinho, Falcão and Dirceu, all playing in Italy, while the majority of the squad were holed up in the customary pre-tournament training camp of extended duration, away from prying eyes.

In reality though, the *Seleção* were already on the radar. A whistle-stop tour in May 1981 had seen the Brazilians emerge with three away wins from a fierce schedule against West Germany, France and England; Éder's dipping and swerving shot against the crossbar and Zico's goal were indelible memories from the game at Wembley, a glimpse of fantasy on a par with the visit of a youthful Diego Maradona in Argentinian colours to London a year before. It was immediately apparent that this was a quite different Brazil to that which had offered marginally the worse of a 1-1 draw at the same stadium in 1978.

Those two matches embody the change in attitude that took place in the country in that intervening period. In 1974, Brazil had been rotten, eliminated by the aforementioned Dutch greats in Dortmund, comprehensively out-thought and out-manoeuvred like never before. For a time, the match was cast as an illustration of how the Brazilians had fallen behind, evidence that they needed to toughen up and adopt the concepts underlying the *Oranje*'s brand of Total Football.

Enter the dour figure of Cláudio Coutinho, an army captain and ultimate roundhead. Coutinho took Brazil to the penultimate stage of the 1978 tournament and while neighbours and rivals' Argentina's 6-0 battering of Peru remains one of the most controversial games in the history of the event, Brazil showed only flashes of their usual brilliance; dull draws against Sweden and Spain in the first group stage and a forgettable shut-out against the hosts being emblematic of the new pragmatism. Coutinho's tactics seemed in-keeping with the chill of the Argentinian winter in which the competition took place.

Coutinho was to perish in a scuba-diving accident, but before that, Brazil turned to Santana, a man who had led Atlético Mineiro to their first national title a few years before. The change was immediate, with an opening 2-0 win over Mexico in 1980 showing signs of a return to the loose-limbed passing and accent on skill of the 1970s greats.

Much has been written about the way Brazilian soccer of the era mirrored the political climate of the country at the time and Coutinho's background in the armed forces wasn't the only martial element at play. A military dictatorship lasted from 1964 to 1985, heralded by the so-called 'new professionalism' of the *Escola Superior de Guerra*, an age of seriousness that saw indigenous and African-Brazilian communities sidelined, roads and dams built to alter the face of virgin rainforest for ever and economic policies implemented in a way that allowed ruling elites to consolidate power.

The gloomy Brazil of Coutinho certainly reflected this reality but the arrival of Santana, while encouraged by the regime because of the positive international image and soft power that would accompany it, did represent a gradual emergence from the slough of despond. The *anos de chumbo* ('years of lead') of dictatorship that stretched from 1968 to 1974 were long since gone; the brutality of the Argentinian and Chilean regimes, including the experiences of 'the disappeared', were not present in the late '70s and early '80s Brazil. An opening up had seen the vote reintroduced for the post of state governor alongside other olive branches to democracy activists, including an amnesty for opponents of the regime. The Brazil of these years was still venal and much of the change was brought about due to international pressure and a foreign debt of $90 billion, but as former *Placar* journalist Juca Kfouri has argued, João Figueiredo's administration was one of *abertura* or 'opening'. In football, as in society, the time was ripe for a return to more natural impulses.

Santana's Brazil raced through the qualification process for the Spanish World Cup in perfunctory but stylish fashion, presented with a series of obstacles in no way comparable with the endless ten-team group of death of modern tournaments. Faced with two of the traditionally weaker outfits on the South American continent in baseball-obsessed Venezuela and Bolivia, the Brazilians cantered to maximum points, even managing to chalk up a victory in lofty La Paz, 3,650 metres up though it is. Among the scorers across the four games were the men who would most convincingly impose themselves on our consciousness at the tournament proper, with Zico and Sócrates to the fore — Zico managed a hat-trick in the 3-1 win over the hapless Bolivians.

After a 7-0 thrashing in Uberlândia of an Éire side packed full of League of Ireland journeymen in one of the most inappropriate friendlies in international football history — the Irish FA had also considered a match against the Chile of Pinochet a viable prospect — Brazil were primed for the trip to Spain, accompanied by hordes of their yellow-shirted compatriots, the country sweltering and Brazil's three first-round matches scheduled for Seville's evocative Ramón Sánchez Pizjuán and Benito Villamarín stadia.

Midfielder Toninho Cerezo had been sent off in the qualifiers, allowing room for Paulo Roberto Falcão to squeeze into the team for the opening match against the Soviet Union. Falcão, dubbed 'the eighth King of Rome' by his adoring fans in the Italian capital, had played only sporadically for Brazil, the demands of club football making his employers reluctant to release him for far-flung internationals. Otherwise, it was close to *the* classic line-up that would face the Soviets, billed as the perennial 'dark horses' and built on the success of Georgians Dinamo Tbilisi, from which republic four of the starting XI hailed.

It was a thrilling game and balm to a 13-year old watching on, having been denied a viewing of the previous night's opening match between Argentina and Belgium due to Falklands War sensitivities. While the very best of this new Brazil was comprehensively showcased thanks to long-range strikes from Sócrates and Éder, the latter after an extraordinary dummy from Falcão, it was also a game that darkly forewarned of the weaknesses to come — lone front man Serginho looking inexpert and frankly 'un-Brazilian' in front of goal and goalkeeper Waldir Peres letting Andrei Bal's opener right through him. At the time though, it just seemed that Brazil's out-and-out excellence would overcome all barriers.

That feeling would continue in the second match against Scotland. Taking place in the smaller of the two Seville arenas, this was a Scotland team full of household names — Graeme Souness, John Robertson, Steve Archibald and Alan Hansen among them. Then, Dundee United's David Narey bent in an unlikely goal that would have satisfied any Brazilian. Nervy for a quarter of an hour, a foul on the edge of the box allowed Zico to reply with the most stupendous of free-kicks — that Scottish netminder Alan Rough stayed rooted to the spot only increased the spectacle. After that, the traffic could only ever be one way, despite the intervention of the interval, and three second-half goals provided the *Seleção* with a handsome win. Oscar's free header from a corner might have been from the playbook of opposite number Willie Miller, but Éder's deft chip and Falcão's rippling daisy-cutter after a sumptuous move were as South American as you could wish for.

New Zealand manager John Adshead remarked in an interview in advance of the final game in Group Six that he could in no way get a handle on who played where in this Brazilian team, with only striker Serginho and keeper Waldir Peres remaining unmoving. So it proved in the final group game, the Kiwis, in Spain thanks to a ludicrous 5-0 away win over Saudi Arabia in qualifying, were cannon fodder. A Zico double, including a picture-postcard volley, set the favourites on their way before Falcão and Serginho rounded things off in the second half. With New Zealand probably the worst team in the tournament, this did give the lie to the 'no easy games' adage.

The XI that emerged as Brazil's first choice in Seville and Barcelona is one of the most storied in the country's folklore, although they only played together for a sum total of four games and 20 minutes. In front of Peres, a crucial part of the mix were the full-backs — Leandro on the right, an elegant talent from Flamengo, and the sublime Júnior, dedicated to the notion of driving forward on the left, bristlingly moustachioed and nicknamed *capacete* or 'helmet' because of his afro hairstyle. He was later to be named one of the ten legends of beach soccer by *France Football*.

In central defence, Luizinho, who would go onto play 537 games for Atlético Mineiro, was one of several in this side who didn't play all that many games for the national selection, 34 in total, while Oscar, previously at New York Cosmos, strode out of defence in a manner that made Britain's nearest equivalent of the time, Alan Hansen look like a clodhopper.

In the centre of the park, it was all about rotation. The nominally defensive midfielder Cerezo would go on to a celebrated career in Europe, while Falcão would also sit relatively deep, albeit with a very unrestricted licence to roam. These two might be considered deep-lying playmakers in modern parlance, while ahead of them, the unparalleled talents of Zico and Sócrates acted as dual 'number tens'. The quartet glided like shifting sands over the surface of the lush pitches, ever rotating, ever dummying and ever creating.

The one wide player in the unit was Éder, possessor of an outlandish shot and stationed for the most part on the left while Serginho operated nearest to goal. Dirceu, a survivor from the 1978 team, filled in for the USSR match.

The column centimetres devoted to Brazil's eventual fate have been lengthy. Some have pointed to a lack of presence on the right-hand side — Antonio Cabrini took advantage of this when bending in a delicious cross for Paolo Rossi's first goal in the match for the Italians — while some commentators, including Rob Smyth and Jonathan Wilson, have tried to rehabilitate Serginho; the former in a dazzlingly written piece in *The Guardian*. That there may have been an element of hunting for the evidence for a pre-existing argument was admitted in a *Guardian Football Weekly* episode in 2020. Yes, the cumbersome striker scored a hatful in the Brazilian Championship, but it was hard to avoid seeing how badly his skill set fitted with those around him. Zico's view, in an entertaining documentary on the world's best international teams aired on YouTube and narrated by another author in this book, Patrick Barclay, perhaps summed it up in that he is damning on the talents or otherwise of both Serginho and Peres, while Cerezo is excused for the ricket that led to Rossi's second goal in Brazil's *Götterdämmerung*.

Then there is the issue of who was missing. It's often contested that Careca, as near as damn it the complete striker as Brazil again excelled four years later in the Mexican World Cup of 1986, would have made all the difference had he not suffered an injury in the run-up to the competition. But, at that point, Careca had played only four times for Brazil and was completely untested, plying his trade at modest Guarani. A more credible alternative was Reinaldo, scorer of 255 goals in 475 games for Atlético Mineiro. His non-participation is mired in rumour and counter-rumour. With his clenched fist salute indicating his pro-democracy leanings, it's said that Reinaldo may have missed out for political reasons and he himself has described Santana as a 'reactionary'. The latter cited injury, but the truth may be more prosaic — Reinaldo had underperformed at the 1978 World Cup and many considered his time as having been and gone.

Elsewhere, Brazil also left their one truly defensive midfielder Batista on the bench, from where he would become chiefly famous for being the recipient of the foul that got Maradona sent off in the first second-round game against Argentina. In reality, his talents were ordinary compared with the first XI, as were those of another substitute, Paulo Isidoro. Perhaps it's obvious to say it now in these days of mass squad rotations, but this Brazil team did not have a lot in reserve.

So to that group to end all groups, played in full at Español's tiny Sarria stadium, an open fount of the clearest sunshine, fans packed to the pitch, Italy and Argentina there because of underperformance in the group stage, that of the Italians most acute after only pipping Cameroon on goals scored. Brazil sat back as their twin opponents crossed swords in the opener — Argentina lacking ideas in the hot, late-afternoon sun, picked off by the Italians on the counter attack, the *Azzurri* showing their first signs of life fuelled by righteous anger and boss Enzo Bearzot's canny move to freeze out a hectoring press pack.

No matter for Brazil. In perhaps the most memorable of encounters between the two South American giants at world football's top table, this was arguably Brazil's most complete performance in the competition. Another incredible set piece from Éder was to cannon off the bar as the industrious Zico followed up, textbook-style to make it 1-0 after 11 minutes and from there, the *Albiceleste* had no answer, Júnior rounding things off with an iconic goal and celebration in a tournament full of them. It ended 3-1 and Brazil needed only a draw to take advantage of the vagaries of the odd three-team group format. Meanwhile, Maradona saw red.

Santana is portrayed as a purist of the beautiful game but his 1986 side had a real steel to them and the odd performance, most notably against France in the quarter-final of that World Cup, is close competition to those served up four years earlier. He would go on to manage São Paulo between 1990 and 1996, defeating Barcelona and Milan to win dual World Club Championships. In 1982, however, his players claim that he would haul anyone off who fouled or played dirty, while his omission of Batista is an indication of an adherence, at least at this stage, to all-out attack.

Vignettes from the all-time classic decider against the Italians indicate the opposing forces at play. Italy, as they proved in subsequent weeks, had moved well beyond the *catenaccio* of previous eras and were a greatly entertaining team when their tails were up, as they had been under Bearzot in 1978. Nonetheless, they were in possession of a notorious hatchet man in Claudio Gentile and as the match progressed, his repetition of the same, nakedly obvious foul on Zico would become wearing.

That said, a delightful drag-back from the Flamengo man outwitted his opponent after Rossi had opened the scoring, leading to Sócrates scoring the goal which, in John Motson's immortal phrase, summed up "the philosophy" of Brazilian football. All seemed right with the world, only for Cerezo to ignore the basic advice of every primary school PE teacher and pass across his own goal. Rossi, a forgotten man due to a ban for involvement in a match-fixing scandal, pounced again to make it 2-1.

From there, Brazil pressed and pressed, finally equalising when Falcão fired in ferociously from the edge of the box after majestic build-up play, veins popping out of his neck as he ran to submerge himself among the benchwarmers. But Brazil kept pressing and a needless corner, combined with Júnior not sticking to the basics of defending, led to Rossi scoring again.

The argument goes that this was the end point of the truest version of *o jogo bonito*. Certainly, Brazil never played with such élan again — not in 1994 and not in 2002, despite twin victories and despite featuring strikers this team would have killed for in Romário and Ronaldo. Writing with hindsight can be easy and attempts to infuse certain matches with deep historical significance can be specious — Cerezo wouldn't have tried that pass 90 times out of 100 — but with the even greater apocalypse of the 7-1 semi-final defeat against Germany in the 2014 World Cup continuing to resonate, and Brazil on the point of being offered congratulations for fielding their thousandth midfielder in the workhorse image of Dunga or Gilberto Silva, it's impossible not to look back wistfully on a side that really might have been the best ever, victory or no victory.

WEST HAM 1985-86

STUART FULLER

'What is history, but a fable agreed upon?'

The most important things are the hardest to say. That was the first line in a letter I wrote, aged 15, to Jo Smith, the object of my affection during the summer of 1985. Back then there was no email, no social network, no mobile phones — the cutting-edge medium for communication was fax. If you wanted to talk to a girl, you asked her for her number and risked having to explain to her parents why you were calling if you dared to ring. So, the safest option was to write a letter. And so I did, still not finding the right words to ask her out — but somehow it worked. First though, let's talk about football.

The record books will show that Liverpool became the first team to complete the domestic double in 15 years in May 1986 when they beat Everton not only at Wembley Stadium to lift the FA Cup, but also over the course of the season to lift the First Division trophy, as it was known back then. But the truth of the 1985-86 season goes far deeper than a two-horse race for domestic honours.

Prior to Leicester City winning the 2015-16 Premier League title having started the season as 5,000-1 outsiders, there had been few clubs outside the 'big six' who had sustained a season-long title challenge. But 20 years earlier, the title could have quite easily ended up in East London on the last Saturday of the season and created one of the most remarkable stories in English footballing history.

Let me take you on a journey back to a more innocent time 35 years ago when, as a fresh-faced young lad, I found love, lust, alcohol and a team that would go down in history as the best team never to win the title. This was the era of the legendary Liverpool side under Bob Paisley and Joe Fagan who had won seven league titles, nine domestic cups and six European trophies in a ten-year period, while across Stanley Park, Howard Kendall's Everton side had just won the league and the European Cup-Winners Cup. The English footballing world's epicentre was firmly in Merseyside.

After a few years of being able to go to West Ham without parental supervision, I was done with football. The previous campaign had seen West Ham finish 16th, avoiding relegation by two points in a torrid season, filled with crushing disappointment. Despite a promising start that saw the Hammers fourth at the end of August, they tumbled down 'like the Christmas decorations' and eventually stayed up by virtue of there being three teams that were truly awful. With the Boleyn Ground at times only a third full, the only bright point was the goals of 18-year-old Tony Cottee. And then came the footballing disasters at Valley Parade and Heysel. Football in England was broken.

West Ham manager John Lyall had been in charge for nearly a decade and his zenith had been and gone. After the FA Cup win against Arsenal in 1980 and then building on that team to waltz through the 1980-81 Second Division, taking Liverpool to a replay in the League Cup final and reaching the quarter-finals of the European Cup-Winners Cup, the club hadn't invested in the squad and the good times had departed E13. Even the mild-mannered Trevor Brooking had had enough by the end of 1983-84 season and retired. It wasn't the hope that killed me, it was the crushing reality that I'd seen West Ham's golden period before I reached puberty.

But then came the summer of 1985, when I fell in love with a blonde and a brunette, and never felt as happy in my life. Everything changed on a sunny day in early June. Days back then were spent playing football and cricket at Hartley Country Club, the oasis for the teenagers in our village. I'd do a deal every week with my elder brother for four cans of Hoffmeister, a pack of Marlboro's and copies of *Razzle* and *Fiesta*, in return for covering for him with my parents for whatever he got up to when he was supposed to be 'supervising' me.

Access to such currency made me very popular among my friends. And it was on one of those sunny days that I met brown-haired Jo, who confidently walked over to us as we sat under the shade of a tree in the club grounds and asked for a light and a look at Beverley, 37, from Hull, whose 'profile' had just been thrown into my lap by one of my friends. Naturally, I went a beetroot colour, tried to explain that it wasn't my magazine and that I had no interest in Bev's natural assets whatsoever.

"Oh it's OK. I've seen it all before. I work in the newsagents so I have a flick through them all when there's nobody in the shop. If you want me to get you some just ask".

I assumed at first she meant cigarettes, but then she suggested I get a copy of *Playboy* to "read the articles", and the penny dropped. She was the girl for me.

It took a few weeks of letter-writing in between seeing her around the village, but my charm finally won her over and she realised I had more interests and conversation than just intimate knowledge of the location of all of the Readers' Wives. Our first date was a trip to Wimpy in Dartford (home of Trish, aged 33) on a rainy day in June where I treated her to a Big Bender and a Brown Derby for afters. There was no expense spared and I was smitten.

A week or so later we ventured up to London to go to Soho, fascinated by stories of the debauchery on every corner. We had grand ideas about going to a 'proper pub' and headed to The Griffin at Charing Cross, a legendary meeting place for football fans that my brother visited before every West Ham home game. We didn't get as far as the front door before a bouncer laughed at us pretending we were 18 and sent us away. As we walked back to the station I saw the back page of the Evening Standard on a news seller's stand. The photo adorning the article was of a blonde. A beautiful blonde. One that would steal not only my heart, but thousands of others. Fortunately, I didn't have to decide between Jo and the golden-locked stunner who was spread across the bonnet of a Ford Capri. I could have my cake and eat it.

Of course anyone who had completed their 1985 Panini UK Football Album would recognise sticker number 525 looking back at them from the sports pages in the newspaper. But to most, West Ham's latest signing — attacking midfielder, peroxide-blonde Frank McAvennie — was a mystery.

Back in September 1979, Lyall had gone north of the border and signed Dundee United's full-back Ray Stewart for a then world-record fee for a teenager and Tonka, as he was nicknamed due to his thunderous right foot, turned out to be a club legend. Perhaps then, in revisiting this strategy, John did still know what he was doing and the previous three seasons of dire football had in fact just been leading up to this moment.

McAvennie had been brought in to replace Paul Allen, one of the best-ever graduates of the legendary West Ham Academy, who was allowed to leave to join Tottenham Hotspur after his contract expired, heaping more pressure on Lyall. But it seems that the club owners, the Cearns family, had found the cheque book and stolen one of the hottest properties in mid-Lanarkshire right from under the noses of Luton Town no less, who had paid for his journey south. Greek philosopher and former Acropolis FC striker Aristotle once uttered "One swallow does not make a summer", but what did a 2,200-year-old Greek bloke really know about Scottish midfielders, or even football for that matter.

Just over a month later I caught three trains and two buses to go and see Frankie make his pre-season debut at Plough Lane against Wimbledon, turning down an evening on the sofa watching *The Karate Kid* and sharing a can of Woodpecker with Jo as her parents were out. He played in a central-midfield position behind the lumbering David Swindlehurst and Tony Cottee in a 4-2 defeat that didn't really fill any of the West Ham fans in attendance with joy or renewed optimism. The talk on the way home from some fans was that our new signing Frankie was spending more time in Stringfellows than at the training ground. That wasn't the West Ham way and Trevor Brooking would have been tutting silently, but very politely, if he was still in the squad.

The biggest event of that summer was Live Aid. Being cocky 15-year-olds, about a dozen of us thought we would try to blag our way into Wembley for the concert of the decade. We tried to think up the ultimate plan for getting in the stadium, ranging from creating our own backstage passes (with no clue on what the genuine design was), offering the turnstile operator cash, or simply attaching ourselves to bigger groups as they entered. Top marks to one of our group, Ian, who was convinced he could blag his way in by saying he was Andrew Ridgeley's cousin (he wasn't). Of course, as soon as we exited Wembley Park station and saw the thousands streaming down Wembley Way we lost our bottle. We convinced little Jo (Joanna/e was a very common name for girlfriends of 15-year-old boys from suburbia in the 1980s) to approach a ticket tout and ask how much for a ticket.

"£200 and I will throw in some Smarties for you and your friends".

"For eight tickets?" You had to admire her innocence, and the tout wandered off laughing loudly.

We hung around outside the stadium for an hour or so before we realised there was no chance of getting in. But I did buy a t-shirt and to this day I still have it, and (whisper this quietly), I haven't ever denied not being there to my daughters when any mention of it comes on the TV. Technically I was there on that historic day.

The 1984-85 season had seen the average attendance at First Division games drop to just over 21,000 and in July, the Government announced some sweeping changes to the game that directly impacted clubs as a result of events that year. A blanket ban on alcohol served in grounds was introduced and there was a consultation exercise launched to consider the introduction of identity cards. Luton Town, who had seen Millwall fans run riot at Kenilworth Road in the previous season, became the first club to ban away fans. Being a football fan wasn't cool, at least according to Jo's Dad, who frowned at me every time I arrived at their front door.

Pre-season came and went. Back in the 1980s, there was no jetting off to the other side of the world to play a team on your doorstep like is the norm today. West Ham's biggest pre-season game was at Brisbane Road against Leyton Orient on a Sunday. Despite bolstering the paper-thin squad with petite winger Mark Ward from Oldham Athletic prior to the game, it was a tired performance from the Hammers which became better known for a fan confronting the team in the dressing room after a 3-1 defeat, calling them a "bunch of tossers". It didn't look good for the next nine months.

And so the opening day of the season was upon us and it was a trip back up to Birmingham City. A few months previous, the FA Cup tie between the two sides had ended in a heavy defeat for the Hammers and some serious crowd disturbances. I'd managed to lose my brother in the crush behind the goal and ended up having to make my own way home. The crowd trouble was featured on the news and so when I walked through the door, solo, after midnight, my parents weren't best pleased and I had to serve a three-game ban on away travel. For the sake of peace at home, I decided not to return to St Andrews.

It was probably just as well. Lyall's ingenious game plan fell apart as early as the 17th minute when striker Paul Goddard fell awkwardly and dislocated his shoulder. McAvennie was pushed up front, but it was to no avail as the season started in much the same way as the previous one had ended — with a limp defeat. I'd promised to take Jo to see *Jewel of the Nile* at the ABC cinema in Gravesend and while she did her best to keep my mind from wandering too far, from 3pm my thoughts were very definitely 130 miles to the north.

To be honest, things weren't going well on the girlfriend front. I could sense that she wasn't onside with the thought of nine months of me sulking about not going to football, and didn't seem keen either on spending her Saturdays outside pubs near football grounds before being expected to jump around a crumbling terrace singing songs about, in her words, someone else's "tits and fanny".

She gave me an ultimatum before the first home game of the season against Queens Park Rangers. It was either her or Frankie. Being a naive chap (and listening to my brother's advice) I chose the latter and despite his two goals on his debut and three points, Jo didn't share my enthusiasm when I tried to serenade her from her front lawn with a bad version of Sister Sledge's number one hit "Frankie" at 11.30pm.

Our relationship was never really the same, and after she missed the 2-2 draw with Liverpool, with McAvennie scoring two again, we split up. When I say split up, I actually mean that I saw her riding pillion on the back of a Yamaha (bike, not organ) with her arms wrapped around the rider. By that time though, I'd managed to source my reading material elsewhere, and why did I need a girlfriend anyway when I had Frank McAvennie?

After a shaky August, West Ham enjoyed a superb autumn that I put down to the fact that Jo wasn't around — she was the unlucky charm, having last seen West Ham when we lost at home to Luton Town. Since that game the team had been on a ten-game unbeaten run that saw them move steadily up the table.

The McAvennie/Cottee partnership just clicked. As the Hammers went into a Milk (League) Cup game at Old Trafford at the end of October, the two had scored 25 goals between them. Not since the days of David 'Psycho' Cross and Bryan 'Pop' Robson had the Hammers had a decent centre-forward and now they had two. The game against Manchester United pitched the two form teams in the league against each other in the Milk Cup, which back then was taken seriously by everyone. Under Ron Atkinson, United had won their first 12 games of the season.

I was desperate to go to the game and tried to get my Dad to drive up, but what with it being a school day and my O-level year (kids, ask your Dad), he wasn't keen to incur the wrath of my Mum. I came up with a cunning plan of getting one of my friend's older brothers (for a fee) to pretend to be from the school and write a letter to my parents about a Geography field trip to Manchester. Of course, my Mum saw through it straight away and rang the school to ensure that my movements on the day were fully accounted for.

In a close-fought game, United took the lead when Norman Whiteside scored with 15 minutes to play. A few minutes later, McAvennie was fouled 30 yards out and the pint-sized pocket rocket Mark Ward smashed the free-kick in, with United keeper Gary Bailey getting fingertips to it. A fine goal to bring the game back to London for a replay.

But no. Referee Frank Roberts claimed that the offence, despite being a foul, was an indirect free-kick and Bailey didn't get anywhere near it. Not one but two slices of injustice — and home team favouritism at Old Trafford … there's a turn up for the books.

Of course, today we would have seen TV replays galore of the incident, but back in the autumn of 1985 there was a complete TV blackout on football after negotiations between the broadcasters (back then it was the BBC, ITV and Channel 4) and the Football League broke down. The previous TV deal had ended with coverage of the tragedies at Valley Parade and Heysel, and it was no surprise that against a backdrop of falling attendances and increasing violence, the deal tabled fell way short of the expectations of the Football League. And so the season started and continued towards Christmas with no football at all on our screens.

With no TV cameras in the grounds, West Ham's style of play went under the radar, although McAvennie was very much above the radar off the pitch, becoming the tabloids' dream when he started dating Page 3 model Jenny Blyth. For most football fans, the first sight they had of McAvennie was on Wogan in the run-up to Christmas — an appearance that led to my Mum becoming a firm fan and even asking my Dad if she could come to a game.

The defeat at Old Trafford was hard to take in the circumstances, but Lyall's men bounced back with seven consecutive wins, lifting them into the top three. Let me just repeat that. West Ham. Winning seven consecutive games. In the top flight of English football. Of course it would never last, but with Liverpool and Everton now also closing in on a faltering Manchester United, West Ham ended the first half of the season with thirteen wins, five draws and just four defeats, almost as many points as they secured in the previous season. Astonishingly, John Lyall had used the same starting XI in 22 of the 26 games they had played, a mere 15 players in total, including one substitute appearance each for Bobby Barnes and a young Steve Potts, who went on to make over 500 appearances for the Hammers.

The spirit within the team could be seen when rather than recovering from the effects of a flight from Australia after playing for Scotland in a World Cup qualifier, McAvennie came almost straight from the airport to Loftus Road in early December to score the winner against QPR. But the haters were in their element when the Hammers took only a point from their games immediately before and after Christmas. Same old West Ham.

January brought new hope for me, for West Ham and for the football-loving public in England. The New Year's Eve disco at Hartley Country Club had delivered a romantic encounter down the side alley (no euphemism) on the stroke of midnight with a girl called Sally I had known since I was five. Sally had flowing, blonde hair, not too dissimilar to Frank's, which was the reason we got together, according to my Dad. My 16th birthday was just a few days away and I was reaching a milestone in my life with a girl on my literal arm. That lasted four days, before she told me she could only see me on Saturday afternoons as she worked on a Sunday — yet another relationship that wasn't going to last. They don't tell you about the crushing disappointment of finally reaching the age of consent, but not being able to take advantage of it unless you give up football.

Some good news though was that football would be back on the TV. Negotiations had started again, and finally a halfway house of an agreement was reached, a short-term deal worth £1.3 million (a thousandth of the value of the last TV deal signed in 2018) for 12 live matches, of which six would be in the league and six would be in the FA Cup. And what better way to kick off the coverage than West Ham's FA Cup third-round derby against Charlton Athletic?

Coming the night after my birthday celebrations in the pubs around Gravesend that turned a blind eye to us having a "shandy", the whole family travelled to Selhurst Park, temporary home of Charlton Athletic, for the game. This was a rare day out for my Grandad who was a staunch Addick and could lay claim to the club's nickname, depending on whether or not you believe his story. He always said that the nickname 'The Addicks' came from the word 'haddock', which was a bonus given to the team if they won in the form of a fish and chip supper, served at his Aunt's pub The Horse and Groom a few minutes away from the ground. That was his standard story, always embellished when he told people.

The game wasn't the best advert for a watching nation desperate to see some football, until McAvennie's last-minute lob hit the bar and Tony Cottee slid in to net the winner.

If anyone doubted whether West Ham had the staying power to remain at the top, then the good news was that they were only defeated once in January and February, away at Anfield. The bad news was that due to poor weather and an FA Cup tie against Ipswich Town that went to extra time in a second replay, played on a snow-covered pitch with the fabled orange ball, West Ham would have to play catch-up in terms of the league fixtures.

In fact, the Hammers ended up playing five consecutive FA Cup games before exiting the competition at Sheffield Wednesday in the quarter-finals, severely stretching the squad.

As a fan today of non-league football, I'm used to seeing clubs who have had a great cup run, normally in the first half of the season, suffer massively due to a fixture backlog as the season gets to the business end. Back in 1986 it was just as bad, with the Hammers having to face nine games in a month, seven of which were at The Boleyn Ground where they had been unbeaten since Luton's (of course) win back in August.

The fans were slowly coming back with a season-best of 29,361 turning out on a Tuesday night in East London for the game against Chelsea. Having embarrassed the Blues on Easter Saturday at Stamford Bridge, winning 4-0, the Hammers looked tired and Chelsea's no-nonsense approach in dealing with the threat of Devonshire and Ward down the flanks stifled the supply to the West Ham front pair, although Cottee did open the scoring before Chelsea came from behind to win. At the time, we didn't realise how costly that defeat would be.

Six days later and West Ham were back under the lights at The Boleyn, with Newcastle United the visitors. If the fans needed a signal that the team hadn't given up hope then this was the chance. And they didn't disappoint.

Three-nil up after just 15 minutes settled any nerves. Newcastle keeper Martin Thomas had come into the game with an arm injury and it was clear from early on he wasn't fit enough to start, let alone continue past half-time when he was replaced by young defender Chris Hedworth, who then dislocated his collar bone on the hour mark. Hedworth carried on, failing, understandably, to keep out a second from Alvin Martin and, with the magic sponge finally admitting defeat and failing to sort out such a serious injury, Newcastle, rather than going for substance over form, stuck 5ft 7in Peter Beardsley between the posts while Hedworth bravely battled on up front.

Beardsley did himself and his team proud, keeping the score down to just eight, with Alvin Martin completing his hat-trick from the penalty spot and claiming a unique treble, with each one scored against a different keeper. To this day I don't think I've seen a more surreal game, which could have easily seen West Ham score double the number they did.

The pressure didn't let up as Everton and Liverpool kept winning. The Hammers won their next two games 1-0 before Ipswich Town arrived, two days after the home victory over Manchester City. Over 31,000 nervously watched the Hammers try to break down a dogged Ipswich side. With three minutes to go and the scores level it looked like West Ham's title dreams were over, but then a typical Mark Ward run into the area was halted in a robust fashion. Penalty. The ever-dependable Ray Stewart stepped up and smashed the ball home and kept our hopes alive.

The win saw West Ham move up to second place as Everton surprisingly lost at Oxford United, meaning that it was all to play for on the final Saturday of the season. Unlike today, when all of the final games are played simultaneously, there was still a potential title-decider to play on Monday if Liverpool slipped up, with West Ham travelling to Goodison Park, both potentially able to win the league.

But it wasn't to be. It is often said that it's the hope that kills you. In the days before mobile phones, apps and instant updates it was also the false rumours. As we stood on the terrace at The Hawthorns, knowing that West Ham had to beat West Brom (tick, 3-2), we heard whispers going around that Chelsea were beating Liverpool. But that was never going to happen. After their win at The Boleyn two weeks previous, Chelsea were determined not to let the title head to East London and once player-manager Kenny Dalglish opened the scoring for Liverpool, it was game over. The title was going back to Merseyside for the fifth season in a row.

The journey back from Birmingham in my Dad's car was as depressing as any car journey I have ever been on. On the way up we spoke about plans for Monday to go to Everton even if we didn't have a ticket. It was a Bank Holiday, so no need to think of an excuse to miss school — but there was no point now. With English teams banned from Europe it didn't make any difference if we finished second or third. We tried to be positive, remembering that just a year ago we'd stayed up by a couple of points, now we'd missed out on winning the title because of bloody Chelsea.

Over the whole season, Lyall used 18 players in the 52 games the Hammers played. Of those, nine players played in 90% of the games — an amazing feat, the like we would never see in the modern game. Frank McAvennie's 28 goals saw him surpassed in the scoring stakes only by Gary Lineker at Everton.

Could life get any better? I'd manage to go out with three times as many girls, albeit briefly, as I had in the previous 12 months and West Ham were everybody's second-favourite team again. I'd started smoking, stopped smoking. Bought a beer in a pub, watched a video (kids — ask your Dad) from 'under the counter' and learned that people didn't read *Playboy* 'for the stories'. Overall, my season got a 9/10, only denied full marks by four points and an 18-goal swing from Liverpool.

A year later and it was business as usual at The Boleyn as West Ham finished in 15th place. Despite the fantastic season, the board hadn't given Lyall any money to strengthen the squad until the New Year, by which time the Hammers had lost as many games as they had in the 1985-86 season in total. McAvennie only managed seven league goals and was heading back north of the border by the end of 1987 to join Celtic, while 40 year-old Billy Bonds, who had missed the whole of the 1985-86 and most of the 1986-87 season was voted Hammer of the Year. Same old West Ham.

History may belong to the victors, but it is in defeat that you become a man ... almost.

NOTTINGHAM FOREST 1990-91
DANIEL STOREY

The 1991 FA Cup final was the last Nottingham Forest game before I attended my first football match. As a five-year-old that had already been schooled by incessant VHS reruns of recorded football, there was never any doubt that August 1991 would bring with it a season ticket and lifetime affinity. But I was — not unreasonably — considered a little young for Wembley. On the morning of May 18, I was packed off to a family friend before my mum left for North London.

Perhaps my mum concluded that Wembley is simply not the place to begin the journey. A cup final must be earned during the winter evenings and long seasons, when the football somehow makes you feel colder. It might take months, years or lifetimes depending on which tribe you are placed into, but the joy of the destination is directly proportional to the length of the journey. The 'good things come to those who wait' principle fuels our loyalty when reason and sense have long given up trying. Win a cup final in your first match and nothing else might ever compare.

Or perhaps she understood just how much that cup final meant to Nottingham Forest and their manager, and could not risk the emotional implications of agonising failure. Nobody wants to spend three hours in a car with a crying child who has only known football in cheerful packaged highlights and thus remained deliberately shielded from sporting failure. The art of good parenting lies in timing — when to allow children to run free into reality and learn from their own mistakes, and when to cover them in blankets and leave them safe in the East Midlands. Lose a cup final in your first match and nothing else might ever make up for it.

One of the great myths of Nottingham Forest's history is that they enjoyed three seasons of unthinkable, unmatchable majesty before quickly shuffling back into the provincial shadows. That notion is attractive to the romantic storyteller, but also to the outsider: in the space of 36 months, Forest won 100% of their domestic titles and 100% of their European trophies. It became the motivator for Liverpool to reinforce their own domestic and continental dominance.

The truth is a little different. While Forest were indeed unable to replicate nirvana following their European Cup defence, that would have been impossible — only Zinedine Zidane's Real Madrid have won three consecutively in the last 40 years. But they hardly reverted to their typical mean.

Between 1980 and 1991, Forest finished in the First Division's top half ten times in 11 seasons, one fewer than they managed between the turn of the century and 1980. They finished third in 1984, 1988 and 1989, and until Manchester City in 2019, Forest were also the last team to retain the League Cup. If Brian Clough's greatest achievement was taking Forest to the pinnacle of European football, then the longevity over which he presided, keeping them towards the top of the English game for another decade, was almost as impressive.

It is easy to bemoan misfortune as a partisan supporter; hard luck generally fills the space that perhaps instead belongs to incompetence or inefficiency. Forest's transfer business during the early 1980s was haphazard at best. Justin Fashanu, Stan Bowles, Mark Proctor and Frans Thijssen were all notable failures sold at a considerable loss. Clough's forte continued to lie in his ability to transform the careers of ageing domestic players and local youngsters. But Forest's post-European Cup success did become defined by a series of situations in which they could justifiably feel hard done to.

The first came in a UEFA Cup semi-final second leg against Anderlecht in 1984, in which the Belgian side were awarded a nonsensical penalty and a tie-clinching Forest goal was disallowed for no good reason. In 1997, it was revealed that Anderlecht chairman Constant Vanden Stock had paid referee Emilio Guruceta Muro £27,000 to ensure that his club would progress and in 2016, UEFA admitted to being made aware of the crime as early as 1993. There is no guarantee that Forest would have beaten Tottenham in the final, but they had finished 13 points above them in the First Division that season.

The ban on English clubs in Europe post-Heysel also affected Forest badly, forcing them to miss out on three seasons of UEFA Cup participation around the turn of the decade. A provincial club in the East Midlands badly needed the financial rewards and transfer market pulling power those cup runs might have provided.

But it is the 1991 FA Cup final that left the most devastating legacy. Forest had beaten three Division One sides en route to Wembley, and scored four times against West Ham after Tony Gale's controversial red card for bringing down Gary Crosby and — in the view of referee Keith Hackett — denying a clear goal-scoring opportunity.

The FA Cup was the one domestic trophy that Clough never lifted and so desperately wanted to win. Until 1988, he had never even reached the semi-finals, an odd flaw on his CV given the prodigious cup record in his first half-decade at the City Ground. For six straight seasons from 1981, Forest never progressed beyond the fifth round of either domestic cup competition.

But in 1988, Forest began to re-emerge as a cup team. They won consecutive League Cups in 1989 and 1990 and the Full Members' Cup too. They reached the FA Cup semi-finals in 1988 and 1989, losing to old rivals Liverpool both times, the second an incredibly emotional affair at Old Trafford three weeks after the Hillsborough disaster. Finishing third in the First Division in both seasons, Clough had somehow manufactured a second era of Nottingham Forest wonder after several years of comparative mid-table mediocrity. The final dream came into focus: prepare to chalk off that last remaining domestic honour at Wembley.

Paul Gascoigne should have been sent off before his infamous lunge on Gary Charles. On the morning of their semi-final against Arsenal, Tottenham manager Terry Venables recalls seeing Gascoigne more hyped-up and tense than he had ever seen him, as if desperate to prove that he merited the lucrative move to Lazio that would soon be announced. Having scored the brilliant free-kick against Arsenal to open the scoring, Venables was not concerned that Gascoigne was in the same mood before the final. Even so, the Tottenham club doctor was sent to the hotel room where Paul was kicking pillows and volleying bars of soap and gave him two tablets to calm him down. We can assume they were Valium.

Gascoigne was in self-destruct mode at Wembley, desperate to prove wrong the accusations from Spurs supporters that he was a mercenary and offer a fitting farewell to English football before his departure for Serie A. Within minutes, he had planted a boot into the chest of Garry Parker, somehow only receiving a ticking off from referee Roger Milford.

"I wish I'd got sent off for the first tackle on Parker," Gascoigne later said to the BBC. "I remember he'd clattered me in one game but I waited two years to get him back. He was one of their playmakers and what you try to do is injure his legs. If you're going to challenge him, make sure he can't kick a ball as well as he can if you hurt his feet or legs. But I nearly took his windpipe out."

Forest fans feel exactly the same. With a one-goal — Stuart Pearce scored from the resultant free-kick — and one-man advantage, they would surely have won the final.

Instead, Gascoigne was substituted for Nayim after the Charles tackle, again remarkably avoiding punishment, and loaded onto a stretcher with what would turn out to be a ruptured cruciate ligament in his right knee. Nayim, meanwhile, would play a crucial part in both Tottenham goals, cushioning the ball for Paul Allen to assist Paul Stewart's equaliser and delivering the extra time corner from which Des Walker scored his own goal.

Clough was incensed, visibly affected by perceived injustice; in his book *The Footballer Who Could Fly*, Duncan Hamilton recalls "his inexpressive marble gaze, as if his eyes were suddenly sightless". In hindsight, Clough had lost control. He had walked out onto the Wembley pitch, hand-in-hand with a bemused Terry Venables as a show of respect or psychological power play, depending on your interpretation. But his perfect vision had been ripped away.

That loss of control was reflected in the performance of his players, which makes sense — this was a young, inexperienced Forest XI. Pearce was the old man at 29, and Crosby the only other player in the starting team older than 25. Mark Crossley, Gary Charles, Steve Chettle, Roy Keane, Ian Woan and Lee Glover were all aged between 19 and 23, one of the youngest FA Cup final teams in the competition's history. Tottenham had the experience and knowhow: Gary Lineker, Pat Van den Hauwe, Paul Allen, Erik Thorsvedt and Gary Mabbutt were all 28 or older.

Stewart was magnificent, running the midfield. Lineker had a penalty saved and a goal wrongly ruled out for offside. Tottenham had the better of the chances in the first half, dominated the second half and were — grudgingly — deserving of their victory. But in Clough's eyes, destiny had been determined in the first quarter of the match.

Those 17 minutes remain some of the most pivotal in English football's modern history. Gascoigne would have joined Lazio without the injury issues and baggage that accompanied his tumultuous recovery. Glenn Roeder, Gazza's friend and mentor, would have accompanied him to Rome as a de facto supervisor rather than pulling out of the arrangement. Gascoigne had other friends that often travelled to Italy, but they did little other than exacerbate his personal demons.

For Clough, victory would surely have led to immediate retirement. "I should have retired after May 18, 1991, the day I witnessed the worst refereeing decision in my 40-odd years in football," he wrote in *Clough: The Autobiography*, a claim backed up by Stuart Pearce in his own autobiography. "The FA Cup final, the only one in which I was involved, Nottingham Forest against Tottenham Hotspur — and Wembley stank to its rafters. Paul Gascoigne committed two despicable fouls."

This was all that Clough wanted, the perfect end to an extraordinary managerial career. By then, alcoholism had already numbed some of his managerial fortitude and eroded his physical and mental wellbeing. The final scene should have seen him completing a Wembley lap of honour, red-and-white scarf draped around his neck as he waved to the travelling worshippers, before walking off into the sunset.

Instead Clough stayed on, desperate to atone for the injustice, but without the faculties to make it likely. His eventual retirement came two years later, tears wiped away on the sleeves of his famous green jumper as he suffered relegation for the first time as a manager after a 2-0 home defeat by Sheffield United. It was also the first occasion that Forest had finished outside the top 12 in Division One since promotion in 1977. I was present on that sorrowful afternoon. Parents can't protect you forever.

Clough's post-match interview with Martin Tyler is difficult to watch back. Stood in the City Ground tunnel with Forest supporters demanding his re-entry to receive their adoration, he begins by repeatedly insisting that he is happy — one last attempt to control the narrative. He speaks of gardening, resting and pride at becoming the very best. Then the mask slips: "I'm also unhappy. We weren't good enough, and somewhere down the line the manager must have contributed to that. I wasn't good enough."

Relegation did nothing to harm Clough's reputation in Nottingham; how could it after everything he has achieved? We understood that it was merely the inevitable end game for a man struggling with the rigours of addiction, managing a squad that failed to replace Teddy Sheringham and asked a young Keane to carry the team on his shoulders, not to mention working in a sport that was rapidly departing from his own ideals. But we might have avoided the long, tortured goodbye. Clough would have been able to live out those two years with the perfect ending secured. Instead it broke him.

Brian Clough as a manager in the Premier League's first decade would have been a deeply intriguing prospect. His comments on managing foreign players, the rise of player power — "Why do you need four fucking cars? You can only drive one at once" — and his admission that "I couldn't compromise to save my life" would have surely been exposed in a league that was changing faster than he could or would have wanted to. He was made for a different world, a staunch socialist in a game beginning its marriage with rampant capitalism.

But it's still extraordinary to see that image of Clough in 1993; the tears in the eyes, the flickers of fight in his spiky responses, the red blotches on his cheeks that provide a map of his personal struggle. A man of just 58 — only five years older than Jurgen Klopp is as I write this — leaving the game for the final time and looking so badly weathered by the experience.

It is also tempting to wonder whether losing the FA Cup final exacerbated Clough's alcoholism. The lack of fairy-tale walk into the sunset clearly ate away at a flawed character, and evidence shows that addictive tendencies are flared by negative triggers. To Clough, control was everything — control of players, control of relationships, control of the media. To have lost control so spectacularly, and unfairly, at precisely the time when he desired it most must have cut him deeply.

But ultimately, it's an unhelpful conversation. Clough's drinking had reached a level at which it was putting his long-term health at risk long before 1991, a product of a drinking culture that permeated English football and an English culture that was too late to realise — or deliberately blind to it until it was too late — its potential impact. Identifying one aggravating factor misses the point; the dependency had already been established.

For me, it's odd to have seen Clough's Forest but never seen Clough in his pomp. That majestic period in the club's history provokes inevitable jealousy in those who missed it and know they will never see its like again. We are sustained by misty-eyed stories of red-tinted glory, but they will forever remain second-hand memories.

Without them though, I may never have gone at all. One of the great unspoken truths of football fandom is that we adore our clubs as if they were immortal members of our close family, but that loyalty is shaped by things entirely beyond our control. Had you been born ten miles down the road, or your grandfather lived 20 miles north, south, east or west, you might adore another.

My mum attended her first Forest match in 1980, with dreams of following the European champions around Europe, before seeing them eliminated in the first round by CSKA Sofia. They haven't returned to the European Cup since, but that was enough. In those circumstances, the ballroom where fate and fortune dance, I must be grateful for what I got rather than resent what I missed.

The same is true of Clough and the FA Cup. Do not dwell on the sadness of the end and the unjust nature of its arrival, but bask in the glow of the remarkable events that even made it possible. If the FA Cup remained the one gap on Clough's CV at two provincial East Midlands clubs who have not enjoyed such sustained success before or since, it is merely one missed stitch. Take a step back and that stitch blends into the glorious tapestry.

YUGOSLAVIA 1992–94

RICHARD HALL

OJ Simpson is in his Ford Bronco on the Santa Ana Freeway. Diana Ross shanks the first of the penalties that would bookend the tournament. Jurgen Klinsmann strokes the ball into the empty Bolivian net to win the opening game. These are the first hours of the 1994 World Cup. And I missed them all.

Ever since I got a first glimpse of tournament football in 1982, the World Cup had been the sun-filled highlight of my sporting childhood. By the time the 1994 edition came around, I was at the end of my first year at university. I didn't care that England weren't there — but I would have been upset had the Dutch failed to qualify. I had spent more time reading tournament previews than I had revising for my end of year exams. First-year exams don't matter much anyway, so I didn't bother to get prepared. But I was fully prepared for the tournament.

In a happy coincidence, my last exam finished at 11am on Friday, June 17. It was the only exam in my life that I left early. I'd done enough to pass and I couldn't wait for the start of the carefree, work-free World Cup summer stretching out in front of me. Nine hours later, as the Bolivians took the kick-off, I was sound asleep in my halls of residence after spending the day, predictably, drinking beer in the summer sun celebrating the end of exams and the start of the World Cup. I missed the big kick-off I had looked forward to for four years.

Looking back now, what else is missing from that tournament? What did it lack?

It had some stand-out performers, like Roberto Baggio, Romário, Hristo Stoichkov and Gheorge Hagi. But no-one dominated like Garrincha in '62, Johan Cruyff in '74 or Diego Maradona in '86. Saeed Al-Owairan's run through Belgium's defence was a fine goal, but the tournament didn't see a clutch of them like Mexico in 1970 and 1986. Argentina-Romania and Brazil-Netherlands in the knockout stages were dramatic games, but they didn't reach the heights of the classics: Hungary v Uruguay 1954, Brazil v Italy 1982, Brazil v France 1986.

Brazil were worthy winners. They were condemned as pragmatic, but they had a better goalkeeper, defence and forwards than their 1982 forebears. They were clearly the best team around in the mid-1990s. Yet the burden of the 24-year wait since their last World Cup victory brought a caution — reflected in the choices of coach Carlos Alberto Parreira — that prevented them from really taking their foot off the brake. Romário apart, the team doesn't stay long in the memory.

Injury and suspension stalked Italy, but Baggio somehow carried them to the final. Argentina's flame burned brightly but briefly before Maradona's exit snuffed it out. And the giant-killing Bulgarians and Romanians entertained us all (or at least those of us bored with West Germany-Argentina finals).

Good, but not great, seems a fair verdict on the tournament. It certainly lacked a great team. But could it have been different? Was there a truly great team that we missed? A team that just wasn't there?

In the autumn of 1991, Yugoslavia clinched their place in the European Championships, to be held the following summer in Sweden. Qualification was assured as a storm gathered in Europe. Over the next four years, it would unleash war and genocide in Yugoslavia, and break up a football team that could have dominated the international game during the last years of the 20th century.

In an era when just eight teams contested the European Championship finals, qualification was no mean achievement. Especially for a team which, in England at least, was not rated highly. Four years earlier,

Bobby Robson's men had blown the Yugoslavs away with four goals in the first 25 minutes of a decisive European Championship qualifier in Belgrade.

Nevertheless, by 1991 Yugoslavia were not a surprise package. They had reached the quarter-finals of Italia '90 with playmaker Dragan Stojković's sublime brace squeezing the team past Spain and into the quarter-finals, where they succumbed to Argentina on penalties. In that quarter-final, the team was deprived of midfielder Srečko Katanec, who was reportedly omitted after receiving a threat of dark consequences if he took to the field (although he maintains he was injured). It was a forewarning of the political turmoil that had been heating up and was about to boil over.

Yugoslavia were among the top seeds in the qualifying group for Sweden, but their roots went deeper than that. Just 17 days before the national team's capitulation to England in 1987, Yugoslavia's youngsters lifted the World Youth Cup in Chile. They took a scratch squad, after suspension, injuries and club priorities had shorn the team of promising players, including Alen Bokšić. Yet after defeating the hosts in the opening match, they marched through the group with two more wins, before 18-year-old Robert Prosinečki, the tournament's outstanding player, inspired his team to victories against Brazil and East Germany in the knockout stages. Prosinečki was suspended for the final against West Germany, but fellow midfielder Zvonimir Boban took up the slack, scoring Yugoslavia's goal in a 1-1 draw, before slotting home the decisive spot-kick in the ensuing penalty shoot-out.

After Chile, the youngsters had to bide their time as senior team coach Ivica Osim set about the task of qualifying for Italia '90 with a squad of established players. Prosinečki, along with fellow members of the Class of '87 Davor Šuker and Robert Jarni, were slowly integrated into the senior squad, and the trio, along with Bokšić, went to the World Cup in 1990 — although only Prosinečki saw significant playing time. Boban did not make the squad. For a very good reason.

Yugoslavia comprised the republics of Bosnia and Herzegovina, Croatia, Macedonia, Montenegro, Slovenia and Serbia, each with distinct political, cultural and ethnic mixes. The country had been welded together in the aftermath of the two World Wars of the 20th century, and a third conflict — the Cold War — kept a lid on the simmering tensions. But when the Soviet empire began to fall apart at the end of 1989, they bubbled up again.

Bosnian Muslim nationalists called for an independent Bosnia; Croats were intent on establishing an independent Croatian state; and Serb nationalists were determined to dominate a Serb-controlled Yugoslavia. All were prepared to fight for what they wanted. With communism swept away in Yugoslavia, nationalism was once again the dominant force. In April 1990, in their first multi-party elections since the 1940s, Croats voted overwhelmingly for pro-independence candidates — incensing Serbs in Belgrade.

Weeks later, Croats Dinamo Zagreb hosted Red Star Belgrade in a Yugoslav league fixture. Nationalist gangs on both sides clashed. Marshalled by warlord Arkan, the Red Star gang attacked, with the police doing nothing to protect the Croats. After violence spread to the pitch, Boban, Dinamo's captain, took a flying kick at a policeman who was beating a Dinamo fan. TV cameras captured the incident, and Boban became an instant Croatian hero. Unsurprisingly, the Yugoslav football authorities took a different view, and he was banned for six months, a period that included the World Cup finals in Italy.

War in the Balkans had not yet broken out but, with the initial loss of Boban and then of Katanec during the 1990 tournament itself, the effect of the coming conflict was already being felt.

The qualification series for Euro '92 began three months after the team's quarter-final exit in Italy. In the first tie against Northern Ireland, Yugoslavia took to the field with four Serbs, two Croats, a Serbo-Croat, a Bosnian-Croat, a Bosnian, a Macedonian and a Montenegrin.

Despite the descent into war, Osim kept the team together, even reintegrating Boban and Katanec later in the campaign. Halfway through qualification, they stood top of the group with maximum points. This included a backs-to-the-wall win in Copenhagen against group rivals Denmark, in which the team's ability to soak up pressure and counter quickly with deadly force was amply demonstrated. The only blemish in qualification was losing the return fixture against the Danes.

But events outwith their control were overtaking Osim's men. In June 1991, Slovenia and Croatia declared independence from Yugoslavia. As a consequence, the team completed qualification without Slovenian Katanec, and Croats Prosinečki, Boban, Jarni and Šuker. They would never play for Yugoslavia again.

Three clean sheets and 11 goals in their last three matches saw Osim's depleted team top the group, with Darko Pančev outscoring the rest of Europe with ten goals in qualification and the Danes booking their summer holiday on the beach. Or so they thought.

Following the declaration of independence, Croats and Serbs engaged in a brutal civil war. By the end of 1991, more than 10,000 people had died. Despite a UN-brokered ceasefire and peacekeeping plan, fighting continued — and Croatia was pulled into the war between Serbs, Muslims and Croats in neighbouring Bosnia.

On May 30 1992, just 11 days before the European Championships began, the United Nations Security Council passed a resolution imposing sanctions on the combatants in the Balkan wars and limiting their participation in sporting events. FIFA suspended the Yugoslav football team from competition, and they were thrown out of the Euros. Denmark picked up their beach towels and took Yugoslavia's place. Less than a month later, the Danes were champions.

Six months earlier, Yugoslavia had been drawn alongside Greece and Russia in the World Cup 1994 preliminaries, but the suspension was still in force by the time the group got under way. They would surely have qualified from a group won by a Greek team that went on to lose all three of its matches in the USA, producing perhaps the worst showing by a European side at any World Cup.

But by now it was too late. The UN resolution did not end the fighting, and wars in the Balkans raged on. Osim offered valuable perspective: "Lots of people have been killed. The country was destroyed. Sometimes there are things that are more important than football."

As Yugoslavia splintered, Slovenia and Croatia competed in qualifiers for Euro '96. The Croats reached England and were eventually eliminated in the quarter-finals by Germany.

Croatia and the rump Yugoslavia qualified for France '98. A Yugoslavia side boasting Stojković, Siniša Mihajlović, Predrag Mijatović and Dejan Savićević reached the second round — where they were eliminated slightly unfortunately by the Netherlands. Croatia, meanwhile, advanced to the semi-finals, avenging Germany on their way. Jarni, Šuker, Prosinečki and Boban all came within touching distance of glory (Bokšić was absent injured) when Šuker gave them a second half lead against the hosts. But for the only two goals in Lilian Thuram's 142-match international career, they would have made it to the final.

While 1990 was too early for the Youth Cup winners, by 1998 both Prosinečki and Stojković were struggling for fitness. Had the team stayed together, it is likely that the 1994 World Cup would have been its peak. How could they have looked when they showed up in the US? And how good could they have been?

Key players were in form. Boban and Savićević were instrumental as Milan dismantled Johan Cruyff's feted Barcelona Dream Team in the 1994 European Cup final. Šuker had scored 24 goals for Sevilla in La Liga. Many of the players had a long history of succeeding together, back to the 1987 World Youth Cup and Red Star Belgrade's 1991 European Cup win. The team was the right age — with an average of 26, the same average age of World Cup winners since 1950.

In 1994, they could have lined up: Ladić (then age 31) — Mirković (22), Đukić (28), Mihajlović (25), Jarni (25) — Boban (25), Jugović (24), Stojković (29), Prosinečki (25) — Savićević (27), Šuker (26).

The likes of goalkeeper Omerović (32); defenders Najdoski (30), Đorović (22), Bilić (25), Spasić (28) and Štimac (26); midfielders Katanec (30), Jokanović (25), Brnović (26), Zahovič (23), Asanović (28) and Stanić (22); and forwards Bokšić (24), Mijatović (25) and Pančev (28) would have provided plenty of options.

Eight of this putative starting XI played in European Cup finals during their careers, collectively racking up eight wins and five runners-up medals. It contains as many European Cup winners (six) as the Italy team that started the 1994 World Cup final, which is remarkable when you consider that during this period of pre-eminence, Italian clubs won half of the European Cup finals between 1989 and 1996. In this starting XI there would have been no place for 1993 European Cup winner Bokšić or Mijatović, who would score the only goal of the European Cup final in 1998.

Strong defenders, abundant midfield creativity and a posse of lethal finishers. This group of players had everything. It at least matches its 1994 contemporaries from champions Brazil for winning pedigree, and its quality arguably runs wider.

But of course, putting together a successful and memorable team takes more than talented players.

Historically, Yugoslav club and national teams tended to prioritise technique and flair over game management, and were often undone at the highest level by more practical opponents. Could they have played smart and stayed resilient through the difficult periods of games that all tournament winners must endure? At that time, no European team had won a World Cup outside their own continent. Would this Yugoslavia team have wilted in the heat and humidity of the US summer? Would they have fluffed their lines at the most important moment like the tournament's actual outsider-favourites Colombia?

The depth of talent among the group of players is incredible, most obviously in creative midfield and attack. But it is also balanced. Štimac and Bilić, good enough to marshal Croatia's defence in their run to the semi-finals in 1998, would have likely been reserves (notwithstanding the latter's apparent antipathy for playing for Yugoslavia). This depth of talent would surely have been enough to cover lapses in form and fitness (even in 1994, Prosinečki's fitness was fragile), suspensions and, importantly in the conditions, afforded the opportunity to rest players when necessary.

In the 1991 European Cup final, Red Star Belgrade, comprising ten Yugoslavs, showed that they could bury their expansive instincts when the biggest prizes were at stake. They were cautious throughout, taking no risks while keeping the Marseille attackers at arm's length. They seemed happy from the start to play for the penalties by which they would win the cup. They carried out a plan. They managed the game. They didn't freeze on the big stage. And the national team would have had the memory of grinding out victory in that Euro '92 qualifier in Copenhagen to fall back on. As for the heat and humidity, it didn't prevent Eastern European neighbours Bulgaria and Romania from thriving in the tournament.

Darko Pančev is sure: "If our generation had had the chance to play in a European Championship or World Cup, we'd have had a big chance," he tells Simon Hart in the Italia '90 book *World in Motion*. "We'd have won a trophy. Maybe not in '92, but '94 or '96. One hundred per cent."

Stojković gave a less emphatic opinion, telling Hart: "Nobody knows. This is just opinions. In football, you can't be sure."

In December 1994, two days before Christmas, a Yugoslavia team drawn from Serbia and Montenegro played a friendly against Brazil's World Cup winners in Porto Alegre. Six of Brazil's starters from the final in Pasadena five months earlier played in the game. Mijatović, Stojković, Savićević, Jugović, Mihajlović and Đukić all started for Yugoslavia. Viola, whose cameo as an extra time substitute had provided the best moments of that goalless final, headed Brazil in front. Then Branco biffed a signature 30-yard free-kick past debutant goalkeeper Goran Pandurović to complete a 2-0 victory.

This coda to the story of international football in 1994 tantalises rather than informs. Watching the game back, it doesn't tell us anything we didn't know. Yugoslavia are weaker than they would have been had the Croats, Bosnians, Slovenians and Macedonians been able to play. This Brazil team is good. It is in the middle of a 40-game unbeaten run in full internationals that would stretch from December 1993 to May 1997.

But it does give us a sense of what we missed. Even this inchoate Yugoslavia team competes and excites. Yugoslavia repeatedly trouble the World Champions. There are skills and tricks, pace and movement. Savićević is especially dangerous, finding space between the lines despite the attentions of Aldair and Dunga. His glorious reverse pass creates a clear chance that Jugović can't convert. Visually, the match is compelling. The bright sunshine. The dark blue shirts. The golden yellow shirts. You don't have to squint much to imagine Porto Alegre as Pasadena. Dunga chasing Savićević. Stojković pulling the strings. Jugović breaking from deep. The World Cup at stake.

Then, in the mind's eye, the picture becomes clearer. This is what might have been. Boban and Prosinečki are helping Stojković take control of midfield. Jarni is driving back the young substitute Cafu down Yugoslavia's left. A tiring Brazil defence huffs and puffs as Pančev and Bokšić warm up on the sidelines. Šuker converts a Savićević through ball. Vice-President Al Gore presents the trophy to Stojković.

Could they? Would they? Stojković is right, of course. Nobody can ever know. Anyway, perhaps winning is beside the point. World Cup history shows that teams don't have to lift the trophy to be considered great.

If you've read, or seen, *The Man in the High Castle*, you'll know that alternative versions of history can be both pointless and captivating. But it's fun to think that a great Yugoslavia side could have provided the ingredient that this World Cup was missing.

The 1954 Hungarians, the Dutch team of 1974 and the 1982 Brazilians are held up as great teams that never won the World Cup. The 'Nearly Men'. At least the teams of Puskás, Cruyff and Zico had a chance. Hungary and the Netherlands ran into West Germany. Brazil were beaten by Rossi. Yugoslavia were denied by history.

MANCHESTER UNITED 1993-98

JOHN BREWIN

I am a lapsed Manchester United fan. I have almost completely lost my passion for a club to which I once devoted so much psychic energy. Well into adulthood, 'United' was often the first thought in my head at the start of a day. My social life and working life were centred around United; I ran a small editorial team for nine years and it was a sore point among the group that I never worked a Champions League evening when United were playing. Sorry about that, chaps. Poor form. Having a birthday in mid-May often meant long-suffering friends having to sit through cup finals to drink with someone not guaranteed to be in a good mood at the end of the match. My sister has no love for football, mostly because of the oscillating effect United's fortunes on the pitch would have on my mood. On reflection, all self-indulgent behaviour of which I am not a little bit ashamed.

What changed? I am most definitely older and perhaps even a tad wiser, and have spent over two decades working in a game that for all its step changes can become a grinding treadmill. There came a point of realisation that football will, as David Mitchell and Robert Webb so immaculately put it, "never be finally decided". How many biggest games ever can there be? How often can United spend obscene money on players for no discernible improvement? At the time of writing, the Premier League has added a new tier of pay-per-view TV fixtures and its leading clubs, with United to the fore, have come up with Project Big Picture, where the endgame of helping out the lower leagues is claiming yet more power over English football's direction. They are also counting up £1.2 billion of spending on transfers mid-pandemic, at a time when many of those lower-league clubs are facing extinction and many people, including myself, are staring down the barrel of a destroyed jobs market. Macclesfield Town, my hometown club, and where my affection had been directed for the last few years, briefly ceased to exist after one final winding-up order and will have to reform somewhere in the depths of non-league.

Manchester United certainly changed too. I was not one of the supporters who refused to enter Old Trafford once Malcolm Glazer's leveraged buyout took place in 2005, though I admired the principles of those who did. A club that was previously a PLC and shipping Ryan Giggs bedspreads to all corners of the world was hardly a socialist paradise, but the club's practices and motives became more cynical at a stroke.

But most of all, I lost the friend I had shared so many of the good times with. During a raucous, smoke-filled minibus trip back across the Severn Bridge from the 2004 FA Cup final in Cardiff between United and Millwall, I received the news that Neil, a pal since he joined my school class when we were both nine, had died in an accident in Thailand. Someone with whom I had shared so much — first gig (his choice, the highly credible Pixies), contrasting success with the opposite sex, teenage package holidays, many many laughs and especially Manchester United — was lost to his friends and his family. He was just 28, due to return to England a few weeks later to train as a teacher. After the final whistle sounded at the Millennium Stadium, my phone had rung and, unable to hear each other, we had both bellowed our celebrations down the line. Within an hour, he had been killed in a head-on collision. I had been in Cardiff on his match ticket.

From that moment, the sight of Ole Gunnar Solskjær's winning goal on May 26 1999 gained an elegiac quality. I still find it very difficult to watch. We had been there together, in the Bayern Munich end after a chase for tickets that took in a missed photo opportunity with Bez from the Happy Mondays and a reasonably priced Bavarian ticket tout in lederhosen. Unable to hide our elation at making it in and the course the match followed, Neil's A-Level German proved little disguise of our leanings to the denim-clad Bayern hordes who surrounded us; their behaviour was exemplary in the face of what must have been a shocking defeat. From a pre-smartphone age, I own just one surviving photograph of a trip, which also took in two days at a Costa Brava holiday resort I never actually learned the name of: Neil, wearing a Barcelona shirt and holding his stubbed ticket a few minutes before kick-off, his huge grin marking our disbelief and joy at actually being at the final.

In the afterglow of victory, in a bar off *La Rambla* where Mani from the Stone Roses gave us an indulgent wink (we never did catch up with Dermo from Northside), the joke between us was that we should give up on supporting United that very night. And as much enjoyment as the club gave me in the coming years, I have occasionally wondered if that might have been the correct decision. Nothing has ever topped Barcelona or the magical realism of the club's journey towards that night.

It was the moment for which we had been waiting, arriving after what had seemed so long. In fact, it had been only six years since the club had ventured back into what was still widely known as the European Cup. Time's arrow travels much slower from the ages of 17 to 23 than in your mid-40s.

As Sir Alex Ferguson often used to remark, United had a habit of making things difficult for themselves and the Champions League, a huge step up from the standard of a Premiership still way off its globe-straddling peak, offered much less margin for error. Galatasaray in November 1993, Barcelona in November 1994, Borussia Dortmund in April 1997, Monaco in March 1998: four occasions when failure on the European stage shook Manchester United's belief in itself, and invited smirking ridicule from just about everyone else. Each of those reverses were televised to a terrestrial ITV audience at a time when a dislike of United was a highly fashionable stance that sold magazines and provided banter material for *Fantasy Football* and *They Think It's All Over.* To be a Manchester United fan in that era, and living in another part of the country — I was a student in Sheffield and then Leeds — was to invite pariah status though it was one that a large part of the club's support enjoyed living up to. Some still do, though it is far easier to large it when your team is the best. See Liverpool in 2020 for details.

The continent was a rather different matter, and hopes of making an instant impact on Europe had been raised by winning the Cup Winners' Cup in 1991, beating a Barcelona team filled with stars like Ronald Koeman and Michael Laudrup that won the European Cup the following year. But a run to the final in Rotterdam past the likes of Pécsi Munkás, Wrexham, Montpellier and Legia Warsaw did not prove much of a grounding for the challenge that faced the Ferguson team that had broken a 26-year title duck in 1993. At a time when European football was, as Ian Rush once had it, "like a foreign country", with only Channel 4's Serie A coverage and issues of *World Soccer* providing much of a window to anyone who did not have a satellite dish, the newly-forged Champions League was saturated with glamour and difficulty. Attending European nights at Old Trafford, where the crowd stood all the way through matches — very much against the advice of Trafford Borough Council — and watching players like Romário, Zinedine Zidane and Alessandro Del Piero skate across the turf remained exotic and other-worldly.

From the vantage point of the Stretford End Lower seat I had occasional and grateful use of, the Zidane of Juventus in particular was an incredible sight, forging past United's young bucks in midfield, plodding along and yet graceful. Even as someone whose career later allowed them to see Messi and Ronaldo play at their peaks multiple times, none have come close to Zidane's aesthetic qualities.

These were midweek evenings of incredible tension. Saturday afternoons at Old Trafford, especially once success in the Premiership became expected, were often quiet affairs, the most noise being made by the types of fans who make it their business to moan their way through matches. Now that United give them so much more to moan about, do these men — always men — regret lambasting a group of players who were achieving their footballing dreams for them? Or was such behaviour actually a deflection of anxieties very probably beyond football?

In Europe, though, the crowd was at one, often too tense to sing anything more complicated than "United ... United". Goals registered as moments of relief, and the biggest, most important goals were an explosion of the senses that took fans into the orgiastic behaviour exhibited when a good batch of ecstasy tablets found its way into the Haçienda. One family friend told the story of celebrating a United goal by hugging someone he vaguely recognised only to realise once his ardour had abated that he had in fact been frotting snooker legend, *Big Break* sidekick and Salford Red John Virgo. United's players had to lift themselves in Europe, and the fans did so accordingly.

That extra tension was a by-product of the failures of United's early forays into the Champions League. Winning the title in 1993 had returned the strut to the club's step, with Eric Cantona to the fore, but exiting at the hands of Galatasaray was a severe jolt. The club's first European Cup in 1968, ten years after Munich, might have been a generation ago but following up league titles with European success was what English clubs, especially Liverpool, had done as a matter of course in the late-1970s and early-1980s. Losing to a Turkish club, even one featuring players of the quality of Tugay Kerimoğlu and Hakan Şükür, was an embarrassment and mirrored Manchester City's only foray into the competition, also in 1968, when the team of Francis Lee, Colin Bell and Mike Summerbee had exited in the first round to Fenerbahçe.

The second leg of the tie in Istanbul remains infamous for 164 fans being detained in frightening conditions, Cantona's post-match red card and a banner saying "Welcome To Hell" that severely underplayed the ferocity of the atmosphere in the Ali Sami Yen. However, it was in the first leg at Old Trafford that the tie was truly lost. Most of the noise was made by the visiting fans and Kurdish separatists staged a pitch invasion. Ferguson's team, much rejigged due to Uefa regulations that meant only three foreign players plus two 'assimilated' players could be fielded, dropped their guard against opposition they had all — and that included the manager — completely underestimated. The sight of 1990 FA Cup final hero Lee Martin playing at left-back instead of Denis Irwin was a rarity not to be repeated. The 3-3 scoreline after a late goal from Cantona rescued an equaliser flattered United, who had scored two quick goals and then found themselves rocked by opposition playing with a far greater sense of purpose.

That foreigner rule tormented Ferguson in those early years in Europe, at a time it had become apparent that the best path to improving the team was importing players from abroad. The following year, the 4-0 group-stage defeat at Barcelona, was one of the deepest humiliations of Ferguson's United tenure. Even with Cantona suspended after his Istanbul explosion, no place could be found for Peter Schmeichel, and instead Gary Walsh, like Lee Martin a member of the first, and ill-fated group of 'Fergie Fledglings' of the late-1980s, kept goal. Like Martin, he would be rarely sighted again.

However, my personal culprit for that disaster in Catalonia is neither Uefa, nor Ferguson and definitely not poor Gary Walsh. Instead, it must be levelled at the feet of Mick Hucknall, the flame-haired *bon viveur*, the voice and muscle behind Simply Red. One of United plc's money spinners of the time was a series of VHS videos, released monthly to document matters around the club, a prototype for the magazine-show waffle that infests MUTV and other club channels besides. The video for November 1994 featured Hucknall cavorting with the players, and at one point he appeared to be pillow-fighting with Ryan Giggs and Paul Ince. Ferguson himself was even seen happily chirruping away with Red Mick. The memory even suggests the horrific sight of Hucknall in training gear, but one thing that remains for sure is that no such pre-match celebrity hobnobbing ever accompanied such a trip again. Ferguson's mood darkened after that night, and took on an even deeper hue when it was followed by a yet worse performance at Gothenburg to kill United's hopes of European progress for another season. Though Ince's tactical indiscipline was later partially assigned the blame for disaster at Camp Nou in Ferguson's 1999 autobiography, there also came the sense that frivolity had been almost completely abandoned.

Many years later, with greater life experience taken on board, it can be uncomfortable to recall the portentous gloom with which I greeted reverses like Barcelona and Gothenburg. It is now little wonder that his humourless grim-facedness and single-mindedness made Ferguson so unpopular with other football fans, but he always got plenty of buy-in from zealots like me. As with many things, he was ahead of his time, since elite football in the 21st century carries little in the way of levity, and the game's followers are asked to treat matches, transfers and even minor rule changes with the same gravity as genuine world events, even when world events have stopped the rest of life happening as normal.

By the time United returned to the Champions League two years later, Ferguson was in charge of a regenerated team, and one that fully shared his missionary zeal. Cantona was still around, and had inspired the likes of Giggs, David Beckham, Nicky Butt, Paul Scholes and the Neville brothers to the Double of 1995-96. They had also grown up under Ferguson's diktat that defeat was a fate almost certainly worse than death, an attitude they shared with the fans. Though United still continue to bring through bright young talent, it is difficult to believe that any future group of players will ever identify so closely again with fans in the stadium as that generation of local lads (plus Beckham, the Cockney Red), with its echoes of the Busby Babes. Here was a group who were relatable and looked like the type of lads you might see down the pub. And it was not unknown to actually see them in a boozer. They held a common touch familiar to the fans who paid to see them, something the self-styled 'Class of 92' lost once they grew up to become a cartel of local tycoons and members of the punditocracy whose agendas and cronyism are these days on open show.

Ince and Mark Hughes, two players loved by fans but who would not bow fully to the manager's demands, had been shelled and the success of the youngsters who replaced them had only deepened the faith in Ferguson. Such ruthlessness would become harder to accept as time went on, as the heroic likes of Beckham, Jaap Stam, Ruud van Nistelrooy and Roy Keane were given the same treatment.

The 1996-97 season and a rather sketchy run to the semi-finals opened up the possibility of United one day soon being able to conquer Europe, though it also closed the door on Cantona. He was slowing down while those around him were surfing an upward curve. His performances in the Champions League never lived up to the elemental brilliance with which he dominated the Premiership, winning four titles and dictating the destiny of another by losing his cool at Selhurst Park. The 4-0 quarter-final home defeat of Porto saw Cantona somewhat on the periphery, despite a goal and an assist for Andy

Cole, with whom he struggled to find the same wavelength. Instead, Ryan Giggs, moved from the left wing into the centre, ripped apart the Portuguese team previously superb in the group stages. This was one of those occasions in which Giggs raised his game far higher in Europe than in the humdrum of domestic football. At Old Trafford, on those European nights, the sight of Giggs at full pelt was greeted with the rumble of seats tipping up as fans got to their feet. Giggs' longevity in the game has very probably shrouded what an exciting player he was in those days. Only Cristiano Ronaldo ever reproduced that same reflex reaction from United fans.

Defeat in the semi-final to Borussia Dortmund was yet another dose of cold reality, and just about the last of Cantona. Shirt off, the flesh of his previously ripped torso showing the hint of a wobble, he left the field after a series of misses in the second leg that bore little resemblance to the player whose finishing had been unerring the previous four seasons and especially at clutch moments. And the defensive quality of Dortmund, for whom the veteran Jürgen Kohler was outstanding, was in sharp contrast to the sloppiness of the goals United conceded in Germany and Manchester.

Meeting Dortmund in the final would be Juventus, whose two group-stage matches against United had betrayed a huge gulf in class and physique. Juve won both matches just 1-0, but though they had been given something of a scare at Old Trafford by Giggs tearing down the wing, their calm and poise placed them a sincere cut above. Later revelations and investigations would reveal perhaps why Italy's champions looked like a bunch of supermen next to the skinny bodies, pimpled faces and sallow skin of the likes of Butt and the Nevilles.

Ferguson regularly labelled Juventus the benchmark and as he often did with those managers whose measure he struggled with, garlanded their manager Marcello Lippi with praise: "He's such a good-looking bastard, he makes most of us look like Bela Lugosi." But the serial Italian champions' return to Old Trafford the following October, and a 3-2 win, suggested United might actually be capable of stepping up to the higher echelons. It remains among the finest matches I have attended, the atmosphere an ear-bleeding squall urging on the team to heights that had so recently appeared unreachable. And it happened with Cantona gone, and Roy Keane absent after his knee had been ruptured by his first, fateful clash with Alf-Inge Håland. United conceded in both the first minute and the last, but in between that they took apart Lippi's team. Giggs was again rampant and Teddy Sheringham, bought as Cantona's replacement, revealed a taste for the big occasion. Both scored fine goals, but it was Scholes putting United 2-1 up that crystallised the belief that he and his teammates might actually be good enough to win a European Cup.

Scholes going on to play 700-odd matches for United has clouded that it actually took him a little longer to break through than his mates from the youth team. Butt, far more of an alleycat, was usually preferred to play alongside Keane, and for Juventus, Butt was paired with Ronny Johnsen in midfield. But after his fellow ginger left the field with double vision towards the end of the first half, Scholes' ease on the ball and creative qualities helped drive Juventus to distraction; Didier Deschamps was eventually sent off for two yellow cards. Scholes' finish, seizing on to a loose ball and rounding Angelo Peruzzi to slot the ball home, was ice cold. It was scored by someone unaffected by the blind panic in the stands. It suggested a team now unafraid of anything put in front of them. And in the stands, we too now flushed with belief.

It was not to be that season, as the absence of Keane and Sheringham's struggles to properly replace Cantona took hold, as did injuries to Giggs and Peter Schmeichel by the time a quarter-final with Monaco came around. David Trezeguet's early thunderbolt in Manchester for an away goal came after another of those still characteristic lapses in concentration. A Solskjær equaliser felt like a consolation even though it came after 53 minutes. A sharp memory of that evening at Old Trafford was a loud barracking of Beckham for failing to score a free-kick from considerable distance in the closing moments. More than a little unnecessary, it nonetheless reflected the wide frustration among United fans that the Champions League was again out of reach. Such angst amid all those reverses would make eventual success the following year all the sweeter. Beckham, Sheringham, Solskjær and Ferguson would find their redemption in Barcelona and United fans, including me, would enjoy the night of their lives. I still haven't had a better one.

To disassociate from something that gave me so much joy and had been so all-encompassing was not a decision taken lightly, or even consciously. But gradually, Manchester United lost its pull on me. Covering the club as a journalist has allowed a look under the bonnet, and I have rarely been happy with what I have found. Beyond the grandeur and mythology, and especially after Ferguson retired, it became a football club like the rest. It swiftly surrendered what made it special and the glory days have become little more than comforting memories.

Seven years on from Ferguson's departure, the owners he vouched for — unforgivably for some — have continued to waste fortunes trying to recreate what they inherited but then dismantled, all while continuing to take their own cut of the loot. The scraps of a club pulled in many different directions are being fed off where once there was a single, clear vision, that of winning the European Cup. Looking back, both the club and my younger self had an innocence that is now long lost.

ROMANIA 1994
EMANUEL ROŞU

The four years that had passed since the Democratic Revolution, which removed communist dictator Nicolae Ceauşescu and his regime from power, managed only to light a match in Romanian society. There was some light, but it was alone in an ocean of darkness. Some became rich overnight, while millions of others were fighting with themselves and capitalism to adapt. The transition wasn't easy and it's still not, more than 30 years later.

Romania didn't open its first McDonald's restaurant until 1995, but if people had known that a year before, they would have queued outside the location to wait for the big moment. America. The United States of America. For the oppressed Romanians who dreamed of escaping communist oppression, America was the supreme ideal of freedom. McDonald's, Coca-Cola, the Dallas series ... you name it, everything that came from America was a marvellous gift from the free world, and the hungry, thirsty and frustrated Romanians would embrace it openly.

Historically, Romanians had been waiting for the USA to help set the country free ever since the communists came to power after World War II. There was the hope of freedom every time a 'suspicious' plane was seen flying over the cities of Romania. Every army plane could have been an American one, part of an armed operation to take the communists out. The Americans were eagerly awaited in Romania for 45 years, but they never came. Instead, a bloody revolution that officially cut short the lives of 1,104 people was what changed history. But although America never came to the rescue, Romania didn't stop dreaming about it.

For the neo-communists (rebranded 'social democrats') who replaced Ceausescu's regime in 1990, the four years after the Revolution were a constant battle. It wasn't a fight to better the lives of the people, or to modernise society, but rather for the conservation of the status quo. The new regime arranged a rebellion by unhappy miners, who came to Bucharest from hundreds of kilometres away to beat and intimidate people that were protesting against the hoax the government was trying to pull. Unofficially, more than 100 protesters died after being beaten by the miners in 1990. And once they were silenced, it was presumed life could go on for the new-old political elite as if nothing had happened. Little did they know that in 1994 a football player by the name of Gheorghe Hagi would become the people's favourite for president of the republic.

In 1994, Romania qualified for its second World Cup in a row, having been part of the *Coppa del Mondo* four years before. In Italy, all the Romanian players came from the domestic league, but the regime change meant the national team had become a free market for agents and clubs. Freed from the communist rule that didn't allow players younger than 30 to play outside the country, many of the stars in the Romanian team went on to find a better life abroad. Gheorghe Hagi, the team's most prominent player, left Steaua and signed for Real Madrid almost immediately. Gica Popescu, Craiova's jewel, could have done the same, but he missed out on the move at the last minute.

"Honestly, I was overwhelmed. I didn't realise how big Real Madrid actually was. I got carried away when I saw the contract and I didn't sign it!", he tells me with a smile on his face. In the end, he left the Romanian league that year to play for Sir Bobby Robson at PSV Eindhoven.

A few days after the Democratic Revolution in December 1989, Hagi and Ilie Dumitrescu, another one of Steaua's young stars, spent New Year's Eve together with other friends in Bucharest.

"I asked Ilie: 'you know what this means?' He was looking at me and I answered myself. Money everywhere! Money, money, money! Everywhere you look there's money. But you have to work for them, you have to fight to make things happen, nothing comes for granted. The Revolution made me realise that not working enough can put me behind others. It was time for everyone to compete," Hagi recalls.

1990 was the signal that Romania had arrived at the table. A very talented generation qualified for the World Cup after a 20-year absence, and made it out of a difficult group, winning 2-0 against the USSR, with goals from Marius Lăcătuș, but losing to Cameroon 2-1.

The game against Argentina ended with a 1-1 draw, putting both teams in qualifying positions for the knockout phase. "Hagi met Maradona in the Romania v Argentina game. We played in Napoli and it was very intense. I think Hagi was better than Maradona that night, he played a great game," Popescu believes.

"We were very good, very talented. I think we deserved more in that tournament, to be honest. We got kicked out on penalties by the Republic of Ireland, but we wasted a lot of chances. Life, you can't complain!" Hagi adds.

Four years on, the ambitions and energies were very different.

Romania's most important players were now coming from teams all around Europe. Hagi had two years at Real Madrid, then moved to Brescia. "After two seasons with Madrid, my contract would have extended automatically had we won the league. We lost the championship to Barcelona in the last minute, on the final day of the campaign. I wanted to try something else. Lucescu, a Romanian manager, wanted to build a Romanian team at Brescia. There were some other Romanians there, the Italian league was the most talked about at the moment and I was convinced to go there," Hagi explains.

It didn't go according to the illusion he was sold. Brescia ended up relegated in 1993, and Hagi wanted to leave. Napoli were at his door and knocking. Hagi, by then 28, was ready to answer, but Brescia blocked him and didn't budge. Nicknamed 'Maradona of the Carpathians', Hagi viewed the opportunity of wearing the number ten shirt at Napoli with stars in his eyes and, upset when the move didn't happen, fell out with Lucescu and Luigi Corioni, Brescia's owner.

"For a few months, I was upset, I didn't play. The team was in 12th place in Serie B, we had been relegated after a play-off game against Udinese. I knew I had to come back to the national team. I found the force inside of me and managed to balance myself. I was very disappointed, but at the same time, I knew I could do more in football. I trained like mad and I felt like a bomb before the World Cup."

The qualifying campaign for 1994 started badly. The Romanian FA had replaced Mircea Rădulescu following a failed attempt to reach Euro 1992. Dinamo legend Cornel Dinu came in, but he was sacked after Romania lost away to Czechoslovakia 5-2, in the seventh game of the campaign. It was time for a Steaua man to take charge and Anghel Iordănescu was at the helm for the last three qualifiers. Iordănescu, who had won the European Cup with Steaua as a player in 1986 and coached the team to a final in the same competition against AC Milan (which Steaua lost 4-0), was 43 and hungry to show the world who he was.

Steaua, the Romanian Army's team, and Dinamo, the Internal Affairs Ministry's club, were the most important teams in Romania during the communist regime. Nothing had changed by 1993, with both clubs retaining their influence in the neo-communist reality. Iordănescu won his first three games against the Faroe Islands (away, 4-0), Belgium (home, 2-1), and Wales (away, 2-1), and made the American Dream a reality for millions of people. Romania topped a group in which they had faced tough opposition from Belgium, Czechoslovakia and Wales.

"I had worked before, at Steaua, with ten or 11 of the players I had at the national team. I knew their character. I added players from Dinamo, who I also knew well, but I kept an eye open for any good player there was. Before I came, there were talks of a wasted generation. Instead, the nickname of that team became 'The Golden Generation' in just a few months," Iordănescu fondly remembers.

Right after they celebrated qualification in the locker room in Cardiff, the Romanian players were brought back down to earth at the airport. In the end, this rather unknown and unpleasant episode actually helped create the team that took the world by storm in the United States, confirming its unity and giving the players the rage to prove themselves. The Welsh authorities launched an investigation after a fan was shot accidentally with a flare gun inside the stadium. Police claimed the shot was fired from the sector where the few Romanian fans were sitting. Despite being told they were detaining the national team, which obviously didn't have anything to do with the incident, the police at the airport didn't care. Hagi, Popescu, Răducioiu, Dumitrescu and Dan Petrescu, future Romanian heroes in the US, were all detained and photographed, held for three hours before the Romanian Embassy stepped in and asked for the immediate release of the players and staff.

The prejudice towards Romania was still there — the players felt it and fought their battle to free Romania of its dark past. It was obvious in each of the games during that campaign. Romania had beaten Wales 5-1 in Bucharest, missing at least five further immense chances to score. Revenge for the Welsh in Cardiff could have left the national team at home. At half-time, Hagi asked coach Iordănescu to leave the players alone for a few minutes. He punched a drawer twice and screamed: "Are these guys going to beat us?! No way! We have to qualify; do you understand this?" Romania were 1-0 up at the break. Dean Saunders equalised in the 61st minute, but Răducioiu, seven minutes before the final whistle, bought Romania their tickets to America.

"Before that game, Iordănescu said something which was very emotional for us. Dan Petrescu and I started crying. It was all or nothing. We didn't care about money or anything else. We just wanted to go to America," former Tottenham Hotspur and West Ham United midfielder Ilie Dumitrescu recalls.

With Cardiff and all the tension around that game left behind, it was time to move on. Romania had made it. They were going to America. Legally! They would have the chance to conquer a country that millions dreamed of reaching while they were living in darkness, without heating or food, under the communist regime. Football players were privileged during communism, but that didn't make them indifferent to the suffering of those around them.

Iordănescu started planning. Before the World Cup, he wanted a long training camp in Italy to get his players to their maximum physical potential. He had them so well prepared that they wanted him sacked. Romania had three head coaches in the two years prior to the tournament — pressure to appoint a fourth just before the World Cup started was hardly ideal preparation.

"There were a few days left until the game against Colombia, our debut at the World Cup in 1994. The FA bosses told me that the players were unhappy with my training methods. They thought I was pushing them too hard. The FA didn't tell me directly, but the decision [to warn me] suggested that they were considering releasing me. I said: 'OK! I have a very good relationship with the players, it's their problem if they feel unhappy. I'm not changing my methods, my planning. Let them come to me if they had something to say.' I knew how players were, moaning because of hard training. It was up to me to make them reconsider what we were doing; we had to get past that moment and then things would settle. That was it!". Iordănescu had another battle, this time against his own team.

His three training sessions per day undoubtedly made some think about leaving the national team if Iordănescu didn't. But the coach didn't budge. He kept the rhythm in Bormio before the tournament, and then when the team flew to the United States. "It ended up helping us big time because our physical condition was the foundation of our results at the World Cup. I had hard boys with me. I managed to make them understand that what we were doing would help them a lot," a smiling Iordănescu, now 70, reveals.

Intensive training wasn't Iordănescu's only problem. Leaving out Steaua hero Marius Lăcătuș from the squad for America seemed like a decision impossible to explain. Lăcătuș, one of the two scorers in the penalty shootout that miraculously won Steaua the European Cup in 1986, over FC Barcelona, was Iordănescu's colleague as a player, then his most valuable goalscorer when Iordănescu moved to the bench. Lăcătuș was 30 in 1994, having returned to Steaua in 1993 after one season with Fiorentina, in Serie A, and two with Oviedo, in La Liga. He had refused to extend his contract with Oviedo one year before the World Cup just to make sure of playing time in his native Romania and to be at his best ahead of the tournament in the United States.

"Leaving Lăcătuş out was one of the biggest mistakes I did. I will regret it as long as I live. I apologised to Marius after we returned from America. I really regret it, I don't even want to remember what I did. I was unfair to Lăcătuş, my soul hurts for that," Iordănescu sighs.

Known as a coach obsessed with detail, Iordănescu prepared for every game like it was his last. The players loved his intuition and the perception he gave them that nothing could surprise them during games. Nicknamed 'The General', Iordănescu was actually given a general's degree in the Romanian Army after his long career at Steaua and his performances at club and national team level.

"I allowed my players to talk whenever they needed to, to express themselves in the locker room, before the game or at half-time. At least from that point of view, I wasn't a dictator," he smiles. Although by then assistant coach at Steaua, Iordănescu made a substitute's appearance in the European Cup final against Barcelona in 1986, despite being 36 and not having kicked a ball in over two years — manager Lăcătuş insisted he should be registered and play in the final to give those around him more confidence. Iordănescu first refused to do it, then agreed in one of the most surprising tactical decisions in the history of the European Cup. Thanks to that, Iordănescu had also added the European Cup to his name as a player.

Europe was one thing, America quite another. Just like his players, Iordănescu was also hungry and eager to introduce himself to the free world, after achieving much, both as a player and as a coach, before the fall of communism.

Romania's group at the World Cup included Colombia, Switzerland and the USA. Ahead of the tournament, Pelé had picked Colombia as his favourites for the tournament. The South Americans had been impressive in their qualifiers, beating Argentina at home 5-0 in the process and going unbeaten through the preliminary round. In April 1994, Colombia's coach, Francisco Maturana, who was on Real Madrid's wishlist to replace Benito Floro, watched Romania play a friendly against Bolivia, which Romania won 3-0. He wasn't impressed. In a press conference organised at the Colombian Embassy, he told the Romanian media that he "was only afraid of Yugoslavia in Europe, but that team doesn't exist anymore". The Romanian players heard him.

At the Rose Bowl in Pasadena, Romania's yellow army showed the world just what their American dream looked like. *Tricolorii* won the game 3-1, to the joy of the 5,000 fans supporting them in a heated ocean of 75,000 people. Hagi scored a fantastic goal, still thought of as one of the most brilliant in the history of the World Cup.

"Everyone in Romania dreamed of conquering America. I think we did it! Some of our biggest sportsmen had success before, it was football's turn to do it now. We were Romania's ambassadors and we're proud of that. We went to America with one thing in mind: to show who we are. We all dreamed of going to America. When we finally did, we were very happy, we felt very good. The coach had a great idea to keep us focused for a month before the tournament, we had time to adapt, to work. It was amazing, we did things the right way," Hagi recollects, seemingly without any memory of Iordănescu's pre-tournament training regime.

"All the talk before the tournament motivated us. We were focused and we believed in ourselves. We knew we were good; we went there to win," Hagi says.

"When I went to the World Cup, I had in mind to win it. Romania did great things, Romania has potential, Romania can do it! I always thought and felt that all the time," Hagi recounts with a proud smile on his face.

He remembers the goal he scored with a geometric diagonal from 40 metres out like it was yesterday. For the millions of fans watching at home, it came as a shocking, fantastic, beautiful surprise that the whole country celebrated, throwing their hands in the air in the middle of the night. His colleagues were less surprised, as was Mircea Lucescu, the Romanian coach Hagi had at Brescia. "Hagi told us weeks before the tournament that he was going to do it. He knew Córdoba was coming out of his goal so Hagi was set to lob the ball past him!" Lucescu remembers.

"It was a beautiful goal, but a very difficult one to score as well! Very hard! I took the risk. I prepared for it. We knew the opponent well. Our goalkeeper, Stelea, can tell you what he did in training because it happened to him a few days before the game. We practiced together. I kicked the ball well like I always did. I had scored before from the half, I scored for Real and Barcelona too, to make them both happy. I had the courage, I believed in myself. That's how that goal came," Hagi confesses.

Răducioiu scored Romania's other two goals, sending tens of thousands of people out of their homes at 4:30 in the morning. Romania wasn't used to taking to the streets in celebration. Previously, such important mass gatherings were either political rallies or a bloody resistance to the regime. It was different now and it was wonderful. Big or small, every town was up all night to live their American dream through the hearts and bodies of those selected for the national team. The World Cup in the USA not only attached even more of an aura to a country that millions were desperate to reach, but transformed Gica, Florin, Dan or Ilie, the players, the boys who grew up in communism, into definitive idols.

Back at the hotel, the players and staff members were greeted by their families. Hagi had dinner with his mum and dad, while others had their wives or girlfriends with them. There was even a small Aromanian orchestra brought over from Bucharest. Aromanians, a minority Hagi is part of, are an ethnic group with roots in Greece and Albania, who have their own language and strong family ties.

Iordănescu enjoyed the time spent with his wife and the players' families, but thinks it was a big mistake. It took the players out of their rhythm and they couldn't focus on the second game in the group, against Switzerland. The fantastic outing against Colombia made people more and more curious about Hagi, Răducioiu, and the enchanting yellows. But the Switzerland match ended in disappointment and a 4-1 defeat. Hagi scored Romania's only goal in the 36th minute to make it 1-1. In the second half, Stéphane Chapuisat proved too hard to handle, scoring in the 53rd minute and constantly threatening the Romanian goal. Adrian Knup's double in just four minutes (68 and 72) sealed the win for Switzerland.

"It was my fault, first of all. I didn't prepare the game well at a mental level. I was too generous, allowing too much free time. I know what I'm saying, trust me. It was more than happiness over there, but I will not go to details right now. I think that Romanian players need to be … let's say under surveillance all the time," Iordănescu says mysteriously.

His assistant during that campaign, Dumitru Dumitriu, doesn't agree. He has his own explanation for the defeat: "I don't think we relaxed. It was a weird game. We played in Detroit, the stadium was like a hall, closed. Not long before the game, they were installing the pitch. The heat was immense, we couldn't breathe. The Swiss had a great evening, it all went in their favour in that game. Their goals were scored easily. Fortunately, that game didn't put us back too much. It all depended on our game against the United States!"

Going into the final game in the group, Romania didn't only lose momentum after the loss against Switzerland. The squad also lost Ion Vlădoiu. 'Charlie' came on as a substitute in the 70th minute of the game and was sent off for a reckless challenge just three minutes later, suspended for Romania's next three games. Iordănescu wasn't happy at all with his player, who would end up taking an early flight home after the game against the United States, the last one in the group stage. Unhappy he didn't get a shirt to swap after the game, Vlădoiu started a big scandal, swearing at assistant coach Dumitriu in front of the whole team. After an emergency meeting, Vlădoiu was given tickets to fly home. His explanations weren't accepted: "I didn't swear, I only told him in front of everyone: 'You're a big coach yourself now, ah?' That's it!" Dumitriu, who was going to be Vlădoiu's witness for his marriage, cancelled the plans, telling the striker to forget about it.

Now, the game. Romania needed at least a draw to be safe in the race to qualify, but the players wanted to beat the United States to prove themselves after the dismal performance against Switzerland. Back to Pasadena, to the stadium which became a myth for Romanian football culture. This time, the goal wasn't scored by Răducioiu or Hagi, those everyone was keeping an eye on. Future Chelsea star Dan Petrescu scored the only goal in the game, pushing Romania into first place in the group.

Romania poured onto the streets again. Hundreds of thousands celebrated the win that put them in the last 16. The team was followed on such a scale that even the Mental Hospital in Bucharest allowed its patients to march around the institution in celebration after they proved impossible to contain.

In the United States, Hagi, Popescu and the others waited nervously to find out who they would face in their next game. Late drama in Group D sent the Romanian troops back to Pasadena: in another shock, Argentina had lost their final group game against Bulgaria 2-0, finishing the group in third place but, with two wins, qualifying as one of the best third-placed sides. The Romanians would face a team without Maradona, who tested positive in an anti-doping test performed after the game against Nigeria.

For the Romanian players, Argentina were the perfect opponent. Hagi told his teammates to dream big, so hearing what happened in the dying moments of the Group D games made everyone smile nervously. "If we do fall, let's fall from the most beautiful peak!" Hagi said to his colleagues.

"We were very sorry Maradona couldn't play. And I was particularly unhappy. I liked playing against him. It happened before, in 1990, at the *Coppa del Mondo*. I played well, I wanted another confrontation against one of the biggest players ever," Hagi says.

Romania had absentees too — Răducioiu, who was suspended, couldn't play. Iordănescu decided he would play the game against Argentina without a striker. The hero came out of nowhere. His name: Ilie Dumitrescu. "I was told I was crazy for playing Dumitrescu after two below-par performances in the group stage. There were voices in the FA who said I only started Dumitrescu because he came from Steaua like me. I'm so happy that Ilie proved everyone wrong and scored two fantastic goals against Argentina," Iordănescu recalls.

The game in Pasadena, Romania's third in the same stadium, was commentated for Argentinian TV by Maradona himself. Afterwards, Pelé said Hagi was the best player at the tournament; Maradona offered the same verdict. Hagi was in the form of his life and he wasn't going to stop performing.

"We created feelings and emotions. Our encounter against Argentina is regarded as the best game of football in the history of the World Cup, which says a lot! There were loads of chances, a lot of energy, sprints, dribbles, everything. Then we had the pass I offered to Ilie Dumitrescu for his goal, also his free-kick and my goal to make it 3-1 in the second half. We dominated the game, we set an example. A game like that sets a model for the future," Hagi believes.

Iordănescu was so tense, he didn't even realise how good the game was. It took him years to acknowledge what his team really did on July 3 1994:

"The game against Argentina confirmed to us that we have what it takes to reach the highest level. I only realised how good a game that really was years after it was played. I knew we played incredibly well, but I didn't know it was so good to watch. Fortunately, I had the chance to enjoy it on TV," Iordănescu laughs.

Apart from the tactical side of things, Iordănescu used a clip with the people's joy at home to motivate his players, showing it right before the game against Argentina. Many of them cried. A match in the last 16 of the World Cup was by far the most intense Romania had ever played in a big tournament. In the middle of the night, Romania lit flares and celebrated. The TV stations, which didn't actually have the concept of live reporting back then, started fighting for the best approach to the historical events they were witnessing. After the game, a TV channel went to Ilie Dumitrescu's block and held interviews with any of his neighbours that opened the door to them. The win could also not be kept out of the political context. All the mass gatherings nationwide had 'Hagi for president' chants repeated over and over again. Surveys presented in the media even claimed Hagi would have won an election, had he decided to run.

Millions were now hoping for a Romania v Brazil match in the semis. But first, the national team had to beat Sweden. It was an opponent that Iordănescu knew to perfection. Romania had played them in a friendly just before the World Cup, which had ended 1-1.

"They couldn't have surprised us, that's what we thought. But they did. They surprised us with a cross in the box," Iordănescu remembers.

Romania had played so well without a striker that Iordănescu thought of leaving Răducioiu out of the first team, even though he wasn't suspended anymore.

"I felt I was going to be kept on the bench for that game. I wanted to start a big scandal if I had been told I wasn't going to start. I was the top goalscorer in the team. No way I was being left out. I decided to fight for my place in the team, it was a normal thing to do!" Răducioiu remembers, laughing. A few hours before the game, he was relieved to find himself in the team: "I did my job, I scored two goals and I also scored my penalty in the shootout!"

Like everything Romania did at that World Cup, the match against Sweden was mad. Brolin opened the scoring in the 79th minute, then Răducioiu pushed the game to extra time a minute before normal time was over. Romania went ahead after 101 minutes thanks to the same player, only for Kennet Andersson to equalise five minutes before the final whistle, with Sweden down to ten men after Stefan Schwarz was sent off in the 102nd minute. Andersson's goal is still talked about in Romania, even 26 years after the World Cup. Goalkeeper Florin Prunea is blamed for his reaction to the cross leading to the goal. It will haunt him and Romanian football forever.

Prunea later revealed he was afraid to get off the plane that took the players home after the World Cup. The plane first landed in Timișoara, on Romania's western border. He needn't have worried — tens of thousands of fans were there to greet the players.

"I didn't want to come out of the plane. I was afraid of people's reactions. Finally, coach Iordănescu talked me into doing it. When I saw the people gathered there, I was ashamed. Fortunately for me, they applauded and sang my name. I was very relieved. That also happened in Bucharest, people had forgiven me. I remember a league game I played with Dinamo after that, a fan was swearing badly at me. I went to have a chat with him. He told me he got a divorce because of my mistake. I told him: 'In that case, go on, I'm sorry!' It is as it is, I can't go back to change anything," Prunea confesses.

The former goalkeeper had the humour to even use his dramatic moment against Sweden during the coronavirus pandemic, asking people to stay in as much as possible to prevent getting infected. In a clip that went viral, Prunea told his followers: "Don't go out as I did against Sweden. Stay in!"

Before the 120-minute-thriller against Sweden finished, Romania's bench thought of making a shock substitution. Stelea, the goalkeeper who started the first two games on American soil, was suggested as a surprise substitute to Prunea.

Gabi Balint, who had been an essential player in the qualifying campaign, had his career ended at 30 because of injury, but travelled to the US as part of Iordănescu's staff.

"Those on the bench were afraid to tell Iordănescu about the substitution they had in mind. They told me to suggest it because I was closer to the manager. Stelea was really good at penalties, so I also thought it was a good idea. Iordănescu said 'no' and Prunea stayed in goal for the shootout," Balint says.

Mild missed Sweden's first shot. Everything was going perfectly for Romania. Răducioiu, Hagi, and Lupescu all scored. Then Petrescu missed, but Dumitrescu scored. 4-4 after five penalties each. It came down to Miodrag Belodedici to equalise after Henrik Larsson made it 6-5. "Belo," the first player ever to win the European Cup with two different clubs, was considered one of Romania's best penalty takers. But Ravelli guessed right, and saved the defender's shot. Sweden were through to the semi-final and would live Romania's dream against Brazil.

"Funny as it is, Petrescu and Belodedici never missed a penalty in training ahead of the tournament. We always had penalty sessions, but they never missed, they were annoying our keepers with their perfect shots," Gica Popescu remembers.

It ended in tears for Romania, but the social impact of that campaign was greater than you could ever imagine. Self-belief, pride, dignity — that's what the national football team brought to the millions at home. The style and spirit of that team, the fact that the tournament took place in America, and that all the players' public statements referred to people's joy at home created a connection for generations between that group of players and their fans.

"A semi-final against Brazil was reality, it was perfectly possible. We knew that we were the only team that could have won against them. We played the same football: we had seven or eight players defending and three very good attackers. That's how you win a World Championship. We had technique, speed and we were in form. We had seven players behind us, they were good football players, they also knew how to play the ball and not only defend," Hagi says.

During that tournament, Johan Cruyff called Hagi. He was impressed by his game and wanted him at Barcelona. The Romanian didn't need a second invitation.

"He said I was the best number ten in Europe. Cruyff was my idol as a player, I loved him and his philosophy. I grew up with the Dutch team and with Ajax in the '70s. I learned a lot from him. When such a big club is after you and gives you the opportunity to work with your idol, you go. I was taught total football by a great manager and a great person. How could you wish for more?" Hagi recalls.

The Romanian ace was told that in the hierarchy for the tournament's best player, he was first after the quarter-finals. He is sure that he could have won even the Ballon d'Or that year if Romania had qualified for the semi-finals. Hagi finished fourth in both the World Cup 'Golden Ball' rankings and the Ballon d'Or race.

"I think I was the most determined player of the tournament. I had to play all the games in order to win the best player award, that's something I sometimes think about. But I left a vacant seat; hopefully, a Romanian player fills it at some time in the future," Hagi sighs.

Talking about the game against Sweden, Hagi turns from energetic to nostalgic: "It was destiny, that's how it was meant to be. Let's take the positives. We left something behind, now it's up for the new generations to beat us. Had we won the World Cup, maybe others would not be motivated enough."

Hagi started an academy in the middle of nowhere, near Constanta, his birthplace. Shepherds used to bring their herds there every day. Hagi paid millions from the money he won as a player to pay football back for all that it's given him. Hagi's Academy is the most modern in Romania and one of the best in Eastern Europe.

"We educate kids to dream, to do important things in life and in football. I'm working to create a generation of players that will win Romania the World Cup," Hagi vows.

That same year, 1994, Romania was rocked by a huge scandal. A pyramid investment fund, Caritas, left hundreds of thousands of Romanians without their life savings, after promising immense revenues for their investments. Desperate parents who sold family homes, pensioners robbed of all their life savings, or people who took out immense loans that they couldn't pay back — they were all on the brink of failure once Caritas suddenly collapsed. After tens of years of sacrifice, then a fake capitalist system and scams that risked to leave people with nothing, Romania finally had a model of how to rise again after being beaten, how to light a match for yourself when others tell you to go on living in the darkness, how to dream and hope. The Romanian team of 1994 was a hearts and minds revolution to millions.

NEWCASTLE UNITED 1995–96

DANIEL GRAY

Snow shrouded the north-east copiously and as if trying to disguise it as somewhere else. It would not have been a surprise to spot penguins advancing on Hartlepool or a polar bear warming his paws on the radiators inside Chester-le-Street Asda. For the Colombian gazing down from an aeroplane window, it must have been a surreal sight. Had *The Snowman* ever been screened in Bogotá, he may have wondered if he were now observing its filming location and ripping loose his in-flight earphones for fear of experiencing *We're Walking in the Air*.

It was February 1996, and as his private jet swooped low over County Durham, perhaps Faustino Asprilla ruminated on how the relatively recent loss of heavy industry had altered this region's landscape. Or, perhaps he was asking his interpreter how to translate 'Warren Barton' into Spanish. Asprilla had signed for Newcastle United on Thursday February 8. His work permit was granted the following day, and now, at 11am on Saturday February 10, 'Tino' was about to touch down on the tarmac of Teesside Airport. For a fee of £7.5m, he had exchanged the north-eastern region of Emilia-Romagna for Tyneside, and Parma for Ponteland. It was that kind of era. The money of John Hall at St James' Park and Steve Gibson at the Riverside Stadium talked, and usually it said: "It's not *that* cold here, and we'll get you some of those fancy beans you like."

Asprilla stepped down from the plane and a gust of snow whipped across the tarmac and into his face. It was a bit like being egged by an entire country. *Bienvenido a Inglaterra, Tino.* The first thing to engulf him was the seal-grey fur coat he wore, which could be filed under the fashion category 'stowaway chic'. The second was a smattering of press photographers and keen Magpies supporters, many of the latter notably and stereotypically coatless. The only fever they had contracted, though, was for Kevin Keegan's new signing, a dynamic and dexterous forward first encountered here in the UK on Channel 4's *Gazzetta Football Italia*. Tino was rock 'n' roll. Tino was impossibly exotic. Tino was going to win them the league.

Kevin Keegan met his new acquisition for lunch at the Newcastle team hotel. That afternoon they would face Middlesbrough on Teesside, snow or not. The Colombian drank a glass of wine and agreed to be named as a substitute. "I explained it was purely so he could get a feel for it," Keegan wrote in his most recent autobiography. "It was never my intention to bring him on."

Ahead of this first ever Tees-Tyne derby at the Riverside, Boro had lost six matches in succession. Heady autumn days of sitting fourth in the table felt more remote than Colombian sunshine. Manager Bryan Robson wore the worried look of a man who had received the wrong kind of advice from a cash machine. Hope rested with his own South American, the Brazilian Juninho, for whom contemporary journalists had dusted off the underused epithet 'mercurial'. On some afternoons, his feet seemed to twinkle in the low winter sun. Today, the weather had calmed and the sky consisted of that murky silver colour which makes men look up, pause and claim: "It feels too cold to snow." It was Baltic down by the Tees and yet Juninho thrived and buzzed in a hectic, restless first-half. Early on, the 5'5" man from São Paolo beat Darren Peacock to a header. Then, he forced Newcastle's John Beresford to score an own goal. 1-0 Boro. Tino who?

In one of those combinations that could only happen during the Premier League's mid-1990s sweet spot of homespun heart and continental innovation, Paul Wilkinson, Nick Barmby and Juninho had Newcastle pinned back. Then Tino rose from the dugout and sauntered up and down the touchline a few times, in a bench coat the size of a factory chimney. The black and white thousands in the away end roared once as he ran, and again when Keegan invited him to remove his abundant jacket. In the 67th minute, Asprilla made the sign of the cross with a gloved hand and entered the bitter fray. Geordies hollered their delight. Teessiders jeered nervously and sang for Juninho. It was an unlikely setting for such Latin American rivalry.

Asprilla's arrival caused spectacular, beguiling chaos. His trickery and lightness, his ability to appear gangly yet deft, languid yet urgent, baffled Middlesbrough. He turned through the home midfield as if on a conjuring spree, his nifty beating of players resembling more a sleight of hand than a footballing manoeuvre. Six minutes after entering the scene, Tino seemed to entwine centre-half Steve Vickers in the manner of a child tying up a sibling during a game of Cowboys and Indians. Vickers must have felt hungover by the time he had looked up and seen Steve Watson plunging the ball into the net. The winning goal appeared shortly afterwards, a trickling effort from Les Ferdinand that somehow beat Gary Walsh, who resembled a clumsy man up a ladder unable to stop its slow descent to earth. Boro had been looking at the stars and feeling ready to notch a rare win. Now, they were in the gutter, and seeking inspiration from Jamie Pollock.

"Tinooooo, Tinooooo", cried the bawling zebras of Newcastle and then, when the final whistle blew: "We shall not/We shall not be moved … ". Their team had escaped thanks to the bewitching powers of a man who had drunk Rioja for lunch. They remained top of the Premier League. To play badly and emerge victorious was a mark of champions. To do it by virtue of a scintillating new signing was poetic. To watch the Magpies was to witness fate unfolding. What could possibly go wrong?

Newcastle upon Tyne cannot help but look pretty. It just has one of those faces. It "is a magnificent city for sheer excitement", offered the great Ian Nairn, "the view that stops you dead halfway along a street, or the flight of steps that sucks you in like a vortex. Too few people know about it; fewer still understand just why the Newcastle pattern is so marvellous." Nairn, a revered architectural critic, was writing on that occasion of the place in the 1960s, though his words still apply today, and did as well to the mid-'90s city that Faustino Asprilla moved among. Back in the '60s, St James' Park was a cosy, if raw, environment; Nairn could never have guessed that it would become one of Newcastle's great architectural diversions, a charismatic temple brooding over its place yet belonging, in their eyes, to its people; the closing bracket to the Tyne Bridge's opener.

It more resembled its '60s self than its modern, colossal state when Kevin Keegan became club manager in February 1992. Though that natural beauty bestowed of being built in a valley was permanent and unflinching, in truth, much of Newcastle now wore a tired, dreary look and was a place of shrugged shoulders and sighs; sighs as the last shipyards fell, sighs as those surrounding coal towns that fed the Tyne were slayed, sighs as the dole line grew longer than the queue for the Gallowgate End at St James'.

"But what do they do all day?/And what are they supposed to say?/ What does a father tell his son?" sings Jimmy Nail in the permanently-moving record *Big River*. It felt like all had been lost. And then, in April, the bloody Tories (for it might as well have said that on ballot papers) were elected again.

The epic time-sweep television series *Our Friends in the North*'s final episode is set in 1995 and it is as close to a documentary as exists about the Big River city in that era. Occasional flutters of hope and signs that regeneration might just benefit more than a few people are littered among the more familiar, hopeless landscapes. The sheer grinding grey of everything from pavement to sky is a heavy, cloying presence, as if the viewer's television has chosen its own settings. Everywhere people are loitering, hanging around by the Swing Bridge with nothing to do, looking at impossible holidays in the windows of Lunn Poly, sitting on the steps by Grey's Monument with no-one to meet and no Metro to catch. To see sadness among such glorious beauty is oddly compelling. There is, too, petty crime — joy riding, shoplifting, car radios prised free with a screwdriver — in this epoch of delinquents and moral panics, of John Major and chips in newspaper wrappers, of chasms where shipyards once hummed and retail parks had yet to fill the land. Often, Newcastle looked like the 1980s had yet to arrive, never mind the 1990s.

This context meant that the arrival of Kevin Keegan and the success of his team were vital. It was not just a happy sideshow in some prosperous multi-club city where football was merely another pastime option; Newcastle United were hope, colour, noise, the future. In many senses, they *were* this city. A winning team invigorated the disenfranchised. It had the stall men of the Grainger Market rolling brown paper bags of pears beneath toothy grins. It gave young lads something to gather for, away towns to visit on dark blue and egg yolk yellow InterCity 125 trains. It even returned to those with not a hope of affording access to St James' some pride and identity, a phenomenon so wonderfully, if bleakly, portrayed in Jonathan Tulloch's novel *The Season Ticket*, and its film adaptation, *Purely Belter*. Government would never do that for the Geordies. Commerce neither. Football could and did.

Shortly after, *somehow*, John Major was returned to power in April, Keegan cast his first spell and kept the sinking Magpies from relegation to England's third tier. The following season, 1992-93, they won the league playing snappy, magnetic football. When Ian Nairn referred to a "Newcastle pattern", he was, of course, referring to the topography of the city. Yet the term could be applied to Keegan's outfit, with their template of lulling in teams and blinding them on the break, and then relentlessly pursuing kill after kill.

It served them well in their first Premier League season, 1993-94. Newcastle finished in third place, their highest ranking since just after the General Strike. Andrew Cole scored 41 times. Keegan's reign invited terms like 'Messiah' and 'Saviour', and there was something religious about the way in which he then proceeded to sell Cole halfway through the 1994-95 season, as if he had received a message from on high. His disciples missed their main goalscorer, and the team finished sixth. There was hunger for more, and Newcastle United had behind them a whole city whose fortune seemed to hang on theirs. The club determined the mood of this entire, dramatic place.

By the summer of 1995, top-flight football had just about completed its journey from societal pariah to celebrated and glamourous darling, though it didn't always feel that way for those of us watching Phil Whelan slice another clearance into the disabled enclosure. Blackburn Rovers' moneyed route to the 1994-95 Premier League title prompted many other clubs to throw around cash with all the abandon of a drunk dad at his daughter's wedding. In came Dennis Bergkamp and David Platt at Arsenal, Ruud Gullit (free, but most emphatically waged) at Chelsea, Savo Milošević at Aston Villa and Georgi Kinkladze at Manchester City. Liverpool paid £8.5 million for Stan Collymore, and Newcastle £6 million for Les Ferdinand. One scored a hatful of goals and achieved legendary status, while the other has lots of opinions.

As witnessed in the Tees-Tyne derby that February, it was, too, a time when the old worlds and the new collided — Duncan Ferguson earning £6.50 a week sweeping prison floors and Bruce Grobelaar on match-fixing charges on the one hand, those foreign stars with their pasta and exotic boot makes on the other. Nothing summed up this blend of shepherd's pie and sun-dried tomatoes more than watching the buccaneering Serbian Saša Ćurčić play at Bolton's charming but dated Burnden Park.

Early in the term, Manchester United's young team were beaten and condemned and Leeds United's Tony Yeboah scored the kind of goals that even Roy Race would have thought far-fetched. Les Ferdinand, backed by wily Robert Lee and the ever-ingenious Peter Beardsley, steamed through Coventry City and Everton. As the season progressed, many other teams would fall victim to the alleged tyrant of the Blue Peter garden. Powered by Ferdinand, Lee, Beardsley and the almost-sarcastically handsome David Ginola, the Magpies won their first four games. By the end of November, they were five points clear at the top. The sight of Keegan and his assistant, Terry McDermott, springing from the bench after a goal, seemingly in competition, like two drunks vying to pay for the last round at closing time, became a terrific, rousing sideshow.

There were shadows and worries, moments of doubt for those many Tynesiders who attached so much to their club. Eric Cantona's return from his kung-fu ban spurred the Magpies' title rivals, for whom Andrew

Cole was now scoring with alarming and familiar regularity. And Newcastle themselves were prone to sporadic, unexpected defeats, often in the capital. A reverse at Stamford Bridge in December left Keegan with time to reflect: "When I get on the bus and I'm taking this team around the country, I look back at the players and I think 'Yeah, I'm proud to take this group of lads down there.' We won't always win, but we're very much on par to win something this year. And we've tried to do it in style." Travelling back north on those occasions, the team coach would stop and the players eat fish and chips at the Wetherby Whaler. Phillipe Albert on the scrap butties and Tizer? These were truly in-between times.

On December 27, Manchester United defeated Newcastle 2-0 at Old Trafford. "It pegs Newcastle back from ten points' lead to seven, which is vital," said Alex Ferguson with a steely glint in his eye afterwards. The Mancunians were tracking and poking the Novocastrians during games and after them. Ferguson looked around the corner and saw a gift waiting. Keegan saw only a dark stranger. Yet he rallied the Geordies, and they him. By early January, Newcastle had extended their lead over the Red Devils to 12 points. "We're in a great position," said Keegan.

If Faustino Asprilla had a newspaper with him on that snowy flight, he may have checked the league table and wondered why Newcastle were sufficiently worried to summon him. Surely such a useful late winter lead at the top would be enough? "It really depends on how Newcastle handle it," Alex Ferguson had said after his team's victory at Upton Park on January 22. "They've some tough away fixtures. We've *had* a lot of tough away fixtures. Once it comes to March … Who knows?" Fergie's team won their next four matches.

After the Asprilla cameo at Boro, Newcastle lost to West Ham United (bloody London …) and drew 3-3 at Maine Road. On March 4, Ferguson's team travelled to play Keegan's on Tyneside. Newcastle battered and peppered Peter Schmeichel's goal. Eric Cantona scored and the Reds won 1-0. "We're still top of the league," said Keegan afterwards, "if we win our game in hand, we're four points clear." Ifs and buts had infiltrated the usual Keegan positivity. It was as if a dad had started to hint that there would not be enough money for Christmas this year.

In the final week of March, Manchester United climbed to the top of the Premier League. Just before Easter, the Messiah took his team to Anfield. After two minutes, the Magpies were a goal down. After quarter of an hour they led. So seesawed this delirious match until the 92nd minute and Martin Tyler's cry of "Collymore closing in … " and 4-3 to Liverpool and Keegan flopped on the dugout hoardings like a sailor vomiting over the side of a ship. "Lady Luck's probably not quite with us like she was early in the season, and that might make a massive difference," he reflected afterwards.

On Easter Monday, Newcastle were defeated 2-1 at Ewood Park. A Geordie, Graham Fenton, scored both Blackburn Rovers goals. Lady Luck, it seemed, had not only absconded, she had bought a season ticket at Old Trafford. "I would like us to finish runners-up if we can't win it. This club has never done that," said Keegan this time. Ambition was fading. He had promised to lasso the moon, but his rope had become entangled on a telegraph wire.

Then, a lifeline: Manchester United lost at The Dell. Newcastle were now three points behind with a game in hand, that magical phrase that bears more hope than four words should be made to withstand. After a narrow Red Devils victory at Elland Road, Alex Ferguson accused the Leeds players of raising their game against his team. "For some of them," said Ferguson, "it's more important to get a result against Manchester United to stop them winning the league than anything else. They're cheating their manager … when they play Newcastle, you wait and see the difference."

At the end of April, the Magpies contested that very fixture. Keith Gillespie, a lesser-heralded craftsman of the wing, scored the game's only goal. Keegan took the Sky television headphones and microphone and combusted, finger-jabbing towards the camera as if its lens were Ferguson's chest. "A lot of things have been said over the last few days, some of them almost slanderous … when you do that with footballers, like he said about Leeds … I've kept really quiet, but I'll tell you something, he went down in my estimation when he said that. We haven't resorted to that, but I tell you, you can tell him now, he'll be watching it: we're still fighting for this title and he's gotta go to Middlesbrough and get something and I'll tell you, honestly, I will love it if we beat them. Love it."

At that point, it was possible to imagine a Glaswegian in a plush Cheshire front room pouring another single malt.

The snatching of three points at Leeds occurred on a Monday night, April 29. Though conventional wisdom now cites Keegan's broadcast eruption as the moment Newcastle lost the title, a draw at the City Ground three days later was the true catastrophe. "You're gonna win fuck all," sang the Forest fans, and even the most bullish away-end Geordie struggled to disagree. On the final day, Manchester United did go to Middlesbrough and get something, a 3-0 victory against a Boro side who gave all the effort and enthusiasm of teenagers at a barn dance. Steve Bruce lifted the Premier League trophy and fans of both clubs sang "Let's all laugh at Keegan".

Forty miles north, men cried into the River Tyne and drowned their sorrows on the Bigg Market. With the reflection that half a dozen pints can bring, they could salute the odyssey that Keegan had taken them on. One man's charisma and his squad's fizzing, irrepressible football had given them back their faith in a club and its city. That city seemed, somehow, like it had a future for the first time in years. Surely this was just the beginning of the story.

ENGLAND 1996

MICHAEL GIBBONS

With so many candidates for nadirs in their history, identifying the actual lowest point of England's men's international side is not the easiest task. Some might point to Belo Horizonte in 1950, where they were beaten 1-0 in the World Cup by a team of amateurs from the United States; others would reach for Nice in 2016, where Iceland shattered their hubris in the second round of the European Championship. In both cases, England led with their chin, presuming victory; the haymakers they didn't see coming left them crumpled on the canvas. Arguably, however, their biggest humiliation came in a game they won 7-1.

England were never going to lose to San Marino in Bologna on November 17 1993, but they did manage to confect a moment of quite wonderful farce straight from kick-off. Needing to win by seven clear goals to have any chance of qualifying for the 1994 World Cup in the United States, England tried to press high immediately. In response, San Marino went forwards and cut straight through them, a move that led to David Gualtieri latching on to a poor back pass from Stuart Pearce to put his side in front after just 8.3 seconds. It was the quickest goal in international football history, and only the third that San Marino — a landlocked microstate in Italy with a population that wouldn't have filled Anfield — had ever scored.

It scarcely mattered that England went on to win. Norway and the Netherlands would have qualified at England's expense regardless of the result. Yet Gualtieri's goal was rich in symbolism, encapsulating just how far England had fallen since their semi-final appearance at Italia

'90. On that run, in that same stadium in Bologna, David Platt had volleyed in the winning goal to put England in the quarter-finals. Now, three-and-a-wee-bit years later, they were failing to qualify for the next World Cup and shipping a goal to a Sammarinese sales clerk in under 10 seconds. It was also just one year on from the launch of the Premier League, BskyB's "whole new ball game". Cowed by the experience, English football retreated into one of its darkest, most introspective moments, but it had to get its act together fast: Europe would soon be coming to visit.

Back in May 1992, England had been awarded the right to host the European Championship in 1996. It was a further demonstration of their re-assimilation into the international fold, following the return of English clubs to European club competitions after Italia '90. Originally envisaged as a continuation of the eight-team format used in the four previous editions, the rapidly changing map of Europe in the aftermath of the break-up of the Soviet Union and the Yugoslav Wars saw the 1996 edition expanded to 16 teams, the biggest ever European Championship. Hosting the competition was a huge responsibility for England generally and the onus would be on the team to deliver too. As the inquest began at the end of 1993, they required a new manager with broad shoulders.

When Graham Taylor resigned after the doomed attempt to qualify for the World Cup, Terry Venables was not a short-odds candidate to succeed him. He'd recently been sacked by Alan Sugar at Tottenham, a bitter dispute that was still not resolved, and was caught up in a morass of legal issues. Members of the FA International Committee selecting the new boss were known not to be fans of his geezer reputation. Yet he was available and, crucially for a cash-strapped FA missing the commercial windfall of the 1994 World Cup, he was affordable. Venables was also the overwhelming choice of people working in the game, a point made to the committee after they commissioned a fact-finding mission led by Jimmy Armfield. It was an uneasy marriage, and would never be anything else, but Venables became England coach in January 1994.

Whatever concerns there might have been over his business dealings, there was little doubt about Venables' abilities when it came to energising football teams. He'd won the 1991 FA Cup for Tottenham with a stylish team built around England's most gifted player, Paul Gascoigne, and before that had been recruited by Barcelona, where he had won them their first La Liga title in 11 years in 1985. After more than three years of mostly long-ball football under Taylor, there was huge hope invested in Venables to transform England into something more technically accomplished in time for the European Championship.

It was a long old haul. With no qualifiers to contest, England ploughed through over two years of friendlies, mostly at a deserted Wembley Stadium against opposition with little more ambition than expending as little energy as possible to secure a stalemate. Venables workshopped a variety of formations and trawled the Premier League for players to suit what he needed. Forty-seven players were used in 18 internationals, 27 of them debutants. Results were in binary combinations, and one of the rare forays away from Wembley was a disaster; England's match with the Republic of Ireland in February 1995 was abandoned after 27 minutes when the neo-Nazi group, Combat 18, rioted, ripping up parts of the Lansdowne Road stadium and using them as projectiles aimed at the Irish fans. It was a stomach-churning sight. Had it not happened so close to Euro '96, it may have seen the tournament taken off England.

Despite those setbacks, Venables would identify the players he needed for that summer. David Seaman would be the goalkeeper, with his Arsenal teammate Tony Adams ahead of him; 21-year-old Gary Neville was the youngest player in the team at right-back, counterbalanced by Stuart Pearce, the oldest, on the left. Partnering Adams in the middle was recent debutant Gareth Southgate, the Aston Villa captain who had lifted the Coca-Cola Cup in March. "Life's just so wonderful at the minute," he had said of that triumph, "that I keep thinking something will go badly wrong".

Out on the wings were Steve McManaman and Darren Anderton, two leather-lunged athletes that Venables referred to as his 'pathfinders'. Alan Shearer was comfortably the best striker in the Premier League and was partnered up front by Teddy Sheringham of Spurs. In midfield, Paul Ince had overcome riling Venables by pulling out of a friendly tournament a year earlier, and a difficult first few months at Inter Milan, to shield England's back four. And then there was Gascoigne.

England had been waiting a long time for their most gifted player to cash in the incredible potential that he'd shown at the 1990 World Cup. Since that landmark summer in Italy, Gascoigne had made barely a ripple in international football. He missed the 1992 European Championship through injury, and lost another year of football to a broken leg during an underwhelming three-season stint at Lazio in Serie A. When Gascoigne returned to the UK in 1995 it was to Glasgow Rangers in Scotland, where he was crowned Player of the Year and won the Double. Yet his propensity to locate trouble like a homing pigeon dogged his first season there and would be evident again on England's preparatory tour to China and Hong Kong just before Euro '96.

The pictures of England's players pole-axed on drink in a Hong Kong nightclub just days before the start of Euro '96 made world headlines. When their Cathay Pacific flight home a day later ended with £5,000-worth of damage to the aeroplane, there was uproar. At the centre of both incidents was Gascoigne, but Venables and his squad opted for a policy of collective responsibility rather than sacrifice their man in accordance with calls demanding he be ejected from the squad. The players adopted a stony media silence thereafter, but their professionalism was under serious question. Just months after Euro '96, Arsène Wenger took over at Arsenal and attitudes to diet and career discipline in English football began to change drastically.

England's nod to the pervasive lad culture of the mid-nineties took the blame for a leggy performance against Switzerland in the tournament's opening game. Shearer scored for England for the first time in 12 matches, but that was the only good news; the Swiss fought back for a draw as England wilted in the second half. Gascoigne was substituted and the subject of intense speculation ahead of one of the biggest games in England's history the following Saturday.

The match with Scotland had been a headache for the organisers for months. It was the first between the two rivals for seven years and required a huge security operation. By some distance it was the biggest game of the group stages, given an extra edge because both teams had drawn their opening matches. Gascoigne was miserably poor in the first half. In the second, England took a 1-0 lead through another Shearer goal but retreated fearfully again as their opponents fought back.

In one unforgiving minute, everything changed. Scotland won a penalty, but Gary McAllister hosed his effort straight at David Seaman, who diverted the ball over the bar with his elbow. While McAllister was still processing the enormity of the miss, England broke upfield and Gascoigne scored the goal of his career to seal the game. That he could locate the composure and skill to lob the ball over Colin Hendry and wallop a volley past his teammate Andy Goram, while having such a stinker, was extraordinary. Given the timing, opposition and occasion, it is one of the greatest goals in England's history.

The margin between triumph and disaster had been painfully thin, but Gascoigne had just about nudged England on the right side of it. At the final whistle after England had won 2-0, the stadium DJ at Wembley played *Three Lions*, the England team song written by David Baddiel, Frank Skinner and the Lightning Seeds. What might have become a kitsch and forgettable novelty single was now on its way to being the most powerfully evocative reminder of the summer of 1996. The first of its many mass communal airings took place that afternoon.

Momentum is crucial in international tournaments and England now had it. The victory removed a huge amount of pressure from their final group game against the Netherlands three days later. Going into the tournament, the Dutch were one of the teams most fancied to win. They had Arsenal's Dennis Bergkamp, and a number of stellar young players from Ajax's Champions League winning team of 1995 that looked set to reinvent football in the '90s. Their future was bright — but the here and now would be England's.

"We thrashed them," Venables reflected months later of the stunning 4-1 victory. "There's no doubt about it. It's nice to say, that's what we did." In general play, the Dutch had more possession, corners and shots on target, but it's unarguable that they were pummelled on the scoreboard. Shearer and Sheringham, now dovetailing as England's most effective front two since the Beardsley-Lineker axis, scored a brace each. The goal that really lives in the memory is England's third, as McManaman, Gascoigne and Sheringham linked up brilliantly to tee up Shearer for a merciless finish.

Three quick goals just after half-time had put England four ahead after just 62 minutes; given how far they had fallen after the 1990 World Cup, it was a night of undeniable catharsis. Some were so caught up that they forgot Patrick Kluivert had scored a goal that put the Dutch through to the quarter-finals at Scotland's expense. "Oh, It's four-nil ladies and gentlemen, it's four-nil!" screamed ubiquitous Radio 1 breakfast DJ Chris Evans to open his show the following day. "Hello, good morning, and welcome to one of the greatest days of our lives." The result was exactly what Venables had been hired to achieve. England executed a well-rehearsed game plan against a technically superior opponent and achieved their most significant result since the 1966 World Cup final.

Looking back through the decade that housed England's greatest sporting triumph was all the rage in that era. Euro '96 took place during the nostalgic frenzy of Britpop and Cool Britannia, where an awkwardly assembled set of figures from across the arts were patriotically marketed as one as they plundered British cultural history for influences and reference points. Yet not everything was about glancing backwards that year.

The people of the UK were just starting to log on and use some strange, interconnected global system called the internet, while mobile phones began to get into the hands of more than just wannabe yuppies. Less than a week after Euro '96, the Roslin Institute in Edinburgh managed to clone a sheep named Dolly. In the usually more mundane world of politics, Tony Blair had rebranded the Labour Party as New Labour. It was a slick-marketed force that was rising unstoppably and was nailed on to end the 18-year rule of the Conservative Party with a crushing victory at the General Election the following May.

All of these retrograde and futuristic forces bubbled around in the same melting pot as a surge of optimism, particularly in young people, swept through the country. The European Championship arrived in England just as this reached its peak. For 11 days, Euro '96 was an Anglo-Saxon offshoot of those self-congratulatory love-ins shrouded in the Union Jack, powered by Venables' rapidly improving England team. St George's crosses were suddenly everywhere, represented in scores of flags and cheap plastic hats at Wembley. They also made it onto the covers of the tabloids, who were reprinting the lyrics to *Three Lions* to literally get everyone on the same hymn sheet ahead of the quarter-final.

Into this increasingly patriotic cauldron stepped Spain, who immediately turned euphoria into cloying nervous tension. David Platt, brought in to replace the suspended Ince in midfield, struggled along with his teammates as Spain's switch to a sweeper system caught England completely unawares. They were comprehensively outplayed, and Spain had two goals disallowed in the first half, one of which was clearly onside. There were also three penalty appeals for the Spanish in the second half that were all good shouts. England were hanging on for dear life and missed a great chance of their own when Shearer implausibly skied a Gascoigne cross straight upwards from two yards out.

That was a close as they got. All of the tactical finesse for which England had been lauded four days earlier was gone; extra time was about sheer bloody-mindedness. The additional half hour was the first time the Golden Goal rule had been used at an international tournament, where the first team to score would win the game instantly. That goal never came, and the man that held England together through that turbulent period was Pearce.

In the shootout, he provided one of the defining images of the tournament when he buried his penalty past Andoni Zubizaretta and exploded in both joy and rage thereafter. Pearce and England both emerged from beneath six years of psychological rubble to win 4-2 on penalties. It avenged their defeat in the 1990 World Cup semi-final by the same method where Pearce had missed; more crucially, it kept England's momentum going despite how horrible their performance had been. Every ounce of home advantage had been required. "You can't play against 11 men, 70,000 fans and three officials," Spain's striker Julio Salinas complained afterwards. "We were cheated."

The boorish undercurrent to England's progress wasn't about to quieten down. Britain was already in dispute with the rest of the

European Union regarding their recent decision to ban the import of British beef for fear of contamination with Creutzfeldt-Jakob Disease. When Germany were confirmed as England's semi-final opponents, the tabloid jingoism zoned in on the Second World War as its running trope in the build-up. *The Daily Mirror* went furthest, with an infamous contribution from then-editor Piers Morgan. His declaration of 'Soccer War' on Germany, a pastiche of Neville Chamberlain's speech declaring actual war in 1939, was a pathetically embarrassing sideshow to the whole event.

And that's exactly what the semi-final had become. The game had the aura of a final, as the country fell silent on the evening of June 26 1996. England measures itself against Germany in football, with an assumption of an intense rivalry from one side met with mostly bemused indifference from the other. They might have lost the 1966 World Cup final between the two with their West prefix, but the Germans had been responsible for much of the hurt in the 30 years of hurt thereafter.

Yet this was a German team at the end of its imperial phase and missing their captain Jürgen Klinsmann through injury. England, re-jigged into a 3-5-2 as Platt retained his place at the expense of the suspended Gary Neville, hadn't had this good a look at beating them in a meaningful match in years. Pearce, Gascoigne and Platt had all had their hearts broken in Turin six years earlier; this was a chance for revenge on a plate.

The pre-match build-up showcased a much better face of supporting England. A spine-tingling version of *Three Lions* reverberated around Wembley before kick-off as the crowd channelled the basic sense of hope in the lyrics. In such an atmosphere, it was almost inevitable that England took the lead in under three minutes through an Alan Shearer header. Equally inevitably, the Germans came straight back and equalised through Stefan Kuntz, 13 minutes later. Thereafter, the two sides settled into a game that comfortably takes its place in the pantheon of classics between the two. For quality, tension and drama, it was comfortably the best match of Euro '96.

It went into golden-goal extra time, where England missed two chances that will haunt them forever. Darren Anderton hit the post, just two minutes into the extra period, before Gascoigne provided the defining moment of agony. The German goalkeeper Andreas Köpke dived at a bobbling Shearer cross and missed it; Gascoigne, who had been anticipating a touch, mistimed his lunge at the ball as a result and just couldn't reach it as an open goal waited two yards away. The guttural cry of agony from the crowd echoed deep into the night. England had planned their celebration beforehand. With the golden goal immediately ending the game, all of the players had agreed to immediately run straight off the pitch and dive into the communal bath in the changing rooms.

Instead, they were in the deep end on the pitch. Kuntz had a goal disallowed just before Gascoigne's miss, and Christian Ziege poked the ball a yard past Seaman's post as the end of extra time approached. The teams couldn't be separated and the game, as in 1990, went to penalties. England had prepared for their first five and scored them all. The problem was that Germany did too, and now England had to find a volunteer. Southgate stepped forward, ahead of McManaman, Anderton and Ince, and saw his effort saved by Köpke. From there, the end was signposted. Andreas Möller roofed his penalty with numbing certainty to put Germany into the final, and peacocked around Wembley Stadium like Mick Jagger.

Everything juddered to a screeching halt. The 11-day lost weekend was over, and it was time for the home team to go home. Rarely has an atmosphere in a football stadium swung so wildly between two extremes as it did at Wembley that night. Gascoigne's miss was the closest England had been to a major final since 1966, and they have not had that gilt-edged an opportunity since. It still troubles the sleep of Venables. "Most nights actually," he told the BBC in 2014 when they asked how often he thought of that chance. "When I'm in bed I have nightmares about it."

The dream of victory came true for Germany, who secured their first major title as a unified nation by beating the Czech Republic in the final four days later. It only cemented England's belief that they would have won Euro '96 had they got through their semi-final. The Germans triumphed despite losing so many players through injury that they had to prepare outfield shirts for their reserve goalkeepers ahead of the final. In a moment of wonderful and thoroughly deserved *schadenfreude*, they celebrated when they returned to Frankfurt by singing *Three Lions* to their adoring public.

Back in England, the Premier League was about to go global. The Bosman ruling had come into effect in December 1995 and on the eve of Euro '96, BskyB signed off a massive renewal deal on their original 1992 investment. English clubs were suddenly flush with cash and could shop and spend anywhere at will. That led to Newcastle United breaking the world transfer record for Alan Shearer and Italy's striker Fabrizio Ravanelli, who had just won the Champions League with Juventus, signing for Middlesbrough. In appeal, make-up and influence, the league was about to transform out of all recognition. Other peripheral forces like mass use of the internet and celebrity culture were in the post and would make the players public figures like never before. When David Beckham scored from his own half at Selhurst Park on the opening day of the 1996 season, it ushered in a new era.

Euro '96 had significant residual power too. The 'football's coming home' refrain of *Three Lions* could be heard at the two huge Oasis gigs at Knebworth two months later, and Blair riffed on it for his Labour Party conference speech that autumn. Yet gradually it came to represent a different era of English football. Gascoigne's England career was unceremoniously ended when new manager Glenn Hoddle dropped him from the 1998 World Cup squad, a decision that had a broader symbolism regarding the changing approach to the English game. Even Wembley Stadium was gone just over four years later. That was replaced — eventually — by a more futuristic version at a cost of £1 billion, as new FA chief executive Adam Crozier busied himself rebranding the England team for the 21st century.

People often speculate on what an England victory at Euro '96 might have changed. One suggestion is that, with the 30-year wait ended, they might have gone on to land more trophies in the decades that followed. It seems fanciful. The 1966 World Cup triumph was a jubilant home victory achieved while London was swinging, but it didn't stop England disappearing into the international wilderness in the 1970s. Had Gascoigne timed his lunge better against Germany and then England had beaten the Czech Republic in the final four days later — itself a haughty assumption — then a second home victory would surely have been the crest of a similar cultural wave rather than the beginnings of a sea change.

The European Championship in England was a moment in time, and one that synced perfectly with its time. Even without the ultimate victory, the tournament formed part of a series of events in the '90s that would revolutionise English football, while blending in seamlessly with the hijinks that sent most of Britain giddy through the middle of that decade. Winning Euro '96 might not have changed anything, but in that particular summer, it would have meant everything.

FIORENTINA 1998–99

GIANCARLO RINALDI

When I was growing up, I had a Fiorentina flag above my bed. Around the club's famous *fleur-de-lis* emblem, it featured illustrations of all the trophies they had won down the years. It probably speaks volumes that it went the best part of 20 years without ever coming close to being out of date.

In fairness, that is not entirely true. There was the infamous 1981-82 season when the Viola lost out on the league title to arch-rivals Juventus in a cruel final-day twist, which is remembered bitterly in Florence to this day. *"Meglio secondi che ladri"*, they spit through grimacing lips — 'better to be second than be thieves'. Don't ask them about the disallowed goal in Sardinia that effectively cost them their chance of making history.

However, I was only really in the process of becoming a fan at that stage of my life, and information filtering back to Scotland was sketchy at best. Over time, I would learn to understand how much it rankled, but I did not fully appreciate the hurt as a first-year student in a Dumfries secondary school. By the late 1990s though, I was a dyed-in-the-Tuscan-wool supporter with all the agonising torment — and sporadic joy — that can provide.

I spent a year living and working in Florence in the run-up to the 1990 World Cup and you really could not have had a more intense experience. The Viola were limping along in mid-table, as they had for much of that era, but went on a glorious UEFA Cup run all the way to the final only to be denied by — guess who? — Juventus.

That pain would be compounded as star player and the only thing really worth watching in the team, Roberto Baggio, would then complete a controversial transfer. His destination? Those evil geniuses in Turin, of course.

I think I bought a book that year as well, a history of the club, written by a local priest. Its title really should have warned me to pick another team but I was in too deep by then. It dubbed Fiorentina the 'joy and despair' of its followers — there was a lot more of the latter than the former in its pages, though.

It would be the 1998-99 season that would really deliver both of those in spades. A bittersweet cavalcade of emotions that, to this day, still makes me both smile and almost weep in nostalgic reminiscence. There was something so special within touching distance, that you could almost feel the significance grow with every passing week. Even the most cynical *tifoso* began to believe that the lengthy wait for the Scudetto — as the Serie A crown is known — might be ending.

You see, in a cruel twist of fate, my favourite team decided to stop winning championships about six months before I was born. That old flag of mine was emblazoned with a few Italian Cups, a Cup Winners' Cup and even a Mitropa Cup — go Google that one. But there were only two league titles: one in 1956, when even my dad was only about 12, and the other in 1969. I didn't come along until nearly Christmas that year. I invented the story to myself — in later life — that this boy born in the south of Scotland was named after a member of that team, Giancarlo De Sisti, even though the reality was nothing of the sort.

So, every year, my age is a cruel and constant reminder of how long it is since Fiorentina finished a season on top of Serie A. Approaching my 30th birthday, I had almost given up hope of ever seeing such an event repeated. But I think I was still young enough to believe — in some hidden corner of my heart — that it might, finally, be their year.

These were the times of the *Sette Sorelle* — 'the Seven Sisters' — a group of teams in Italy reckoned to be up to the task of challenging for the title. Juve, of course, were among their number, along with the kings of Lombardy (Milan and Inter), capital outfits Roma and Lazio and *nouveau riche* Parma. Incredibly, on the back of lavish spending by cinema producer owner Vittorio Cecchi Gori, the seventh sister was the team playing at the Stadio Artemio Franchi.

And, after the setback of falling into Serie B a few seasons earlier, what a team Gori had assembled. Time would tell us that the whole thing was built on financial quicksand but — at that moment — we were blissfully unaware. We just drooled every time goal machine Gabriel Batistuta, graceful playmaker Rui Costa, and madcap Brazilian Edmundo took to the pitch. They couldn't finally deliver, could they?

I was working as a journalist with the local newspaper in Dumfries at the time, going out with the beautiful young woman who is now my wife and had just had my second book published. I think I was still labouring under the misconception that the world was at my feet and anything was possible. It probably encouraged me to dream that I might be catching a flight to Pisa that spring, in order to speed to Florence and join the celebrating hordes in the Piazza della Signoria. Looking back, I feel a bit like Tom Waits writing his wonderful song *Martha*: "We were all so young and foolish — now we are mature."

But it is nice to dream, isn't it, and back then it genuinely seemed the Tuscan club meant business. One of the first signs of this tougher approach was the hiring of Giovanni Trapattoni to replace the amiable Alberto Malesani. Anyone who has ever followed Italian football will know that the wily and idiosyncratic old coach was synonymous with just one thing — winning. There was something symbolic in turning to him anyway, as his greatest successes on the bench had come at Juventus. This showed that there was no intention of letting old rivalries stand in the way of the pursuit of glory. If the Viola had a weakness, it was probably in defence and that was where the legendary Trap was expected to work his magic.

The main signings that summer probably hinted as much. Tough old Tomáš Řepka, the hirsute Moreno Torricelli and versatile Jörg Heinrich were primarily about stopping the opposition scoring rather than providing more firepower. Mind you, when you had Edmundo, Batistuta and Luís Oliveira at your disposal, with Rui Costa pulling the strings, you didn't really need more attacking options. Even in a golden age for Serie A, this was still one of the most special goal-scoring units on the premises.

These were the days when my Calcio watching was split between *Football Italia* on Channel 4 in the UK and a satellite dish beaming in coverage from Italy. Every weekend I would sit down, mostly with my highly-strung father, to suffer through another Fiorentina game. If you think Trapattoni is animated and twitchy during a match, you should probably try spending 90 minutes next to my dad. He is a stream-of-consciousness talker through matches, constantly jumping to his feet or gesticulating for the 90 minutes of even the most mundane encounter. Nowadays, he tends not to watch big games because he gets too agitated, but back then he was my constant companion for Viola clashes and the Italian national team. No wonder my nerves were shot through by about the age of 12.

We started off the season well enough — dispatching Empoli and Vicenza — but it was in week three that I first remember thinking this team might be the special one that could actually make a serious challenge to finish at the top of the table. A visit to the San Siro and a resounding victory courtesy of a Batigol hat-trick sent the boys in purple clear at the top of the table. Milan were a yardstick back then of title credentials and we had displayed that we were not out of our depth. At the very least, I thought, this was going to be fun.

The thing is, those of us who have followed Fiorentina for any length of time usually expect the wheels to come off pretty quickly. Instead, we continued to set the Serie A pace. There were setbacks — defeats to Roma, Parma and even Piacenza spring to mind — but we showed a resilience that had rarely been witnessed in my youth. When we beat Juventus shortly before Christmas to go four points clear, there was no doubt we were as good as anyone else in the division. There were plenty of teams breathing down our neck, but we seemed able to hold our nerve. This was not the kind of composure we supporters — both long-distance and nearer to Florence — were used to witnessing.

They make a big deal in Italy of the team crowned *Campione d'Inverno* — 'Winter Champions' — as the side leading the way at the halfway stage of the season generally goes on to win the Scudetto. A study by *La Gazzetta dello Sport* showed recently that more than two-thirds of the teams to hold an advantage at that point go on to take the championship. If nothing else, it gives a boost to the belief system, having played everyone else in the division and seen what you are up against.

But if my belief in the dream started with Milan, it probably also snapped against the *Rossoneri* too. The return game in Florence in February was a closer affair than the away match had been as the Viola strained to see off one of their main rivals. From a sofa in south-west Scotland, it felt like this was one of the key moments in chasing that elusive third title. Then came the horrible episode that, in hindsight, killed off those hopes.

It was Batistuta, of course, who was single-handedly trying to batter down a stubborn *Rossoneri* defence when something snapped. Trying to race onto a long through ball late in the game, he fell to the ground grasping desperately at the back of his leg. A stadium, a city and a young-ish journalist in Dumfries and Galloway all held their breath. We had a strong squad and all that but, to paraphrase Sinead O'Connor singing Prince, nothing compared to Batigol.

Our hopes of some miracle immediate recovery would be forlorn and our talisman would be missing for a month. When he returned, his team had gone from three points clear before the Milan clash to four points behind Lazio. The impact of his absence was only compounded by the fact that fellow hitman Edmundo disappeared to the Carnival in Rio — as per an apparent agreement with the club — and also missed the dismal defeat by Udinese, which followed the game with the *Rossoneri*. Some in Tuscany have still never forgiven him for that party time in Brazil.

A trouncing by an Alvaro Recoba-inspired Venezia on Batistuta's hurried return all but sealed the deal. Belief seemed to fizzle out of the side and by the time they thumped Perugia with four games remaining, the title was long gone and had become a battle between Milan and Lazio. It would be the *Rossoneri*, in an ironic twist, who would take the crown. It was hard for Fiorentina fans not to feel that was even more painful, given the manner in which they had dispensed with Alberto Zaccheroni's side early in the season. They were a good team, yes, but not a great one and, but for one attempted run by Batistuta, could perhaps have been outlasted. Third place — quite a distant one in the end — did not feel like much consolation.

At the time, certainly, it burned like the worst home-brewed grappa. This had been a one-off alignment of star players and coaching staff, which would slowly unravel alongside the financial affairs of the club's owner. Within a few years, the side which had threatened to take the title would be playing in Italy's fourth tier under the name Florentia Viola. How the mighty had fallen. Perhaps, we wondered then, if Trap had spotted the effort our Argentinian hitman was giving in that ill-fated Milan match, he might have subbed him before his injury and kept him fit for the run-in. No coach, though, can see the future and, in the end, he was trying to kill off a team he knew to be a serious contender for the Scudetto. He was certainly right about that.

Easy enough, then, to write it off as yet another season of disappointment in Florence. A closer failure than most, perhaps, but a failure nonetheless. That would only be compounded by defeat to Parma in the two-legged Coppa Italia final that year. Their coach? The recently jettisoned Mr Malesani, of course. Even in a history of sinking feelings, this was a new low.

And yet, at a distance of more than two decades, why does that period still seem so special, despite the absence of trophies? Fiorentina would win a few cups but they never got closer to a league title than they did in that campaign. So there is still something magical about reading the names of Francesco Toldo, Sandro Cois, Anselmo Robbiati and all the other players who were part of that topsy-turvy procession of feelings.

That's the thing, you see, at least for us fans of not-quite-elite clubs. It is not only about the winning, it is about — to steal a phrase from those awful reality TV shows — 'the journey'. A few seasons after seeing a team that was 'too good to go down' get relegated, huge crowds were at the Stadio Artemio Franchi to witness the chance of history being made. From a distance, in Scotland, you could tell that this was a never-to-be-repeated moment for the club.

But what pleasure they gave us, despite not getting to stitch that daft little green, white and red shield to their shirts that signifies title winners in Italy. If I close my eyes I think I can still see Rui Costa swaying through defences and the chant of 'Bati-Bati-Bati-Batigol' coming up from the Curva Fiesole. The thing that followers of big clubs don't understand is that we can be happy with memories, even if they did not deliver anything concrete at all.

Serial winners like to look down their noses at those of us who have to satisfy ourselves with near-misses. They lap up their open-top bus celebrations and ridicule us with social media posts about our commemorative videos for finishing runners-up or going close to victory. That is the nature of sport, of course, but those of us who enjoy success less often have become connoisseurs of much smaller portions of delight. We don't need their all-you-can-eat buffets of triumph that they gorge themselves on almost every season. Instead, we are happy with a little fine dining every 20 years or so, or even less.

Breaking through the barrier of my 50th birthday just about coincided with celebrations to mark the half-century anniversary of Fiorentina's last league title. It only underlined how unlikely they are to enjoy such success again in a footballing landscape which has changed enormously since the late 1960s. Championships have become — even more than they were back then — the preserve of the few, with the rest of us having to press our noses up against the windows of their fancy stores, in which we cannot afford to shop. The gap between the haves and have-nots is much wider than the River Arno.

I am still working away as a journalist in the south of Scotland and torture myself most weekends by watching the Viola struggling along in mid-table, with the occasional big win just about getting me through. My hopes of writing a best-seller have just about been extinguished but, whisper it, I still keep a little hidden dream that one day I might find the time to scribble down something that will touch the souls of millions and allow me to jack in the day job and buy that bolthole in the Tuscan hills, where a dusty old typewriter and a bottle from my own vineyard await. Meanwhile, though, I try to satisfy myself with being a half-decent husband on my good days and a father who is more proud than he could possibly express of how his now teenage daughter and son have turned out. Words will always fall short of capturing how much my family means to me. And, just to punish my boy, I have done my best to pass on my passion for Fiorentina — and Queen of the South — to him. A lifetime of torment awaits him, while my daughter was smart enough not to fall for football at all. It has taken the coronavirus pandemic for me to realise just how much my life revolves around the game and all that it has given me. Others will scoff at the lack of silverware, but I genuinely look back and don't mind that I didn't get to party back in 1999.

It would have been nice, sure, to get my trip to Florence to dance beneath the Duomo and join the jubilant under Giotto's Tower, but that team and that season still gave me so much. Nostalgia is defined as a sentimental yearning for the happiness of a former time or place, and those epic battles provided fuel for that by the bucket-load. Not in a bad way, I like to think, where one despises the present, but rather in a more mellow, soul-warming fashion. This provides something akin to the afterglow from a fine bottle of Chianti, when all is right in the world despite all its shortcomings. I may never see a Scudetto in my lifetime but that is OK, really, because there is more to existence anyway. My dad and I dreamed for a while, Lulu Oliveira danced and the scooters coming back from the Franchi tooted their mad celebration song on more than one occasion. That might not be enough for you, but it's good enough for me. *Grazie Viola*.

04

BAYER LEVERKUSEN 2001–02

TERRY DUFFELEN

"I am proud of what we have achieved this season, but we have played so hard and it hurts us to end with nothing."

It's May 15 2002 and Klaus Toppmöller is putting a brave face on a crushing loss. His team have just been beaten 2-1 in the Champions League final by the great Real Madrid. Just four days earlier, they had been beaten in the final of the DFB-Pokal, the German Cup, and it had only been 11 days since they had missed out, yet again, on another Bundesliga title in the last week of the season. Within the space of a month, this provincial factory club from the Rhineland had almost achieved football immortality.

I suppose, in a way, they still did, albeit not necessarily the good kind. The club's unofficial nicknames of *Vizekusen* or the more Anglo-friendly 'Neverkusen' is well-earned. This is a club that is defined by being almost, but not quite, good enough.

Their emergence as a force came at a time when German football was at a crossroads. Bayern Munich were being challenged by a Borussia Dortmund club that was spending more money than it had. The German national team, despite reaching the final of the 2002 World Cup, were acknowledged to be in decline and were still stung by their wretched defence of the European Championships in 2000. German football needed reform, and reform it got, with a programme of youth development that, in time, yielded a generation of great young German players. It is possible that Leverkusen's prominence in 2001-02 can partly be explained by this moment of preoccupied flux in German football. However, in my view, the club's success was achieved as a result of patient recruitment and effective use of a generous budget from its corporate backers.

For me, the Bayer Leverkusen team of 2001-02 was the team that wiped the smile off Manchester United manager Sir Alex Ferguson's face during their Champions League run that season. The first ever German replica shirt I owned was a Bayer Leverkusen one. I bought it from a discount rack in a shop in Cologne in 2004. That was my first ever football trip to Germany and it was a trip that had a profound effect on my life.

In one weekend, I watched Borussia Dortmund and Schalke at the Westfalenstadion and Veltins Arena, respectively. I was blown away by the atmosphere and the fact that you could drink beer while watching the game. In the years that followed, I started blogging and podcasting about the Bundesliga. I eventually settled on Dortmund as my adoptive club. But, in spite of my allegiances, I continued to play five-a-side football in that Leverkusen shirt every Thursday for years.

Bayer 04 Leverkusen, officially nicknamed *Die Werself*, which translates as 'company XI', are not a well-liked club in Germany. They are regarded somewhat contemptuously by neighbours FC Köln and Borussia Mönchengladbach, whose fans prefer to focus their hatred at each other and not the comparatively small 'plastic' club just outside Cologne.

The term 'plastic' is reserved for clubs in Germany that rely on a wealthy benefactor for their income rather than their fanbase. The Bundesliga's 50+1 ownership rule, which (with some exceptions) only lets clubs play in the league if its members own more than half of its voting rights, is a model to be admired and envied. However, it has generated a snobbery from fans of *Traditionsverein* (traditional clubs) towards those that are essentially owned and bankrolled by a single entity — in Leverkusen's case, the Bayer international pharmaceutical group, whose headquarters are in the city. 'Plastic' also suggests a faux quality, lacking in tradition and history, and while that accusation can be perhaps justifiably levelled at other clubs like Hoffenheim[1] and Rasenballsport (RB) Leipzig, Leverkusen — founded by Bayer employees — has a history that goes back to the early 20th century, 1904 to be precise.

A lower regional league club much of that time, Bayer 04 finally gained promotion to German football's top flight in 1979. For the early part of the 1980s, they existed as a 'grey mouse' club (a nondescript, mediocre club that, were they English, would be permanently last on *Match of the Day*). It wasn't until Erich Ribbeck took over as coach in 1985 that Leverkusen started to make waves. Ribbeck led the team to UEFA Cup qualification and success in 1988, beating Javier Clemente's Espanyol side on penalties after a 3-3 draw over a two-legged final.

Bayer's next and last piece of silverware was lifted in 1993 when Ulf Kirsten scored the only goal in the Olympiastadion, Berlin, against Hertha's amateur side in the German Cup final. Kirsten, a classic goal poacher, would experience the club's 'nearly' moments throughout the period that has defined their character, his 220 goals in over 400 league, cup and European appearances making him the club's all-time top scorer. His arrival at Leverkusen was thanks to the club's CEO Renier 'Calli' Calmund, who recruited the young Kirsten from Dynamo Dresden in 1990, just after German reunification.

Calli first joined the club as a stadium announcer at the BayArena in 1976 and enjoyed a longstanding association with Bayer in a variety of roles. His gregarious nature served him particularly well as a player recruiter and made him a charismatic frontman for the club. To this day, he still enjoys minor celebrity status and is no stranger to the TV cameras. On player recruitment, he once said that it was not about being the biggest fish in the tank, but the quickest.

His approach was certainly effective. Calmund is credited with bringing Rudi Völler, Bernd Schneider, Ulf Kirsten, Michael Ballack and Dimitar Berbatov to the club. He also established a fruitful pipeline

---

1. *While Hoffenheim was founded in 1899, it was a village club, playing in local leagues, and remained that way for over a century. Software billionaire Dietmar Hopp took control of the club in 1990. In 2005, Hopp increased his investment, taking the club into the Bundesliga and relocating it to a brand new stadium in Sinsheim. Many feel that without Hopp's intervention, Hoffenheim would still be a village club and would not be able to sustain themselves were they working under the 50+1 rule.*

of South American players, such as Paulo Sérgio, Jorginho, Emerson, Zé Roberto, Lúcio and Juan.

Calmund's departure from Leverkusen in 2004 was sadly under something of a cloud after unexplained cash payments were made to a player's agent. However, he left an enduring legacy for the club. Their South American connection lives on, most recently in the shape of Charles Aranguiz from Chile, the Brazilians Wendell and Paulinho, plus the Argentine striker Lucas Alario. Their ability to sign and develop young domestic players, such as Kai Havertz and Julian Brandt, is also undimmed.

The Bayer Leverkusen line-up of players in the mid-90s was hard to dislike. The coach of that team was Christoph Daum. A Bundesliga winner with Stuttgart in 1992, Daum joined Leverkusen in 1996 and injected some real dynamism into a hugely talented squad. Bayer 04 under Daum were one of the best teams to watch in Germany.

The tragedy is that they have nothing to show for it. For three separate seasons in the final decade of the 20th century — 96-97, 98-99 and 99-2000 — Bayer finished runners-up in the Bundesliga. The most heartbreaking was in 2000, when they needed just a point at unfancied Unterhaching on the final day of the season to clinch the title. "We are programmed for victory," said Daum before the match. "No one will stop us." He was right. They stopped themselves.

Leverkusen put on an abject display, losing 2-0, the first being an own goal by Ballack. According to Philipp Reich, who wrote about the match for *Watson.ch* in May 2020, the real Bundesliga trophy travelled with Bayer to Unterhaching in anticipation of them being crowned champions. Bayern Munich, who won the title, paraded a replica around the Olympiastadion that afternoon.

Daum was unbowed and vowed to fight on. Sadly, he was sacked for cocaine abuse in 2000. The incident also cost him his job as German national team coach — a position he was due to take up when his contract at Leverkusen expired in October of that year.

The disgraced Daum was replaced for the start of the 2001-02 season by Klaus Toppmöller, a player of some distinction for FC Kaiserslautern; he's still the club's all-time top scorer. As a coach, he enjoyed moderate success at Frankfurt, Bochum and Saarbrucken.

With his crop of curly silver hair and unashamed smoking habit, Toppmöller cut a figure closer to that of a '70s football manager than a modern trainer. All that was missing was a sheepskin and perhaps a fedora.

Armed with one of the most balanced squads in the league and, it turned out, Europe, for the 2001-02 season, Toppmöller would set up his team in a 4-1-4-1 formation, or a 3-5-2 if he fancied an extra striker. The goalkeeper was Hans-Jörg Butt, an experienced custodian formerly of Hamburg. He would go on to serve as an able back-up keeper for Bayern Munich. The defence, whether a three or a four, would always include Lúcio, Jens Novotny and Carsten Ramelow.

Nicknamed 'O Cavalo' (The Horse), Lucimar Ferreira da Silva, shortened to Lúcio, was possibly one of the best centre-backs ever to grace the German top flight and certainly one of the most decorated. While he would miss out on glory in his time at Leverkusen, there was nothing nearly about this man. He became a World Cup winner for Brazil in 2002 and added three Bundesliga titles and three DFB-Pokals with Bayern Munich after leaving Bayer. Lúcio was also part of Jose Mourinho's great Inter side that, as part of an historic treble, beat Bayern in the 2010 Champions League final.

Ramelow, meanwhile, was much-loved by the Leverkusen fans and it is easy to see why. The uncompromising defender and sweeper was a fixture of the Leverkusen backline for 333 games. And club captain and legend Jens Novotny was a tough, disciplined centre-back who was not ungraceful, could read the game, anticipated the runs of his teammates and would frequently be the door that slammed in the faces of opposition attackers.

On the left of the defence (although this was such an attacking team that 'defender' seems a pedestrian description) was Diego Placente, an Argentine signed from River Plate the preceding summer. On the right was Zoltán Sebescen, enjoying a season that amounted to the high point of an injury-blighted career. He retired at the age of just 29.

Staffing the flanks of the midfield was the 'White Brazilian' Schneider on the right and an actual Brazilian, Ze Roberto, on the left.

An indisputably classy midfielder, Schneider was so good that he had two nicknames, the other being 'Schnix' — from the German '*schnixeln*', meaning dribbler. Another recruit from East Germany, he was a dead-ball specialist, superb crosser and could drift past players. In full flow, Schneider made the game look easy. It's a tragedy that a player of his class didn't collect any silverware in his distinguished career.

Some guy on the *FourFourTwo* website (it was me) once described José Roberto da Silva Júnior as "easily distinguishable by his explosive pace, intelligent running and reliable crosses". Ze Roberto, as he was known, could play as a full-back but was deployed in Leverkusen as an all-action attacking midfielder.

Down the middle were Ballack and Yıldıray Baştürk. In a World Cup 2002 preview, Turkish International Baştürk was defined in *The Guardian* as "a schemer and a prober, with a deadly pass over any distance and quick feet, while he can tend to be a little over-indulgent at times". The report added that "nevertheless, he's got a bit of battle in him, too, as Didi Hamann will testify. The Liverpool man had a harrowing time trying, and failing, to contain him the night the Reds went out of the Champions League in Leverkusen". Less flatteringly, Arsenal coach Arsene Wenger said that he "should play in a swimming pool because he dives so often". Meow.

What can be said about Michael Ballack that hasn't been already? A world-class, dedicated professional who was blossoming at this point of his career; he turned 26 in September 2001. Ballack finished the season as the club's top scorer with 23 goals in all competitions from midfield in what would be his career-best tally. The German international was seen as a tragic figure following his own goal two seasons earlier and that bad luck would continue, past the 01-02 season and into the World Cup in South Korea and Japan. Ballack was one of the national team's best players in the tournament, but was suspended for the final against Brazil. It's worth pointing out that Ballack had a Bundesliga winners medal as a Kaiserslautern player in 97-98, but he only made 16 appearances. However, once he left Leverkusen, he would enjoy great success at Bayern Munich and Chelsea.

The frontman of this spectacular ensemble was Oliver Neuville, who scored 22 goals in all competitions that season. Talented but with a visibly strong work ethic, the Swiss-born German international was one of those nice guys who deserved more from this season and his career. It's a mark of his professionalism that he is fondly remembered by both Leverkusen fans and at nearby Mönchengladbach, whom he served with just as much distinction.

Regularly deployed from the bench was the veteran Ulf Kirsten and a young and callow Dimitar Berbatov. The Bulgarian still had much to learn, but his creativity and technical skills were well deployed by his coach.

For me, unburdened by the domestic philosophical debates and internal politics of German club football, this Bayer Leverkusen side was a breath of fresh air. Moreover, they were a plucky underdog that toppled two of English football's mightiest and most storied football clubs: the north-western giants of Liverpool and Manchester United. As a fan of neither of those clubs and an active hater of the latter, the sight of a po-faced and miserable Sir Alex Ferguson denied the chance to play a dream final at Hampden Park in his native Glasgow was nourishing. I imagine that there is a German word for it ...

Given the season Leverkusen had, it's easy to allow bitter memories to overpower the sweet. It is worth emphasising that the 2001-02 season was mostly gravy for Leverkusen fans. This is a team that fought back from 2-0 down to draw 3-3 and deny Schalke a win in their first Bundesliga match in their fancy new stadium. There were satisfying wins against local rivals FC Köln in the league and in the semi-final of the DFB-Pokal, plus a thumping 4-0 defeat of Borussia Dortmund, the eventual champions. Of the 19 Champions League nights, wins over Barcelona and Juventus were among the most memorable. The best of them was the comeback win at the BayArena in the second leg of the quarter-final where Ballack (twice), Lúcio and Berbatov saw off Liverpool by virtue of a 4-2 win.

However, they weren't all-conquering. They never beat Bayern that season, which is obviously not necessarily a requirement of winning the Bundesliga, but is usually a hallmark. They shipped four goals in matches against Arsenal, Juve, Lyon and, most damagingly, Schalke. However, if you chose to forget the last few weeks of the season, you'd remember a club that played adventurous, fast-paced football and that won far more games that they lost. But we are not here for that.

After nine consecutive matchdays at the top of the table as the season drew to a close, it looked like the curse would be lifted and all the hard work and heartache of previous years would pay off. However, the sheer number of games in the Bundesliga, DFB-Pokal and Champions League was about to suddenly take its toll. That and the fact that although Leverkusen spent so much time at the summit, they could never extend their lead, which would have allowed them to relax and prioritise. Their nearest title rivals, in terms of points, were Dortmund, Bayern and Schalke, all of whom kept Toppmöller's team honest.

A draw against Hamburg with four games left shortened the distance to five points. But two straight defeats, 2-1 to Werder Bremen and then 1-0 to FC Nürnberg, suddenly saw Borussia Dortmund — who had kept winning — top of the league by a point, with a game remaining. "There will be no second Unterhaching," Toppmöller had declared after the Bremen loss. "Fear does not exist for us. We believe in ourselves and will not bury our heads in the sand. We have a two-point lead, which should be enough to win the title." Sadly, it was not.

Either side of that Nürnberg defeat was the punishing and highly emotional two-legged semi-final against Manchester United, a tie in which Leverkusen prevailed on away goals. Ballack and Neuville silenced the Old Trafford crowd in a 2-2 draw. The second leg was a belligerent 1-1 draw in Leverkusen. That semi-final would be Ferguson's biggest regret. He claimed that his team were unlucky and later joked that the referee didn't grasp the concept of 'Fergie time'. But perhaps he made his own bad luck. In a press conference prior to the tie, Ferguson kept referring to Leverkusen as 'Kaiserslautern' and admitted to scouting for hotels in Glasgow before the matches took place. However, as tough as it was for the legendary Scottish coach at the time, the match may well have brought about the downfall of Leverkusen's season as well.

Amid the scenes of jubilation immediately after the game, the portents looked bad. Sebescen, Lúcio, Ballack and Neuville all played with knocks during the game. Nowotny, injured in the first leg, lasted less than 10 minutes in the second. "All of them fought for their lives, although nearly all were handicapped by injuries," said Topmöller afterwards. "We lost Jens Nowotny, and then Zoltán Sebescen wanted to be substituted and Lúcio, too. I just told them they *must* continue."

Worse still, Ze Roberto's dreams of playing in the final were shattered by referee Kim Milton Nielsen (famous on UK shores as the man who sent off David Beckham against Argentina during France '98) who took exception to something the Brazilian had said and booked him. The player's first yellow card had been against Red Star Belgrade at the beginning of the campaign 18 games earlier. Referees really are the worst sometimes.

Emotionally and physically suffering, it all began to go wrong for Bayer Leverkusen. They managed to rouse themselves the following Saturday and beat Hertha BSC 2-1 on the final day of the Bundesliga season, but Dortmund beat Bremen by the same scoreline to snatch the title at the death. The Leverkusen players, having experienced the emotional high of beating United in the semi-final only days before, were disconsolate

A week later and it was a trip to Berlin for the final of the DFB-Pokal at the Olympiastadion. The opponents were the current cup holders, Schalke. Bayer were the better team in the first half and were more than worth the 1-0 lead given to them by Berbatov, standing in for Kirsten who was on the bench. When Schalke coach Huub Stevens was sent to the stands just before half-time by referee Günter Perl for letting his emotions get the better of him, it looked good for Leverkusen. But Schalke stormed back with four unanswered goals. Toppmöller also took issue with referee Perl's officiating and he too was sent to the stands after 76 minutes. Ulf Kirsten came off the bench and netted a consolation but the team could not be consoled. Another week, another lost trophy. Up next, Glasgow and the small matter of the Champions League final against football royalty.

Real Madrid's band of *Galacticos* were heavy favourites to win. Real also had the portents of history on their side. Hampden Park was the location of their famous 7-3 victory over another German side, Eintracht Frankfurt, back in 1960. Surely this team of modern-day greats would vanquish another team of Germans on their return to Glasgow?

That said, Leverkusen could also lay claim to the glimmer of an omen. Hampden was the place where Germany claimed their first European club trophy, when Stan Libuda's lob hit the post, rebounded off Ron Yates and into the net for Borussia Dortmund's Cup Winners Cup win against Liverpool in 1966. But history doesn't win football matches, players do. Specifically, those Real Madrid players. Mind you, they had to work for it.

"We got hammered by Leverkusen in the last 10 minutes," Real's Steve McManaman told ESPN. "Iker Casillas came off the bench and he was the man of the match, he made that many saves. We were hanging on for dear life and the relief at the end was palpable. There was danger every minute."

We all remember Zidane's volley and rightly so but Toppmöller blamed the goalkeeper Hans-Jörg Butt for not saving it: "It was a fantastic hit," he recalled to ESPN years later, "but the ball didn't really go to the left or the right, it was close to the middle of the goal. At that elevation, he could have got to it. Every German football fan said that if Oliver Kahn had been in goal, he would have saved it." He also added, unkindly: "We would have won three titles with him [Kahn]. I was disappointed with Butt, but not me alone. It was everybody."

At the opposite end of the field, it's important to acknowledge Casillas's triple save from Baştürk, Kirsten and Schneider, any one of which going in could have produced a different result. And I suppose that is the point. It is small margins that decide games at the highest level between two well-matched opponents, and for this season none of those margins benefited Bayer Leverkusen. Or as Michael Ballack put it: "The football God is not from Leverkusen".

After the game, Calmund said: "We are proud of our team, even if we ended the season without the league, the cup and the Champions League. Zidane alone is as expensive as our entire team. There is a good saying: 'Don't spend more than you have and don't piss higher than you can.'"

Leverkusen fans that reflect on how they emerged from this season with nothing may look to those Bundesliga near misses in the late '90s and feel that fear of failure affected how they played in the crucial final weeks of the 01-02 season. In spite of the injuries and concentration of fixtures towards the end, it is baffling given the positions they were in that the team failed to yield at least one trophy. Losing the Champions League final is understandable — Real Madrid had the pedigree and the players. However, to have missed out on the DFB-Pokal and the Bundesliga is harder to accept. How would Oscar Wilde have put it? To lose one domestic trophy may be regarded as a misfortune. To lose two looks like carelessness.

The following summer, Ballack and Ze Roberto left the club. They would be followed later by Lúcio, and all went to Bayern Munich, where they would not only win the Bundesliga and DFB-Pokal the following season, but repeat that feat in 2005, and again in 2006 and 2008. That trio played a significant role in Bayern's success in the noughties. Had they stayed at Leverkusen, who knows. Perhaps it would be they who could boast a few league titles or cup triumphs. This sort of speculation is common among Bundesliga clubs who see their best players sold to 'Buyern'.

As it was, Leverkusen went into an understandable, if modest, decline. Toppmöller was sacked in 2003. His next club job, at Hamburg, where many a good coaching career has run aground, was his last.

It's possible that had Bayer won the treble, they would have been permanently elevated to the European top table, perhaps preventing the rise of Klopp's Dortmund and mitigating the impact of Bayern on the Bundesliga over the last decade. That's a counterfactual for another time. However, what we can say is that as traumatic as that one fateful month of May 2002 was, it didn't destroy them. The club continues to win more games than it loses, they are regular participants in the Champions League and continue to be well run, yes, in part thanks to mega-rich owners, but also with a great scouting and recruitment strategy. It is highly unlikely in the modern football landscape that Bayer Leverkusen will ever scale the same heights they did in 2002. However, assuming they keep their funding and stick to those principles laid down by Calmund all those years ago, they will continue to be a relevant, if unpopular, football club.

04

ARSENAL 2005–06

NICKY BANDINI

The floor of Charles de Gaulle airport is not a comfortable place to sleep. There were no seats left to slump in at 2am on May 18 2006, and no luggage to rest a head on either, for the slow but steady stream of Arsenal fans trickling into the departure hall.

Any night flights back to England had long since taken wing and it would be hours before the check-in desks reopened. Where else was there to go, though, for supporters who had come to Paris for the Champions League final without booking a hotel room?

Travelling to follow your team is an expensive business. With even the budget airlines charging close to £600 for return flights from London's least accessible airports, savings had to be made. There were many here who had told themselves that they could enjoy a night in the city regardless of the game's outcome, pushing through from post-game pint to coffee and croissant.

But that was before they knew how events would unfold. When you are shaken awake from a beautiful dream, it is natural to want to go straight back to sleep.

Arsenal were not the best team in Europe in 2006. They were barely the best team in north London. For the first time in a decade under Arsène Wenger's management, they found themselves trailing Tottenham Hotspur late in a Premier League campaign. The Gunners actually fell behind their neighbours in December 2005 and did not overtake them again until the final weekend, finishing fourth with the help — so the story goes — of some dodgy lasagne.

Even then, this was still the first time Wenger's Arsenal had finished outside the top three. A team that had swaggered to the 2003-04 Premier League title without losing a single game crashed this time to 11 defeats. They were beaten by Middlesbrough, who finished up getting relegated, and drew with 17th-placed Portsmouth, scoring 19 fewer goals than in the previous campaign.

Wenger's squad hardly lacked talent. Arsenal still had Thierry Henry as their frontman, with Freddie Ljungberg, Robert Pires, José Antonio Reyes, Dennis Bergkamp, a young Robin van Persie and the newly-signed Alexander Hleb as support acts. The first-choice defence was the same as it had been for those 'Invincibles' two years before, with Jens Lehmann in goal, Lauren and Ashley Cole at full-back and Sol Campbell paired with Kolo Touré in the middle.

Yet this was a team in transition. Arsenal's captain, Patrick Vieira, had been sold to Juventus in the summer, leaving the armband to Henry and command of the midfield to an 18-year-old Cesc Fábregas. Bergkamp, another defining figure of that first Wenger era, celebrated his 36th birthday that May, and had started just 12 games in this, his final campaign before retirement.

It was a delicate moment for Arsenal, their final season at Highbury before moving to Emirates Stadium. The club wanted to leave its old home on a positive note, but could not afford to spend lavishly while servicing the debt incurred building its new one. Even Henry seemed concerned about the club's direction, and was stalling over a new contract amidst reports of interest from Barcelona.

The timing was especially uncomfortable. From 1997-98 through to 2003-04, the Premier League had been a two-way carve-up between Arsenal and Manchester United; a competition defined by the rival ideologies of Wenger and Sir Alex Ferguson. But now José Mourinho's Chelsea had arrived, and the terms of engagement had changed.

It was not simply that they had broken the duopoly, winning their first league title in half a century, but the way they had done it. Chelsea's triumph was both emphatic — they finished 12 points clear of Arsenal on a then-record 95 points, losing only a single game — and expensive, made possible by Roman Abramovich's lavish outlay. The Blues had hoovered up Didier Drogba, Arjen Robben, Petr Čech, Ricardo Carvalho, Paulo Ferreira and Tiago Mendes in the previous summer alone.

Now they were trying to lure away Arsenal's homegrown talent. Chelsea and Mourinho were each fined for 'tapping up' Cole, as was the player himself, after a meeting engineered without his employer's consent in January 2005.

It would be another 19 months before the defender switched clubs, but the impact on Cole and his teammates in the meantime cannot be ignored. His subsequent autobiography, with its much-mocked account of "nearly swerving off the road" at a contract offer of £55,000-per-week from Arsenal, instead of the £60,000 he sought, may support the suggestion that his head was no longer in the right place. In Cole's own words: "I suppose it all started to fall apart for me from then on."

Injury, in any case, would keep him out of Arsenal's line-up for an important chunk of the 2005-06 season. Cole fractured a metatarsal in October and did not play again until January. His replacement, Gaël Clichy, suffered the same injury a month later. Wenger had no choice but to force square pegs into round holes as he fielded the likes of Kolo Touré and Mathieu Flamini at left-back. That meant more games for Philippe Senderos and Pascal Cygan in the middle.

Premier League opponents were ruthless in exposing the weak links. Arsenal lost consecutive games against Bolton, Newcastle and Chelsea in December — the first time they had lost three in a row since Wenger became manager.

Progress through the Champions League group stage, though, had been serene, aided by a gentle draw. Arsenal dropped just two points in six games as they finished ahead of Ajax, FC Thun and Slavia Prague. Henry supplanted Ian Wright as the club's all-time record goalscorer when he grabbed a brace away to the Czech side in his first game back after a six-week injury layoff of his own.

It was a welcome moment of positivity, in a difficult start to the campaign, but hardly evidence of a side about to power through to the final. The consensus was that Arsenal should not expect to go any further after they were paired with Real Madrid in the last 16.

By the time the first leg rolled around, the Gunners' defensive options were looking even more sparse. Lauren sustained a knee injury during the League Cup semi-final against Wigan in January that would keep him out for almost a year.

That same month, Sol Campbell walked out of a defeat to West Ham at half-time — asking to be substituted and then leaving the stadium without waiting for the game to end. He did not play again until April, as stories swirled about difficulties in his private life — something Pires had alluded to in post-game interviews.

So it was that Arsenal turned up for their first-ever competitive game against Madrid, away at the Bernabéu, with a defence made up of Emmanel Eboué, Senderos, Touré and Flamini. Those first two players, aged 22 and 20, respectively, had never started a Champions League game before facing Thun in November. The last was a right-footed reserve midfielder filling in reluctantly at left-back.

It looked like a recipe for disaster, against opponents whose starting XI featured such 'Galácticos' as Ronaldo, Zinedine Zidane, David Beckham, Roberto Carlos and Robinho. On the day of the game, *The Guardian*'s Richard Williams reflected once more on Patrick Vieira's departure, pondering what difference his steel and leadership might have made on a night like this.

Wenger, he wrote, could yet forge another great side built around the likes of Fábregas and van Persie. "What does not seem within Wenger's scope," he added, "is the ability to devise an interim solution to the sort of challenge that will be posed tonight by Real Madrid."

No English club had ever beaten Madrid on their own turf. The hosts, meanwhile, had won all seven games they had played at the Bernabéu to start 2006. Arsenal's run of four victories in 12 matches looked a little less impressive — especially when you considered that one of those came in the second-leg of the League Cup tie with Wigan, and failed to save them from an aggregate defeat.

This is all a long-winded way of saying that the game in Madrid should have been a rout. And at first, it looked like it might be. Just not for the team everyone expected.

Arsenal created three clear goal-scoring opportunities inside a scintillating opening 10 minutes, with Henry at the centre of all of them. He played Reyes and Ljungberg through on goal, only to see both thwarted by Iker Casillas, before thumping a header of his own just wide. Williams had pondered whether the captaincy was weighing too heavily on the Frenchman. Here, the responsibility seemed to inspire him.

Madrid's only real opportunity of the first-half arrived when Senderos gave away possession carelessly on the edge of his own area. Beckham swapped possession with Ronaldo, but Lehmann was off his line sharply to block the Englishman's shot.

The game stayed goalless at the interval but in the 47th minute, Henry took a pass from Fábregas and accelerated through a gap between Ronaldo, Guti and Álvaro Mejía. He drilled a low shot into the far bottom corner, unfazed by Sergio Ramos's late lunge.

Madrid still could not respond. In the fourth minute of injury time, Henry knocked the ball beyond Ramos and sprinted away from Roberto Carlos, hurdling a challenge from Mejía and strolling to the corner flag, where he held off that last player for a while longer before winning a throw-in. He had not just dominated these opponents, but humiliated them.

At full-time Henry acknowledged that it had been a "long time since I've seen an Arsenal team play like that". Wenger allowed his own insecurities to show when he spoke of the future, saying: "I hope the quality our young team has shown will persuade [Henry] to stay."

The return leg at Highbury finished goalless, though it is hard to fathom how. Ronaldo missed a header from five yards out, Fábregas's shot was deflected off-target at the last moment by Michel Salgado and Reyes hit the bar from close range. Raúl, restored to Madrid's starting XI, had one effort ricochet back to him off the inside of the post before Lehmann made a lightning recovery to claw away his rebound.

Madrid had come to Highbury knowing they needed to attack. Arsenal, starting with the same patchwork defence they took to the Bernabéu, simply chose to. The result was 90 minutes of glorious end-to-end action. Even in the dying moments, Roberto Carlos produced a superhuman effort to run down Pires's half-court shot after Casillas had come forward for a corner.

Arsenal's European adventure continued. Next up were Juventus, with a certain former Gunners captain in midfield. "We welcome Patrick back to his favourite ground," said Wenger before the first leg in London. "But we will make sure it is not easy for him."

Once again, Arsenal were the underdogs. Juventus had topped their own group ahead of Bayern Munich, and were eight points clear in Serie A with seven games left to play. The *Calciopoli* scandal that would eventually see them stripped of the domestic title had not yet started to publicly unfold.

On paper, their team looked imposing, with Gianluigi Buffon in goal, Lilian Thuram and Fabio Cannavaro at centre-back, Vieira in the middle and David Trezeguet joining Zlatan Ibrahimović up front. On the Highbury pitch, though, they were meek. Arsenal dominated down the flanks — exposing an out-of-position Adrian Mutu on Juventus's left wing and an overwhelmed Mauro Camoranesi on the right.

Wenger's team were winning every duel, including some that his own players would never have dared to imagine. In the 40th minute, Pires dispossessed Vieira with an immaculate sliding challenge before launching a counter-attack that ended with Fábregas opening the scoring from the edge of the box.

The memory of that tackle would delight Pires long into his footballing retirement. Asked if he remembered it during an interview with *Off The Post* in 2012, he struck the table with glee. "Of course," Pires exclaimed. "I did this one tackle in my career!"

Arsenal's European run was starting to have that feel about it, of something unprecedented, inexplicable, unique. They went on to beat Juventus 2-0, their second goal scored by Henry after a dazzling exchange of passes between him, Hleb and Fábregas.

The extent to which Juventus's spirit had been broken was brought home as Camoranesi and then Jonathan Zebina each got themselves needlessly dismissed in the space of three minutes at the end of a game that was already lost. Vieira had collected a booking that would keep him out of the return game, too.

There could be no more laments in North London for a captain departed. Instead, Italy's leading sports newspaper, *La Gazzetta dello Sport*, reflected on Pires's tackle as a turning point, defining Vieira as "the first brick to fall in the crumbling wall of Juventus".

The teams drew 0-0 in Turin, sending Arsenal through to their first Champions League semi-final under Wenger. Their next opponents were Villarreal, another team who were never supposed to get this far. The Yellow Submarine was headed for a seventh-place finish in La Liga, but had torpedoed Inter in the previous round.

For the first time in the knockout phase of that year's tournament, Arsenal began as favourites. Villarreal had Diego Forlán in attack and Juan Román Riquelme to pull the strings behind him, but at the other end, they were a mess. Their goalkeeper, Sebastián Viera, was suspended for the first leg in London, while both starting centre-backs — Gonzalo Rodríguez and Juan Manuel Peña — had been injured in a bruising league game against Barcelona.

In their last-ever European game at Highbury, Arsenal put in a mature performance, taking the lead through Touré in the 41st minute and, for the most part, avoiding unnecessary risks. They were fortunate not to give away a penalty when Gilberto Silva brought down José Mari on the stroke of half-time, but Henry had also seen a goal wrongly disallowed for offside at the start.

Wenger vowed that Arsenal would attack in the second leg, seeking a killer away goal. Instead, they found themselves overrun. Ironically, it was injuries to that makeshift defence which seemed to undermine them — with Senderos ruled out before kick-off and Flamini limping off after nine minutes. The returning Campbell and Clichy were superior players, but their lack of match practice was glaring.

Lehmann had to be at his sharpest to thwart Juan Pablo Sorín, Javi Venta and Riquelme. Guillermo Franco and Forlán blazed presentable chances off-target. Arsenal were desperately poor, but still had every right to feel aggrieved when their opponents were gifted a penalty in the 88th minute, after José Mari went down theatrically under Clichy's challenge.

As Riquelme waited to take the penalty, Henry walked over to speak with Lehmann. It was a calculated act.

"There was a penalty against Charlton [earlier in the season] and I knew that [Paolo] Di Canio would sometimes chip the ball from the penalty spot down the middle," the striker would later explain. "On that day I didn't speak to Jens about it. After the game I said to Di Canio, 'If you had seen me talking to the keeper would you have changed your plan?' He said, 'Yes.'

"I've seen Riquelme taking penalties and when it was an important one he put it right in the middle, waiting for the keeper to dive. So I told Jens that usually when Riquelme's under pressure and he's scared, he puts it in the middle. So maybe when he saw me talking to Jens, he thought that's what I was saying to him. Maybe, therefore, he changed."

Instead of shooting down the middle, Riquelme tried to place the ball to the keeper's left. The shot lacked conviction, struck with neither power nor precision. Lehmann blocked it, and Arsenal claimed their place in the final.

It had been the most improbable of journeys. Arsenal had not conceded a Champions League goal since they went to Ajax in the second round of the group stage. Ten consecutive clean sheets — a record for UEFA's club competitions — achieved despite starting the last six games without a recognised left-back.

Their opponents in the final were Barcelona. Frank Rijkaard's team had easily won La Liga, finishing 12 points clear of Madrid. They had already eliminated Mourinho's Chelsea, as well as Benfica and Milan, in the knockout rounds. A front two of Ronaldinho and Samuel Eto'o had combined for 12 goals and eight assists in the tournament so far.

Arsenal were at least safe in the knowledge that they would return to the Champions League the following season. For months, it had seemed that their only path to qualifying would be to win the whole thing. They entered the final week of the Premier League campaign knowing that even three victories in six days would not be enough to crack the top four unless Tottenham slipped up.

In the end, of course, Spurs did exactly that. Their defeat to West Ham was a story all of its own, with a number of players coming down sick on the morning of the game. No cause was ever proven, despite extensive club investigations that included taking stool samples

from players, but Arsenal fans were only too happy to embrace the
legend of a bad lasagne, and turn it into a terrace chant.

On they went, to Paris. Arsenal's starting XI for the final looked
more robust than it had all season. The patchwork defence that had
carried them this far was gone, with Cole returning at left-back and
a renewed Campbell reclaiming his place at centre-half.

Might it have been the loss of familiarity in that group, though, that
led Arsenal to disaster in the 18th minute? Touré and Campbell both
stepped forward to confront the run of Ronaldinho, allowing Eto'o
space to run in behind. The Brazilian played a simple ball through
to his team-mate, who was brought down crudely by Lehmann on
the edge of the box.

If referee Terje Hauge had not been so quick to whistle, advantage
could have been played and a goal awarded — Ludovic Giuly rolling
the ball into an unguarded net. In that circumstance, a yellow card
for Lehmann might have sufficed. Instead, with a free-kick awarded
on the edge of the box, it had to be red.

The implications of that decision went beyond a single game. Lehmann
coming off was one thing, but now another player would have to
make way for his replacement, Manuel Almunia. Wenger chose Pires.

A decade later, the winger would still recall that moment as the
bleakest of his entire career. "It was a nightmare. I remember it like
yesterday," he told *L'Equipe*. "You know a player has to come off,
but I never thought it would be me."

Pires refused to even look at Wenger as they passed on the touchline,
or to commiserate with him at full-time. Arsenal had hoped to persuade
him to sign a one-year contract extension. Instead, he agreed to join
Villarreal the next day.

The players who remained on the pitch were defiant. Henry had
missed a golden chance to put Arsenal ahead in the second minute,
freeing himself from Rafael Marquéz's marking with a sumptuous
touch but failing to beat Victor Valdés from six yards. Even with
ten men, though, they still found a way to get their noses in front
before the break.

If Hauge had seen things clearly in the 37th minute, then Arsenal
could have been down to nine men. The already-booked Eboué took

a scandalous dive as he moved past Carles Puyol just outside the Barcelona box, and was rewarded with a free-kick. Henry's delivery found the head of Campbell, who thumped it into the corner of the net.

Arsenal's impossible dream had never felt so vividly real. They made it through half-time and survived the first wave of frantic Barcelona response. As the second period progressed, their ten men began to carve out chances for a second goal that might have sealed the win.

Ljungberg stole the ball from Oleguer and sprinted through on goal but could not find the angle to beat Valdés at his near post. Hleb released Henry for another one-on-one but, for the second time in the game, Arsenal's captain fired too close to the keeper.

And then, the bucket of cold water. Barcelona scored twice in four minutes to turn the game on its head, Eto'o and Juliano Belletti making good on brilliant assists by the substitute Henrik Larsson.

Somewhere in-between, the skies opened over the Stade de France to leave Arsenal both literally and figuratively drenched.

Two days after the Champions League final, Henry signed a new four-year contract. He confessed that he had thought about leaving, but said that Arsenal's performance in the Champions League final had reassured him of the team's potential to rise again. "I've never played in Spain and I never will," he said. "This is my last contract."

Wenger struck a similarly optimistic note. "I had two aims at the start of the week: to win the European Cup and then to make Thierry stay," said Wenger. "I only managed one of those but, for the future of the club, that's certainly the best one."

A year later, though, Henry was gone, joining Barcelona at the end of an injury-hit 2006-07 season in which he scored only 12 goals across all competitions. Arsenal, who had won five trophies in the preceding four seasons (seven if you count the Community Shield), would not claim another until 2014. Wenger never got another league title, nor made it to another European final.

As those fans resting tired heads on cold tiles at Charles De Gaulle airport knew all too well, a dream cannot be forced, nor is it easy to return to. Arsenal's 2005-06 season had been glorious, but it marked the end of an era. It was not just Henry but Cole, Pires, Bergkamp, Ljungberg and Reyes who departed over the following 15 months. Wenger had to build a whole new team.

Going to a Champions League final can indeed be a costly business. Only those who made the journey can know if it was worth it despite an eventual defeat, and all the discomfort that came next.

MIDDLESBROUGH 2005-06

JOHN NICHOLSON

Middlesbrough and European football are not two things any football fan might expect to say in the same sentence, unless that sentence was "Middlesbrough never play European football".

But in 2006, Boro almost won the UEFA Cup. Yes, you read that correctly.

OK, they lost 4-0 in the final to Sevilla, but in some ways, that is irrelevant because the journey to Eindhoven was the sort of fairytale story that all fans of small, out-of-the-way, unfashionable clubs in small, out-of-the-way unfashionable places dream of. Even though we didn't collect the silverware, reaching the final was reward enough.

Now, 14 years later, with Boro having just escaped relegation to the third tier, it seems like a fevered cheese dream to think of such an unlikely scenario. Given the financial disparities now disfiguring the English game, rendering the Premier League dysfunctional while poisoning the clean waters of the rest of the pyramid, it seems unlikely that Middlesbrough will ever repeat this feat. This is a lofty peak in a mountain range we can no longer climb.

The first European campaign in the club's history had played out the previous season courtesy of the 2004 League Cup win — our only silverware since winning the Kirin Cup in 1980 in Japan and the Anglo-Scottish Cup in 1976.

In the 2004-05 season, the club entered the UEFA Cup in the first round and made it all the way to the quarter-final before losing out

4-2 on aggregate to Sporting Lisbon, but beating Lazio along the way. This was but a taster, an amuse-bouche for what came next.

Boro qualified for the 2005-06 UEFA Cup by finishing seventh in the league. This is where the fairytale really begins. In the last game of the previous season, Mark Schwarzer had saved a last-minute penalty against Manchester City to preserve a 1-1 scoreline. Had Boro lost, there would've been no European campaign. On such narrow margins are legends forged.

First, there was the knockout game to negotiate against Greek side Xanthi. In front of just 14,191 fans, goals from George Boateng and Mark Viduka secured the win and a 0-0 draw in the away leg sent Boro into the group stages.

It's important to note at this point that, in truth, when the UEFA Cup run started, most fans were not overly fussed by it. Like all good love stories, it started out with indifference or disdain and ended in a passionate embrace. It was widely seen as the poor cousin to the Champions League and was in its death throes as a competition, soon to be replaced in 2009 by the Europa League, which has rarely proven any more popular and given, at last count, you have to play about 193 games to win it, is often seen more as a burden than a privilege.

So when Boro were drawn into a group alongside AZ Alkmaar, Litex Lovech, Dnipro Dnipropetrovsk and Grasshoppers, there wasn't exactly dancing in the streets. The home game against the Ukrainians pulled just 12,953 through the Riverside turnstiles to see an easy 3-0 win. The game against Bulgaria's Litex Lovech fared even worse, with just 9,436 watching the 2-0 win. When you've got 35,000 seats to fill, it hardly made for a sizzling atmosphere. Typical Boro.

Boro topped the group with three wins and a draw, but this was greeted with little more than a shrug of the shoulders. OK, we'd beaten some teams that most hadn't even heard of, so what?

In February 2006, the knockout rounds began with a game against VfB Stuttgart, who were one of the best teams in the competition. They had played in the previous season's Champions League, only losing their quarter-final with Chelsea by a single goal.

Middlesbrough fans are not, by nature, optimists. It comes with mother's milk. We're built to cope with failure, not success. Built to dodge the punches, not to expect the hugs. So when we got Stuttgart in the draw, we thought that was it. Boro would have no chance. We pretty much always think that about every game, though. Typical Boro.

The away leg was first and thanks to Jimmy Floyd Hasselbaink and Stuart Parnaby goals, Boro emerged with a 2-1 win.

This made us all raise our eyebrows in surprise, which is about as hysterical as we Boro fans normally get. Maybe we had a chance after all. So, this time, 24,000 turned up to see the home game — still leaving the Riverside about a third empty, but an improvement all the same.

Naturally, just when we thought we might be any good, Boro lost. Of course they did. 1-0. Typical Boro. But we went through on away goals. Only Boro could win by losing. Stuttgart had scored early on but couldn't get a second. Gareth Southgate was man of the match as he marshalled a backs-against-the-wall performance in the second half.

So it was that for a second season we had got to the round of 16. Now our opponents were Roma, who were very good and would go on to finish second in Serie A. Too good for the Boro, surely. Much too good. The home leg was first and, in one of our best performances to date, a 12th-minute Yakubu penalty actually won the game for the Teessiders. Even so, the Riverside was still 10,000 short of its 35,000 capacity. We still did not really believe. And we'd get beat in Italy, wouldn't we? Of course we would. Boro winning in Rome? No chance.

And we were right. Of course we were. Six days later they played a blood and thunder game and Boro lost. They lost 2-1, to once again go through on away goals, a 32nd-minute Hasselbaink strike doing the job nicely thank you very much. It was a game designed for one Mr Lee Cattermole's talents of being relentlessly combative and fearless. Despite being booked early on for kicking the ball away and thus being ruled out of the next game, he and keeper Mark Schwarzer kept the Italians at bay for what felt like eons. Winning by losing. Typical Boro.

So who's next then? After beating two cracking sides in Stuttgart and Roma, Basel looked like an easy win. For a moment, the traditional Boro cynicism lapsed. We can do this. Basel are Swiss and so can't be any good. Nowt good comes from Switzerland except Toblerone. Everyone knows that. They would surely be an easier prospect than either of the previous ties.

The first leg was away. What did Boro do? They bloody lost, didn't they? Of course they did. Typical Boro. In a poor display, they went down 2-0. No away goal here.

Just when we thought we had a chance, it was lost. See? That's what comes of having hope or believing in the Boro. Don't make that mistake again. While the team was dangerous going forward with Mark Viduka, Hasselbaink and Yakubu, and Stewart Downing on the wing, we were shipping too many goals. Winning the return tie 3-0 was unlikely to say the least. There was no way we'd keep a clean sheet.

So a week later, with the return game almost certainly lost, the Riverside had just under 25,000 in it to see Basel score early, making it 3-0 on aggregate. Aw, Boro man, what the hell are yer doin'? This is typical Boro this is, we grumbled to each other, knowing in our steel hearts that it was all over. Now we needed to score four without reply. Impossible.

Yes, OK, Viduka had got one back by half-time, but even at 1-1 we were still obviously going out. Boro started the second half well, playing fluent, spirited football. A second Viduka strike on 57 minutes sent the Riverside into molten eruption.

We looked at each other. Nah, it's not going to happen, is it? Nah. At least they're giving it a go though. Fair play to them for that. We still needed two goals … but had over half an hour to get them.

For a moment, it was on. It was, wasn't it?

But when 20 or so more minutes had passed without further scoring, we'd lapsed back into our default cynicism. Hope was being snatched away from us, as usual. No, it wasn't on. We had been lulled into a false sense of optimism. Typical Boro.

It was at this point that Jimmy Floyd Hasselbaink received the ball on the edge of the D and without much backlift of his right foot, quite nonchalantly belted it into the top left-hand corner of the net to make it 3-1.

He barely even celebrated. It was one of those moments when you think something has gone wrong. It was a too-easy strike. There must've been a foul. It'll be disallowed. Everyone just stood still for a moment before screaming.

Now it's really on y'know, it bloody is, it's on. C'mon Boro! With 11 minutes to play, now we believed again, but the fourth wouldn't come even though Boro were all over Basel. The Swiss were out on their feet and Boro were a relentless wave after wave of red. C'mon Boro, man.

It fell to the unlikely hero in the shape of Massimo Maccarone to score the winner in the 90th minute. He'd been signed as a promising Italian striker, but hadn't done much of note, and after this season was over wouldn't do anything else of note at the club either.

Fábio Rochemback, a chunky Brazilian the club had signed the previous year, advanced on the ball 30 yards out and hit a hard, low shot. Rocky had put much of his not inconsiderable weight behind it. The keeper parried it out to the left of his box. Maccarone advanced on the ball. It was immediately obvious he'd get to it before a defender could block it.

Physicists say time travel is not possible, but I've long felt it happens at football. I was up celebrating that winning goal before the Italian had struck the ball. It was as though I went forward in time by two seconds, saw it hit the net, and was already celebrating the goal when it actually did hit the net. He struck it clean and true beyond the diving keeper.

When the final whistle went, we were shocked as much as overjoyed. This didn't happen to Middlesbrough FC. This was the sort of heroic performance we always dreamed of but never saw. It went against the grain. It was the football equivalent of brushing a cat's fur up the wrong way. There was something unnatural about it.

Legendary local radio commentator Ali Brownlee called it "the greatest comeback since Lazarus".

So it was to be Romanian club Steaua Bucharest in the semi-final. 'Dracula's boys' as Ali would later call them, though there was no evidence any of them sucked anyone's blood, or were particularly vulnerable to crosses for that matter.

The away leg was once again the first game. We all hoped for a draw. A draw would do it. We were all certain we'd win the home match now. All the old doubts and negativity had vanished after the Basel game. Like someone casting off a heavy winter coat and pulling on their swimming cozzy, we embraced the golden sun of positivity for once in our Boro lives.

Of course, Boro lost the first game. Yes, of course they did. We laughed about it. We laughed and laughed. Losing 1-0? That was almost a win for a Boro side that could score four at home. No trouble, son. No trouble at all.

But a week later and 24 minutes into the return leg, all that fresh hope and positivity was gone. It evaporated like summer's morning mist. The Romanian side had already scored twice and we'd lost our defensive rock, captain Gareth Southgate, to injury.

Now we need to score four. That'll teach you to feel cheerful. Typical Boro.

We knew in our pig iron hearts that we couldn't do it again. We couldn't. No chance.

Then Maccarone scored in the 33rd minute — the exact same time that Viduka had netted in the Basel game. It was an uncanny coincidence.

Was something weird in the air? Some sort of loop in the space-time continuum? We searched for some cosmic significance to prove this was the start of the comeback.

As half-time came, I convinced myself that this game would be a blueprint of the Basel game. So when over ten minutes had gone by without us scoring in the second half, I wasn't worried.

Viduka's second in the game against the Swiss had come in the 57th minute. History was obviously going to repeat itself. But the 57th minute came and went. No goal. In our chemical hearts, we now knew this was a different game and there'd be no such glory again.

But the XXL Aussie striker waited merely seven more minutes to score, this time in the 64th minute. The noise from the 34,622 fans that had crammed into the Riverside this time was immense. Like the roar of the smelting plant that the town was founded upon. Ironopolis was born again.

It was like coming up on mushrooms as the psilocybin rushes into your bloodstream. Everything becomes hyper-real, the vibration of the molecules of existence now available to see, touch and taste.

When Chris Riggott scored in the 73rd minute, it felt somewhere between surreal and hallucinogenic. Now, no-one didn't believe. Now was our time. All those years that had passed with the working class's Teesside dreams being dashed. All those years of fight and struggle on and off the pitch. The ups and the downs and the downs and the downs. All those long years of Typical Boro, all were forgotten now.

I doubt a single one of Boro's fans felt we wouldn't go on and win. It seemed certain. Seventeen minutes plus injury time was easy enough.

Time ticked away.

Don't do this to us Boro. Don't … just … just don't.

89 minutes on the clock.

Downing crossed the ball, but it was headed out and away. Boro knocked it back in only for it to be well-defended again. A Romanian player took control of the ball about 30 yards out from his own goal and passed it to his right, but he put too much pace on it and it was collected by Stewy Downing once more. Here we go.

This time he cut inside to his right, then took it left outside the defender, beating him easily. Now he was free. Boro had three strikers in the box against four defenders as Downing's cross came in. But crucially, Maccarone had got ahead of his marker. Downing's ball dropped right in front of him, but was too far away to kick without putting it over the bar.

So what did he do?

What did he do? I'll tell you what he did. The bald billiard-ball-headed Italian left the ground for no more than two seconds, stuck his head on the ball while actually flying horizontally through the air like a flightless bird momentarily aloft.

Goal. A fucking goal. A fucketty-fuck-fuck goal. Fucking hell.

Even writing this now, I am reduced to tears, once more.

It was absolute bedlam in the Riverside. As the final whistle blew following a couple of nervy minutes of added time, it was a shining moment of transcendence.

All those generations of supporters who'd gone to Ayresome Park since the 19th century, season after season in the bitter easterlies that blow in off the North Sea. This was for them.

For the Boro industrial working class who laboured too hard, for too long, to make an elite rich with their sweat, spit and snot, with their brains, brawn and bastard hardness, had come and gone, all hoping for a night like this. This win was for all of them and although Ayresome was gone a decade previously, all their ghosts were somehow suddenly present in the Riverside. You could feel them. The might of Ironopolis, the infant Hercules, the Steel River people who were born and raised to serve their steel mother. It was what they were taught and all they ever knew. And they believed that she would keep their children, even though not a single word was true.

This was a moment for all of us who left and for all of us who stayed. For the Teesside diaspora flung to all corners of the world, in just the same way its steel was, from Sydney Harbour to San Francisco Bay.

To understand the magnitude to fans of this run in the UEFA cup, which climaxed as Maccarone flew through the air like a bullet, you have to understand the mentality of the supporters; the Teesside hive mind, if you will.

It's a region that has suffered economic decline since the early '80s and has long felt abandoned and misunderstood by governments of all stripes. You get your head down and you get through. You don't expect any help. It has forged a gritty, resolute population, one with a gallows humour and a fondness for a drink to medicate life.

We are built to survive disaster, not to expect success. This is why that night is still such a powerful and emotional thing. For once, the stars were aligned and for once, everything that normally goes wrong, went right.

It was a time like no other. The side had been expensively assembled and would be disbanded over the coming 24 months. It had put the club deep into the red, an unfortunate truth that within a couple of seasons had to be addressed, especially after relegation. But that didn't matter. As long as the club did what it had to do to survive, that was fine. It is still fine.

Because that night, the steel river's burning heart was alight once again and all the pain, the hurt, the heartache, the crushing weight of economic oppression, state negligence and too many home defeats, was all gone.

For once, it was Untypical Boro.

ARGENTINA 2006-2014

MARCELA MORA Y ARAUJO

"Casi casi. Alegrias imposibles de atar a un resultado."

Santi Cañizares was a goalkeeper at the height of international acclaim when, in early 2002, he dropped a bottle of cologne on his foot, the broken glass slicing through a tendon. He missed that year's World Cup, obviously, and when I was flown over to Spain to interview him on "the worst thing that ever happened to him", the charming peroxide blonde laughed at me. "Hombre!" he exclaimed. "I had a great year! Professionally achieved so much, and also my first son was born. Almost-playing-in-a-World Cup-and-then-not is a minor blip, not a tragedy."

Jorge Valdano also had to sit out a World Cup as a young man in his prime when he caught hepatitis shortly before the 1982 finals. Unlike the wiser Cañizares, Valdano was very depressed by the shattered dream implications of his 'nearly'. Years later, he told me that if he had known then that the following World Cup he would lift the trophy having scored in the final, his convalescence might have been easier to endure. Hindsight is a wonderful thing.

Almost being there, almost winning. Almost scoring. The phrase *'si no es palo es gol'* comes to mind — difficult to translate, but essentially stating that when the ball doesn't hit the post, it's a goal. The 'if' clause almost turns it into an ongoing rule; not a depiction of a single instance, but rather a truth about the laws of physics and the game; 'if, then' renders it sort of timeless, the 'either-or' rhythm implicit: it's either post, or goal. Almost in. A close call. *Casi*. Football is a game spiced with '*casi, casi*', a serial of 'ifs', of split seconds where the ball can define history one way or another.

A football-revering nation, we have had our fair share of *casi* moments ingrained in our collective memory. Some are on-the-pitch incidents, others broader in scope. The Maradona years of which Valdano was part and parcel kicked off in 1979, in a Youth World Cup, and although the era sustained the nation's adrenaline until 1994, when Diego exited the world stage with an ephedrine-induced bang, many still think of the 1978 World Cup — our baptism as a force to be reckoned on the worldwide field of dreams — as the one a young promising talent by the name of Maradona *almost* played in. *Casi*. The World Cup in 1978 was also the one in which Holland *casi* scored us out of our hour of glory, further cementing their reputation as the 'nearly' international side to dwarf all others.

A victorious Argentina entered a new chapter in its footballing history. Our chain-smoking, long-haired intellectual Cesar Menotti, who had chosen to leave Diego out of the squad, chose now to demote himself and take over the youth international squad for the Japan Youth World Cup. I am one of millions of a generation that watched matches at dawn, growing up with this new crop of talent, among them our very own six-million-dollar-man who, by the beginning of the next decade, was already one of the most controversial and gifted talents ever to grace this most noble of games.

There were no 'nearly' moments in 1986 — the task was completed. Our delirious belief in a deity that shared our national flag as an emblem of belonging firmly established. God was Argentinian. So it was not a surprise for us as a nation to reach the final match of the 1990 World Cup as well. The football didn't merit it, but playing forever was the least we expected, and the bitter taste of defeat in the last game is always sweetened by being there at all. As the saying goes: 'In order to lose a final you have to reach it.' In a sense, every final is a chance at 'almost'.

Then came 1994, the beginning of the Americanisation of soccer. The Mexican waves and the Valderrama wigs and the corporate hospitality packages made all us week-in week-outers turn up our noses as the game of the people was grabbed by the commercial free world, and sponsors and rights brokers gained more and more control. On the pitch, our Diego was once again as delightful as he was grotesque — but kicked out in disgrace, as the grotesque trumped the narrative.

The good news was that enough good men continued their daily work in child and adolescent development all over the nation's vacant lots and kiddy-tournaments. From the mountains to the sea they nurtured raw ability and a craving for the ball with strategic training of control in reduced spaces, meticulously entering little boys for the various relevant competitive stages that corresponded. The eternal factory of dreams never ceased, and if the 1998 World Cup didn't quite pan out as hoped (Michael Owen and Ariel Ortega conspired with the cosmos; David Beckham and Diego Simeone did the dirty work), it did give way to a true revolution in standards.

The Argentine Football Association (AFA) decided to change the way youth development was handled and ceased the old tradition of having someone appointed by the first-team manager overseeing the kids. They invited proposals and a thorough and meticulous project presented by José Pékerman was picked. An outsider in the football elite, Pékerman brought a seriousness and respect for the game that hitherto had been absent. His focus on fair-play, and the all-round wellbeing of the youngsters, was as important as on-the-pitch performance. His aim was to establish a long-term m.o. which would serve to educate and nourish the formation of young men, not just players. It was a break away from the 'resultist dictatorship', as he called it, valuing process more than scorelines. He appointed men who shared these values: Marcelo Bielsa, another outsider, to manage the first team, and Hugo Tocalli to assist the work with the youth.

While Tocalli and Pékerman's various categories did incredibly well at international level, Bielsa's stint at the helm started out promisingly, but saw the first team crash out of the 2002 World Cup with unprecedented speed. A conspiracy of bizarreness saw the team, who had qualified earlier than any in their group, undefeated, leave equally early after just three games. Michael Owen, again, had a stellar role in Argentina's demise. Beckham and Simeone, again, played out a sort of duel in which Beckham was hungrier for revenge.

Bielsa looked like he wanted to quit, but stayed on to win an Olympic Gold medal, as he had vowed — perhaps a promise more to himself than anyone else — to win 'something'. When he stepped down, Pékerman, who had already distanced himself from the AFA and was managing Levante in Spain, agreed to take charge of the first team, now ready to work with several generations of youngsters who had come through the ranks of his own programme; the Pékerman Boys, as we still call them.

Lionel Messi wasn't a Pékerman Boy in the same way the others were. He had moved to Barcelona at a young age and had barely played in Argentina, not even in the super-organised kiddy tournaments. In fact, he 'nearly' wasn't ours. He 'nearly' played for Spain.

The Pékerman project had devoted years to setting up a solid structure, finding kids from all over the country and embracing them in the national enterprise with the assistance of nutritionists, psychologists and education experts. Legend says Messi's father, Jorge, compiled a VHS tape of Lio's best moments and personally took it to Bielsa during one of his many visits to Barcelona. Bielsa, who doesn't really 'do' chatting to agents, never met Jorge, but his assistant Carlos Vivas apparently did. They viewed the tape and requested entire matches. Jorge Messi delivered. Upon arrival back in Buenos Aires, Vivas went straight from the airport to the Ezeiza complex where Argentina trained and handed the tape to Tocalli.

Another version is that Pékerman, by now officially separated from Argentina and managing in Spain, went to watch a game and then introduced himself to Messi. Bielsa and Pékerman tried to influence Tocalli, who was reluctant to bring an outsider into his carefully balanced group. But, as word spread that Spain were about to call Messi, and Barcelona denied a first summons on the grounds it clashed with a club game, AFA supremo Julio Grondona intervened.

Spain's interest in calling Messi intensified and Argentina upped their game. Suddenly, a friendly against Paraguay's under-20s was hastily arranged, along with all the relevant paperwork needed in order for it become an 'official' Argentina international match (one which would tie Messi into forever bearing the national strip under the then rules).

I didn't know any of this until a few years ago, when journalist Andres Eliceche carefully reconstructed the operation for *Anfibia* magazine. He interviewed the photographer sent by the *Clarin* newspaper with the instruction "the game doesn't matter, the kid's called Messi", as well as the referee, who remembered being surprised that official FIFA documentation was required to register a sudden youth-category friendly. But Messi came on and scored a seventh goal against an improvised Paraguayan under-20 side assembled at the 11th hour. Andres Eliceche summarises the goal ("still bouncing around on YouTube") thus: "Lionel got the ball from the left in the centre of the pitch, controlled it with his left leg and changed velocity, already eyeing up the goalkeeper. Two Paraguayans watched him close up, unable to stop him. Six touches with the left, and one with the right, a dummy and the shot in six seconds."

Fittingly under the radar, this orchestrated baptism as a national treasure with barely 200 spectators served to seal his 'Argentinian-ness', but didn't really make waves beyond the memories of the few who knew.

It was his superlative performances with Barcelona, maybe especially the Champions League match against Chelsea, that made so many of us sit up and take note. His connection with the club and his firm link to Europe preceded his international standing, even after winning the under-20 World Cup — Tocalli now fully embracing the genius so small they called him 'the flea'.

That Messi might be unveiled in Germany 2006 was a tale foretold — more by the sponsors than the football connoisseurs, as massive billboards and murals on the sides of buildings announced his impending presence. But Pékerman had a carefully orchestrated symphony to play out, and a labour of love and many years was delicately timed. The seeds he had harvested were flowering, and he gave Messi and Tevez their first minutes of play on a World Cup stage almost at the same time, a few games into the tournament. After the unforgettable 24-pass goal against Serbia & Montenegro, in which a group of young men seemed to be gliding joyfully, as if showing the world what it meant to have fun playing football, the pressure came on more intensely. The stakes were high by the time they faced Germany in Berlin; the pressure unbearable.

We could maybe think of that quarter-final match against Germany as Messi's first flavour of 'nearly' … he was visibly grumpy, sat on the bench, and as the game spiralled into a battleground, the players losing their cool and their collectedness, Messi turned more and more into a disgruntled teenager. He never played, and Argentina were knocked out.

There was a universal call for Pékerman's head after that. He resigned during the press conference, in the mixed zone. Everyone was screaming from the rooftops demanding to know why he didn't play Messi. Personally, I find it understandable that managers with the emotional intelligence of Menotti and Pékerman are able to make the call when they see kids as 'not ready'. In a world of clamour for their talent and little concern for their wellbeing, it's pertinent to wonder what they know about them — what could Menotti tell about the young Maradona that made him think "not yet" in 1978 and step into the role of youth manager in 1979, just so he could take the boy to new heights? What could Pékerman tell about the young Messi, who over the next World Cups we would learn routinely vomited pitch-side before big games? Perhaps rather than near misses, these exclusions were necessary conditions to allow both players to go on to become the icons they are.

Unlike Maradona, who could be nothing but an Argentinian folklore legend, Messi has a universality about him that makes it hard for him to be easily identified through stereotype. Also unlike Maradona, who thrives on conflict and is fuelled by a sense of combat and being in constant feuds against everything, who feeds off opposition, Messi is an evolutionarily more advanced type, who needs cooperation rather than competition to succeed. He functions best as part of a well-oiled machine and is clearly comfortable with familiarity and order. Throughout most of his professional life, Barcelona have given him that. Argentina has not.

When Messi missed a penalty against Chile in the final of an 'extra' Copa America invented as a centenary celebration in 2016, his frustration and exasperation took hold. Ten years on from the beginning of his international dream in Germany, he broke down. Not a man to generally explode emotionally, he announced his retirement from Argentina in tears. It brought the national conversation to a head; the country was divided between those who questioned his 'loyalty' and those who were just grateful for the beauty and the joy. I like to think of myself in the latter camp, wanting to believe that if Messi represented Uruguay, or Congo, Spain or even Catalonia at international level, I would love to watch him play just as much.

I interviewed Messi once, long before, and what struck me was how low-key he is. How unassuming. He's not a great talker and many who have interviewed him more than once comment on this, some going so far as saying they would decline further interviews. I didn't get that. Observing him was fascinating, truly as if talking to a child. He enjoyed looking at a picture book, and got animated when he understood the sense of a line of questioning. He enjoyed recalling how much winning mattered to him even as a young child, so much so that his siblings would let him win at any game they played because his tantrums if not were not worth it for the family. He even said for a while he wasn't sure if he was truly that good at football because as he mostly played with his older brothers and cousins and their friends, he thought maybe they let him score. Maybe they were making concessions because he was the little one. When I asked him if he had learnt to 'contain' his emotions, as a professional, if he had any mechanisms now to curb his frustration at not winning, he just said "contain?", and I couldn't tell if he didn't understand the word or if the idea of having to contain his emotions was so alien to him he couldn't even fathom the thought.

It was shortly before the 2010 World Cup, with Maradona the unexpected manager. Either some kind of magic realism would kick in, and a cocktail of unruly genius in charge of the ruly would take us places no football fan had ever been before, or the entire enterprise would be exposed for the sordid unplanned fiasco of earthly mediocrity it most likely was. One or the other. *Palo o gol.* As it turned out, there were some instances of pleasure, mostly cameras catching Diego and Lio passing the ball around in training, smiling, enjoying the playful essence of their art. Maradona hogged the limelight and it wasn't the disaster many feared, but for Messi and Argentina it wasn't even a 'nearly' event. Once again, Germany extinguished the dream, and when Spain picked up the cup, Messi himself might have wondered what could have been.

Finals, as I mentioned earlier, are always 'almost' events. Anything can happen, the ball can cross the line, everyone who reaches a final can certainly claim to have come close to the target. Messi's Argentina have reached a handful, four Copa America and the 2014 World Cup. And won none.

Sometimes it feels like the Argentine flag, the national anthem, the strip itself, weighs Messi down, like an albatross around his neck, or an unpaid debt. Sometimes people write that Messi owes us nothing, that Argentina owe him — and then the debate gets ignited again. 'Why should we owe him anything?' many proclaim, outraged.

It's a question of eternal interest and elusive answer — what does it even mean to be from the same country as someone who accomplishes so much? How does the trophy of one individual get to be relished so by the compatriots who are but onlookers? And more puzzling to me still, why doesn't all the gold and silver collected for Barcelona count, then? If he belongs to us, why don't we just delight in his victory, as a consummate elite athlete? But we don't. And more to the point, he doesn't. It's like he might never be satisfied unless he wins with Argentina, for Argentina, because Argentina …

By 2018, the institutional collapse of Argentina's structures was total, and whatever happened on the pitch and within the squad, the grotesque had once again prevailed over any magic or beauty or playfulness. It was painful to watch, to report, and to be within the crumbling entity. The players looked like they were being subjected to some form of punishment, and the fans back home were equally disengaged. Emotionally, we had all been drained.

Yet Messi, who nearly quit two years before, continued to delight — his moves, each and every one an eternal instant. He can become intertwined with several other players, often twice his size, he can wriggle from under them like a worm, and fly upwards as he turns into a butterfly. He can create space, pass perfectly, dribble, assist, hang his head down, slouch his shoulders, and rise again. The film-maker Lucrecia Martel once gave me a beautiful description through her cinematographer's eye: "Contrast the long-shot with the close-up," she said: "When you take a distant view you can see how everything on the pitch appears still, like the waves on the sea from a plane, you can't make out any movement bar Messi's silhouette swaying along and the ball going into goal". And then imagine, "you zoom in: you can literally see the speed, the decision-making in every muscle, a body that thinks".

I can never unsee that. Messi's a perpetual motion machine, his feet and the ball are as one, a single curve, a single figure, a dancer and a warrior.

There's no 'nearly' about it. The guy is the best there is. Even now, in his mid-30s, and extending his frustration and his desire to quit toxic situations to Barcelona, even now, with nothing to play for, one imagines, he continues to leave football lovers open-mouthed with his flashes of brilliance. Out of this world. Moments of joy untied to results. Surely, that's what counts.

Argentina's trophy drought continues, and for the first time in decades, the export of players is declining. A new generation of development experts needs to emerge and find its place in a country — a world even — in which the old structures are falling apart before new ones have risen. Some may ask if Messi has another World Cup in him, I personally wonder if there will ever be another World Cup as we know it. In many ways, it doesn't matter.

It's almost a philosophical position, for me personally. The trophies, the cups, the medals, the scores are less relevant than the game itself. And the game is infinite, to paraphrase Borges. As I write, I hear that Santi Cañizares' son has been given a call by Zinedine Zidane, for Real Madrid's first team. Generation after generation will forever play, cheer, weep and laugh, chasing after the ball, or watching. The vacant lots of Argentina, the organised kiddy schools, from the mountains to the sea, will burst with children dreaming of becoming the next Maradona, the next Messi. Little girls are starting to be allowed the same dream, an exciting prospect indeed. No '*casi casi*' about it — Messi completed the task.

GHANA 2010

BROOKS PECK

A month before the 2010 World Cup began, FIFA announced the different slogans that would adorn the team buses for each of the 32 participating nations. They ranged from the charmingly cheesy (New Zealand's "Kickin' it Kiwi style") to the vaguely morbid (Slovenia's "With eleven brave hearts to the end"), but Ghana's transport rallying cry was particularly unique; "The hope of Africa." It was the only one that invoked the spirit of not just a single country, but an entire continent. It was the only one that carried as much expectation as it did optimism.

By the time the tournament kicked off in South Africa, Ghana's bus slogan felt more like a cruel joke. Then 32nd in FIFA's world rankings — only sixth best among African teams — Ghana announced on May 27 that midfielder Michael Essien, the team's best player, wouldn't be fit for the tournament having suffered hamstring and knee injuries months earlier. That news came on the same day as a 2-0 tune-up win in a friendly against Slovenia, the first of three they had scheduled before the World Cup started. They then lost 4-1 to the Netherlands and only managed a last-minute goal against Latvia to salvage a 1-0 win before travelling to South Africa. Ghanains had taken to calling the team the 'One-Goal Project', which might sound like a lofty mission for unified hope, but was actually a sarcastic jibe referencing how the Black Stars hadn't scored more than one goal in any match — aside from that friendly against Slovenia — all year, nor had they won any matches in which they conceded first.

"When you wear the Ghana shirt, you have to die, you can't wear it and not want to die," right-back Samuel Inkoom, who made his World Cup debut in 2010, told ESPN in June 2020. "This is what Ghanaians expect."

A lesser team would have crumbled under the pressure, the loss of its star player, and the challenge of a difficult group that included sixth-ranked Germany, 15th-ranked Serbia and 20th-ranked Australia.

"Going into the group games, people were like, 'Oh, Germany and Serbia will qualify (for the knockout rounds),'" says centre-back Jonathan Mensah, who goes by just 'Jonathan' to avoid confusion with fellow defender John Mensah, his older and more established teammate in 2010. "We were determined to go out there and perform and I think that's what we did."

Not only did Ghana perform, they made history, and came within touching distance of taking African football to new heights — only to be thwarted by one of the most controversial actions ever in a World Cup. Ten years later, this proud achievement cruelly remains a painful memory for many Ghanaians, most of all for the team itself.

Ghana qualified for their first World Cup four years earlier, in 2006, making an impressive debut that took them to the round of 16. With rising expectations, the country was certain that hosting the 2008 African Cup of Nations would bring their first AFCON title since 1982. But despite going unbeaten in the group stage, the performances were widely criticised by Ghanains, with particular scrutiny on then 22-year-old striker Asamoah Gyan. He scored from the penalty spot to set up a narrow victory in the opener against Guinea, yet after a 1-0 win against Namibia in their second group-stage match, Gyan and his older brother Baffour nearly walked out on the team as their family had to be issued police protection due to death threats from fans angry about squandered scoring chances (in matches Ghana won). The brothers ended up playing on, but the team was vilified further after losing to Cameroon in the semi-finals and finishing third.

To correct the course, the Ghana Football Association named 54-year-old Milovan Rajevac manager of the team, touting his "superior football coaching certificate from the University of Belgrade". Rajevac had just taken then Serbian SuperLiga side Borac Čačak from relegation playoff participants to UEFA Cup qualifiers in one season.

"The only time I'd been to Africa was when I travelled to Libya with Red Star Belgrade for a friendly," he later admitted. But the Serbian's appointment had more to do with where he was from than where he had been, as he shared a nationality with Ghana's manager in 2006, Ratomir Dujković. "I have to thank Dujković because the Ghanaians were specifically looking for a Serbian coach," Rajevac said in 2010.

While a tactically-focused new Serbian settled in with the senior team, Ghana began to assert itself at the youth level under Ghanaian coach Sellas Tetteh. They won the African Youth Championship at the start of 2009, then beat Brazil on penalties to win the nation's first under-20 World Cup title later that year.

For the African Cup of Nations in early 2010, Rajevac mixed established players like Gyan, Essien, midfielder Anthony Annan and the steadying presence of goalkeeper Richard Kingson with youth-level champions in standout winger André Ayew, defenders Inkoom and Jonathan, and striker Dominic Adiyiah, plus other emerging talents like defender Isaac Vorsah and creative force Kwadwo Asamoah.

Almost solely reliant on Gyan to score goals, Ghana refined a defensive discipline that resulted in clean sheets in three of their five matches, making the 'One-Goal Project' viable. However, in the final, Egypt scored in the 85th minute to break a scoreless deadlock and win a third consecutive AFCON title.

Despite that heartbreaking conclusion, Ghana's tournament successes in 2009 and early 2010 built a level of momentum and confidence for the players that the Essien news and lacklustre friendly performances just before the World Cup couldn't derail. While outsiders doubted them, their spirits remained high, and they were ready to show the world what they could do.

Rajevac's 2010 World Cup squad included nine changes from the AFCON finalists. Though Essien was lost, three of Ghana's biggest talents and team leaders John Mensah (the elder), full-back John Paintsil and midfielder Stephen 'Tornado' Appiah were now fit. Then Inter midfielder Sulley Muntari was also brought back into the fold after being excluded from the previous tournament due to disciplinary issues. Plus there was the addition of German-born midfielder Kevin-Prince Boateng, who parachuted into the team after completing a switch to represent Ghana in May 2010.

"We had a little bit of everything on that team," says Jonathan, then just 19 years old and in his first World Cup squad. "We had experience, we had young guys, we had skillful guys, fast guys — we had everything, and the cohesiveness in that team was never seen before."

They even had a little bit of Essien, as Jonathan opted to wear his number 8 for the tournament.

"I wore it a couple of times for training and I said, 'I like it,'" Jonathan says. "I liked the spirit in it and I went with it. ... He's like a big brother to me, and he was proud of me wearing it. We actually went into the tournament playing for him and the country, and that's what we did. (He was) talking to us after every game, and we were encouraged by that."

Despite the changes, Rajevac's disciplined tactics carried over. A slew of defensively skilled midfielders ensured that Ghana would again provide a brutal challenge for any opposing attack, while Boateng's ability to push the ball forward and Asamoah's deft passing would help Gyan be slightly less isolated up top than in the previous tournament. What made this Ghana team so formidable, however, was their exceptional versatility and positional fluidity while maintaining their formation, making them a terror to try to man-mark and profoundly difficult to break down at the other end of the pitch.

Rajevac's familiarity with Serbia, Ghana's first opponent in the 2010 World Cup group stage, helped the Black Stars follow a well-practiced script. A scoreless match turned in Ghana's favor when

Serbian defender Aleksandar Luković was sent off in the 74th minute, then Gyan coolly scored the match's only goal from the penalty spot after a handball in the 84th minute. At full-time, Rajevac refused to celebrate the win against his homeland, while Gyan ran the length of the pitch, proudly flying Ghana's flag over his head.

Belief in the team was instantly restored. The other participating African nations — South Africa, Nigeria, Algeria and Cameroon — all failed to win their opening matches. But the strong start didn't ensure a smooth ride through the rest of the group stage for Ghana. Injuries to both starting centre-backs, John Mensah and Vorsah, in the opener forced Rajevac to use Jonathan and Lee Addy, a pair who entered the tournament with six caps between them, against Australia.

Around midnight on the eve of the team's second match, Rajevac knocked on a sleepy Jonathan's hotel room door to tell him he would be making his first World Cup start the next day.

"I was nervous when I was sleeping because I got the news very late," Jonathan remembers. "As a young player you always want to play, but this is a big, big game — big stage — and I was anxious at best, but the day of the game, I was starting to get calm. The coaches spoke to me and said, 'Go out there and have fun, and make sure you play safe.' At the start of the game I was a little bit nervous, but 10-15 minutes into the game I kind of settled down and my teammates also helped me a lot."

Australia scored early, though it wasn't the young centre-backs who were to blame. The normally reliable Kingson, wearing the armband with John Mensah out, parried a bouncing free kick from 30-yards straight back in front of him for Australia's Brett Holman to fire into the net. Maybe it was the *Jabulani* — the tournament's notoriously unpredictable match ball. Maybe it was the fact that Kingson had failed to make a single appearance for Wigan over the previous club season before they released him ahead of the tournament. Either way, the one-goal deficit put Ghana in a position from which they had not managed a win so far that year.

In the 24th minute, Ghana's opponents were reduced to ten men for the second straight match, again for a handball — this time called on Australia's Harry Kewell, whose shoulder stopped a certain goal from Jonathan after he was set up for a shot from point-blank range by Ayew's dazzling display of skill to twist a pair of defenders into pretzels along the byline. Gyan slotted the ensuing penalty home to equalise.

Though Ghana seemed sure to find another goal with such a prolonged advantage, they were only able to put six of 22 shots on target, and Australia goalkeeper Mark Schwarzer made tremendous saves on the shots that did require his efforts. The match ended 1-1. With Serbia rebounding to beat Germany 1-0 the day before, Ghana found themselves atop Group D with a match against a now stunned German side left to play.

But any joy in the group was immediately overwhelmed by a displeased Sulley Muntari pushing the team to the brink of chaos.

"After the game we were in the dressing room, Sulley ... was not happy about the result," Kingson told Ghana's Max TV in July 2020. "He was talking in Twi and Italian and he didn't understand why we should draw with an Australia team with one man down.

"So when we went back to the hotel, news came in that the coach said he wanted Sulley out of his camp because he had insulted him. ... He said Sulley had to leave, and we said no, he should let Sulley stay — he can decide not to play him, but shouldn't sack him from camp. The man still insisted Sulley must leave, and we kept begging him, even including (then president of the Ghana Football Association) Mr. Nyantakyi. He was there, (Nyantakyi's deputy) Fred Pappoe was there, including some of the senior players and the interpreter of the coach. We begged him. The coach kept insisting Sulley leaves, and if Sulley left, it was also going to affect us, so finally, I told him that if Sulley leaves then I will also leave."

The next day, France's players thoroughly overshadowed Ghana's dressing-room drama by refusing to train in protest against striker Nicolas Anelka being sent home early because of a half-time dispute with manager Raymond Domenech.

Unlike France's mess, Ghana's situation was quickly resolved. Not only was Muntari allowed to stay with the team after Kingson's ultimatum, he was the first player to come off the bench in the 64th minute of the final group match against Germany, shortly after Mesut Özil scored with an unstoppable shot from outside the box.

Though heavily favoured, Germany only won 1-0, putting them top of the group with six points. Ghana's four points were enough to advance to the knockout stage, edging out Australia on goal difference.

Of the six African teams in the group stage, only Ghana made it through. Now, as their team bus had been claiming for a month and a half, they truly were the hope of Africa.

Although Ghana finished the group stage with a loss, the performance against Germany, an eventual semi-finalist that year, gave the Black Stars a confidence boost going into the win-or-go-home phase of the tournament.

"Going into that game, (people) said that they're going to beat us 4-0, 3-0 and all that, but we went into the game determined and we matched them boots to boots," says Jonathan. "It was an incredible game even though we lost, and (the German team) actually said that was one of the toughest games for them. … Going forward we knew we were doing something right, and if we continue to play together as a team, we have a chance of going further into the tournament. And that's what we did."

In the round of 16, Ghana would face a familiar World Cup foe: the United States. Four years earlier, Ghana beat the US 2-1 to seal a place in the knockout stage and send the Americans home winless and at the bottom of a group that also included Italy and the Czech Republic.

Ghana had no fear of the US and it showed when, in just the fifth minute, Kevin-Prince Boateng took the ball from the halfway line to the edge of the box almost wholly unimpeded, sliding a shot past goalkeeper Tim Howard to make it 1-0.

Ghana were a better team than they were in 2006, but so were the US, and the Americans would test Ghana's confidence in the second half. Near the hour mark, Clint Dempsey nutmegged a flat-footed John Mensah for a clear view on goal. With Dempsey wide-eyed and salivating, Jonathan tried to avenge his namesake by clattering into the American while poking the ball away. The referee blew the whistle, the US had a penalty and Jonathan was shown his second yellow card of the tournament. Landon Donovan then chipped his spot kick into the net. It was now 1-1 and the US had momentum, finishing the half with several chances that required Kingson to make big saves, as he had done throughout the match.

In extra time, Ghana again quickly hit the US with a dizzying counterattack. Gyan split centre-backs Carlos Bocanegra and Jay DeMerit to chase down a looping long ball, somehow chesting it down while getting shoved in the back and lofting a shot directly over Howard to score, as if it was the most natural thing in the world. Gyan then ran past the corner flag, arms outstretched — not to soak up the adulation, but more to say, "Can you believe that just happened?" before breaking out a now trademark celebratory dance.

Ghana weathered the US's best efforts to find a second equaliser and won 2-1. Tired and proud, they were through to the World Cup quarter-finals, a feat only two previous African teams had achieved: Cameroon in 1990 and Senegal in 2002. Not only that, the One-Goal Project was no more. Granted it required extra time to do, but the two goals — both with the run of play, and one even scored by someone other than Gyan — offered further reassurance after just two Gyan penalties in the group stage.

"Ghana are a talented team and their coach has them well organised," then US coach Bob Bradley said after the match. "They are capable of moving on."

Those were the positives. On the other side, both Jonathan and Ayew would be unavailable for the quarter-final against Uruguay due to yellow card accumulation, and Kevin-Prince Boateng was a doubt after suffering a hamstring injury that forced him out of the US game in the second half. But feeling fresh would be a challenge for everyone who played that match.

"It felt like we played for four hours," Jonathan told the *Columbus Dispatch* in June 2020. Meanwhile, their quarter-final opponents, Uruguay, had dispatched South Korea 2-1 in regular time.

No amount of fatigue or concerns for the starting XI could outweigh the joy of the situation for Ghana, though. This was their chance to go further than any other African country ever had in a World Cup, and to do it on African soil. Many South Africans adopted Ghana as their own, tweaking the South African team's 'Bafana, Bafana' ('The boys, the boys') nickname to dub The Black Stars 'BaGhana, BaGhana'. The African National Congress, South Africa's ruling political party, issued a statement thanking Ghana "for salvaging the image of the continent in this tournament. … You are our pride."

"The mood in the camp was so high, as we knew that our destiny was in our own hands to make history for Africa and Ghana," Ayew told ESPN in June 2020. "Now, I honestly don't want to even look back to that game (against Uruguay), it still hurts."

The constant, deafening buzz of the vuvuzelas made it seem like there were even more than the 84,000 people packed into Johannesburg's Soccer City stadium on that cold Friday night. With Jonathan and Ayew unavailable, Vorsah made his first start at centre-back since the opener against Serbia, and Muntari, who could have been watching this match from home had his teammates not intervened a couple of weeks earlier, made his first start of the tournament.

Uruguay came out strong, twice forcing Kingson to make exceptional saves early on. But when their captain, center back Diego Lugano, exited in the 38th minute with an injury, the match shifted. Muntari made sure his presence was appreciated just before half-time. Uruguay gave him the space to take an ill-advised shot from 40 yards out that split four defenders, narrowly missed a ducking Gyan and took a swerving bounce outside the six-yard box before beating goalkeeper Fernando Muslera to the bottom corner. Ghana held their improbable lead until a stunning Diego Forlán free kick in the 55th minute again made use of the *Jabulani*'s unpredictable path and forced the match to extra time.

As the only team to go to extra time in both the round of 16 and quarter-finals, Ghana faced the mighty task of persevering through total exhaustion. Yet Rajevac only made two of the three substitutions available to him — Appiah for Inkooom in the 74th minute, and Adiyiah, the Golden Ball and Golden Shoe winner at the previous year's under-20 World Cup, for Muntari in an attempt to give Gyan help up top and find a winning goal. However, all this did was push the opposition into an act of desperation that would carry devastating effects for years to come.

In the final seconds of the second half of extra time, Ghana had one last chance to avoid a penalty shootout when they were awarded a free-kick deep into Uruguay's half. Paintsil delivered a perfect cross into the area, which was headed right in front of goal, forcing Muslera to come out and thwart an attempted header with his fist. The ball went to Appiah for a half-volley towards an open net that ricocheted off Luis Suárez's legs, who had alertly moved to the centre of the vacated goal line. With the ball suspended in the air, time all but stopped. Adiyiah forcefully headed it back toward goal, only to have Suárez push it away with his hands while Uruguay left-back Jorge Fucile made his own desperate attempt to swat the ball with his arm. Muslera caught the ball and held it over his head, unsure as everyone else on the planet as to how it was in his hands and not in the back of the net.

"I was in the VIP stands and I was going crazy, and I was like, "Oh my gosh," says Jonathan of that moment.

After being shown a red card for the obvious infraction, Suárez trudged off the pitch in tears. And for the third time of this World Cup, Gyan lined up the spot kick awarded for a handball offence.

This time, Gyan swayed back and forth as he stood over the ball, his eyes glancing from side to side. His run-up was faster than the previous two, more rushed. Fuelled by adrenaline, anticipation and raw nerves, he blasted the ball off the crossbar and up into the South African night. Gyan's hands immediately covered his face while Suárez, watching from the mouth of the tunnel, went from peeking over the collar of his shirt to baring his teeth and pumping both his fists.

Prior to this, Gyan had only missed one penalty in eight career attempts — a shot against the Czech Republic's Petr Čech at the 2006 World Cup in a group stage match that Ghana won 2-0, thanks in part to an earlier goal from Gyan. To miss a match-winning penalty was a completely foreign horror to Gyan, a player who had carried the burden of his nation's footballing hopes from a young age. And he had to experience it in the biggest moment of not only his country's World Cup history, but the entire African continent's.

"We know how penalties — especially last-minute penalties — how it goes, you know, tension, full stadium, the vuvuzelas are blowing, and all that," Jonathan says. "And to be able to take charge of a penalty like that takes a lot of courage. So I'll give Asamoah Gyan that. He's a strong guy. And in that moment obviously he was our penalty taker, so we had a lot of confidence in him, but it was tough."

With Uruguay reborn, Ghana in shock, and the vuvuzelas somehow getting louder and more forceful, Forlán opened the shootout by casually and confidently poking the ball into the net. Then, displaying an incredible mix of bravery and desire to press on from a waking nightmare, Gyan took his side's first attempt. His movements steadied and an unshakable determination now in his eyes, he had the absolute gall to pin the ball into the top corner.

Though Gyan had made a quick recovery, his teammates did not. Mensah took no run-up and delivered a weak shot that Muslera blocked with ease. The 20-year-old Adiyiah put his in virtually the same place as Mensah, with the same result. Uruguay won the shootout 4-2 when Sebastián 'Loco' Abreu skipped up to the ball and chipped it in.

"We did our best," Jonathan says. "But our best wasn't enough. So we gave credit to them, but obviously the Suárez incident, you know, we were very mad."

Emphasising his innate ability to fuel such anger, Suárez told reporters after the match that "the hand of God now belongs to me," referencing Diego Maradona's famous handball goal against England in the quarter-finals of the 1986 World Cup. "I made the save of the tournament," he added.

"At that moment, he did that to help his team win, even though it was a foul play in our standards," Jonathan says, "but at the same time … Yeah, we all know, the whole world knows that wasn't fair, and he is known to be like that. He's not fair. … In our game some people play fair, some people don't play fair, and, with all honesty, it's one player that doesn't play fair. We know he's had a couple of incidents in big games — biting (Italy defender Giorgio) Chiellini (at the 2014 World Cup), fighting other players — this is something that we've seen him do and people weren't surprised."

Surprised or not, opinions remain deeply split on Suárez's action a decade later. Even among members of that Ghana team.

"I can't forgive him because it was not an accident," defender Hans Sarpei, who started all five of Ghana's matches in South Africa, told the BBC in July 2020. "He knows what he has done. We were crying and you see someone who has cheated us is celebrating. How can I forgive him? Never. Never ever."

"That is what patriotism looks like, you have to be there for the country," Inkoom told ESPN. "If it was me, I would do the same. He did it, and it works for him."

That this is still a point of contention after all this time is largely down to it happening in the internet age, though. In 1966, Jack Charlton used his hand to save a shot on the goal line during England's semi-final win over Portugal, and in 1990 Maradona did similar in a group match against the USSR. The first resulted in a penalty kick converted by Eusébio, the second went unnoticed by the match officials. But both have largely been forgotten, while Suárez's handball seems likely to live on for decades to come.

No man has been more haunted by the events of that night than Asamoah Gyan.

"Sometimes when I'm alone, I get up and put the DVD on and start watching that game," Gyan told *The National* in 2014. "Probably watched it 20 times until now. I wish the match could happen again because it really hurts me every time when I'm alone. It's something that I can never forget. I watch it over and over and over again and hope one day I can turn things around and make people happy."

In 2020, now 34 years old and his playing career winding down in the Indian Super League, Gyan takes his hope for redemption a step further.

"I know this is something that will haunt me for the rest of my life," he told TV3. "I accept that because there is nothing I can do about it. I went there to save my country, but I ended up being the villain, which I accept because I know how people feel. … All I was telling myself was to get another chance because I knew I could redeem myself even if not football, something else. But even if I don't, my kids will do it one day."

Gyan had another chance at a penalty in an important moment in the 2012 African Cup of Nations. It was early in Ghana's semi-final against Zambia, but a look of panic similar to the one that night in Johannesburg came over him. He made a stilted run up to the ball and delivered a low shot that the Zambian keeper easily saved. Gyan stood still in the middle of the penalty area, glancing around as if he suddenly didn't recognise his surroundings. Zambia went on to win 1-0.

After the match, he apologised to Ghana fans. "It's now two of the biggest penalties in my country's history and it's difficult to take," he said. Ten days later, he informed the Ghana FA that he planned to "take a temporary break" from international duty.

"Mr. Gyan is frustrated over the verbal abuse he has received since playing for the country at the 2012 Africa Cup of Nations," the GFA's statement said.

By the 2013 African Cup of Nations, Gyan had returned to the fold, but announced before the tournament that he would never take another penalty for the national team, saying that before his mother died several months earlier, she had told him not to do it anymore.

Mubarak Wakaso converted three penalties at the tournament in Gyan's place, but Ghana lost their semi-final to Burkina Faso after the side missed three of five attempts in the shootout, with neither Wakaso nor Gyan taking one.

Gyan then served as Ghana's captain for the 2014 World Cup. They went winless, including a 2-1 loss to their old US foes, and finished bottom of their group, though Gyan scored twice.

After five years, Gyan finally took another penalty for Ghana in a July 2017 friendly against the US. Again it was saved, again he froze in disbelief. He hasn't taken a penalty for Ghana since.

The 2010 World Cup proved to be the crest of a wave for Ghanaian football. Improving from their first ever qualification in 2006, then going home winless in 2014 and failing to qualify altogether in 2018, the hope of sustained excellence has been lost to rampant corruption in the GFA that resulted in FIFA issuing a lifetime ban for former president Nyantakyi.

The way the ensuing years have played out has made the painful end to Ghana's proudest footballing achievement all the more unthinkable. While it's still too much for some members of the 2010 team to bear, others consider what could have been had they advanced to face the Netherlands in the semi-final instead of Uruguay.

"It was gonna be big," says Jonathan. "We were gonna go into that game very very determined and strong, nothing to lose. We've come this far, so what do we have to lose? Nothing. So we would go at them and put everything on the line. But, unfortunately, it didn't happen for us."

Paintsil took it a step further. "For me, we would have been in the final, and we would have won the World Cup, because our confidence levels were very high," he told ESPN. "Against Spain, they like to play ball, they're not direct, they don't do silly tackles, and they were a decent side — but we were, too, and that final would have been beautiful."

It's easy to dismiss such a thought. That Spain team in 2010 was one for the ages, in the middle of a historic run of success. But had they played the first African team to reach a World Cup final and done it on African soil, rather than an uninspiring Netherlands side, could that run have been interrupted? It's a thought that offers a bit of hope. It takes the focus off of Suárez's hands and puts it where it belongs: on an exceptional team that played with joy, skill, passion, and unbreakable unity. A team that proudly carried the hope of Africa.

BENFICA 2012-13
FILIPE D'AVILLEZ

A PASSION PLAY IN THREE ACTS

PROLOGUE

I understand that most readers will be from Christian-majority countries, but in my experience, one should never underestimate the religious illiteracy of the modern man, so please bear with me.

Good Friday is one of the holiest days in the Christian calendar. It marks the day Christ was taken into custody by the Jewish religious authorities of his time, sentenced to die, handed over to the Romans — because under the law at the time Jewish authorities were not allowed to carry out death sentences — beaten, ridiculed, crowned with thorns, then forced to carry a heavy beam of wood up a hill, called Calvary, nailed to a cross and left to die. This suffering of Christ is called his Passion, and over the centuries has been represented during Lent through Passion plays.

Good Friday is a day of sadness and contemplation, of sacrifice and fasting. The only day in the Catholic calendar in which mass is not celebrated, out of mourning. The liturgy and the general atmosphere are of death and desperation.

All this lasts no more than 24 hours. Benfica's Passion lasted 14 days, between May 12 and May 26 2013.

ACT 1: KELVIN

I was in the Azores, on the beautiful island of São Miguel on May 4. I had been sent by my media group to interview American Cardinal Sean O'Malley, who was the Vatican's point man on fighting sexual abuse in the Church. Heavy stuff. With the interview out of the way, I promptly returned to my hotel room and accidentally deleted it as I tried to transfer it from the recorder to my computer. I wrote up as much as I could from memory, but there was nothing else I could do before returning to Lisbon, where an IT technician would try and recover the file. Praying quietly for a positive solution, I headed out alone for dinner.

I sat in a restaurant and watched FC Porto easily defeat Nacional, from Portugal's other archipelago, Madeira. I had been hoping our northern rivals would drop points in what is usually a tricky away game, but no luck. I texted my friend Lazar, from Serbia, about the result, but told him that it was ok: we were still five points clear provided we beat Estoril at home on Monday evening, which should not be complicated. This meant we could even afford to lose to Porto away in the second last game of the season, and we'd still clinch the title if we won our last game at home against modest Moreirense. Our main concern at the moment was getting our hands on tickets for the Europa League final in Amsterdam against Chelsea. With the Taça de Portugal (Portuguese Cup) final to look forward to as well, we could end the season with three new pieces of silverware.

I returned to Lisbon and our trusty IT pals managed to recover the interview, so things were looking up. I had it all finished by Monday, leaving me free to go to the home game against Estoril.

The atmosphere was charged, the stadium packed. After a stunning first year with the club, manager Jorge Jesus had disappointingly lost the title to Porto over the past two seasons. This year, however, we were playing well again and on the road to success. I suppose the Apostles must have felt that way when they dined with Jesus in the upper room following his triumphant arrival in Jerusalem, then went off to the Garden of Olives to sing psalms, as was the custom, in that festive paschal season. Little did they know that disaster was about to strike. Nor, for that matter, did I.

We started feeling a little edgy as the referee whistled for the break. Still 0-0. But Benfica were crushing the small coastal club and it seemed like a matter of time, despite an injury to Argentine midfielder Enzo Perez, who was replaced by Portuguese international Carlos Martins after just half an hour.

In the 58th minute, however, Estoril scored. Bad, yes, but we had over half an hour to recover. Fiery Maxi Pereira — one of those players you'd swear would die for his club colours but then ended up trading us for Porto a couple of seasons later — drew us even at 68 minutes and then, just when we needed to keep a cool head, Carlos Martins' ridiculously ill-timed challenge earned him a second booking, leaving us with ten men and making Estoril's job that bit easier.

The Canaries, as they are known for their blue and yellow kits, held out until the final whistle and their hundred or so fans celebrated as if they had won the title themselves. I left as quickly as possible, got myself home, mumbled something to my wife and kids and headed downstairs to my bedroom where I knelt by my bed and began to pray. "Please Lord, not this," I kept repeating to myself. "I know you don't decide football games, but please, not this." I might as well have asked him to take this cup of sorrow away from me.

As things stood now, a defeat in Porto the following week would leave the Blues in the perfect position to win their third consecutive title. "Please Lord, not this!"

I was going to miss the Porto game. I had seen Benfica away at Porto for ten years in a row, including at least one cup game. We lost all of them but two; both 1-1 draws. Then, in 2005, I had to miss a game because of a wedding — not my own — and we won 2-0. I still tried to go back a couple of times but following a 3-1 defeat against ten men and a 5-0 humiliation, I gave up. I was clearly the problem. I've never been back since.

So, I sat this one out and watched it quietly at home with my wife and a cousin who usually accompanied me to matches. The three kids we had at the time pottered around us. We took an early lead, which was promising and even made us entertain the idea that we might win the title there and then. But Porto equalised very soon afterwards through an own goal by Pereira.

Then we pretty much took control of the game. Porto didn't come close to scoring and we seemed happy with the draw and locked down our defence. In the 66th minute, Jorge Jesus took off Nico Gaitán and put in the young and inexperienced Roderick Miranda to strengthen the defence. With Porto still no closer to scoring, they subbed in an equally young and inexperienced Kelvin. It seemed like an act of despair.

We were into stoppage time, and I had finally begun to relax. Just a couple of minutes to go and my three-year-old began to clamber over me. She saw we were watching Benfica and so she started chanting "Goal! Champions!" I turned my eyes from the screen to smile at her and that was when I heard my wife and cousin curse and exclaim in disbelief. When I looked up all I saw was an ecstatic Kelvin running across the pitch, as Porto fans eluded stewards to race up to him. Jorge Jesus was on his knees. I didn't see the ball go in, but I know now that it was Roderick who failed to block the shot. I have never seen a replay or highlights. I hope I never will.

"This, Lord, this is exactly what I was asking to avoid."

Needless to say I hardly slept, but the following morning at 8am there I was at the stadium, patiently waiting in line to buy a ticket for the cup final a couple of weeks later, and wondering if all of this was healthy for me.

ACT II: BÉLA GUTTMAN STRIKES AGAIN

There was no doubt that we'd lost the title, even if mathematically there was still hope. But before the last game of the season we still had to play the Europa League final against Chelsea and a European title was just the thing to help us recover.

Of course, there was a glitch in our plan: a long-dead Hungarian Jew by the name of Béla Guttman who led Benfica to back-to-back European Championships in the early '60s and allegedly cursed the club when he was dismissed in 1962, saying that without him we wouldn't win another European title in a hundred years.

There are doubts as to whether he actually ever said anything of the sort, but there is no doubt that Benfica have gone on to lose the eight European finals they have participated in since then.

Before leaving for Amsterdam, I texted the Rabbi of the Jewish Community of Lisbon, an Italian with a wonderful sense of humour, and asked what we could do to lift a Jewish curse. I added that I was only half serious, but that the half that was serious was deadly serious. He replied that we would have to gather the Sanhedrin, the same institution that sentenced Jesus to death for blasphemy in the early hours of that Good Friday, so long ago. Not much chance of that, I reckoned.

By the time we reached Holland, the atmosphere had changed, with the streets crammed full of Benfica fans, many from the Portuguese diaspora, including friends of ours who had been forced to leave because of the financial crisis, which had hit the country so hard.

There were a few spots of trouble between opposing groups of fans, but nothing too serious, and overall it was like a large outdoor party. As the alcohol levels rose, so did our confidence that this was going to be the year we broke the damned curse.

The players seemed as confident as we were and showed it on the pitch. At half-time, my brother, watching the game in a pub in London with the same cousin who had watched the Porto game with me a few days earlier, confirmed what we seemed to be experiencing inside the stadium; we were dominating Chelsea, but seemed to be hesitating too much in and around the box, instead of just taking shots at goal.

The game recommenced and Chelsea scored in the 60th minute, but Benfica didn't surrender and Óscar Cardozo sent a penalty into the back of the net on 68 minutes, putting Benfica back on track.

As the 90th minute approached, both teams started slowing down, clearly expecting extra time. The fans braced themselves for another 30 minutes of play, at least.

But then Chelsea were awarded a corner kick in the second minute of stoppage time. I remember thinking to myself that we were safe, because there was no way the same thing would happen to us two games in a row.

The ball whistled over the box, just beyond the far post, where Ivanovic headed it in … could this actually be happening? I was at the other end of the stadium, so I still had some hope that it had hit the side netting and fooled the Chelsea fans who had awakened from their game-long silence and were now celebrating raucously.

I turned my head to the right and saw a good friend on his knees, back turned to the pitch, in absolute anguish. I was wrong. It was happening. It was real. Groundhog Day.

The final minutes were a frenzy of support, as we hoped that we might be able to win the game with sheer passion. Cardozo still had one shot, if I remember correctly, but I think it hit a defender. I'm not sure, and there is no way I'm going to watch the highlights of this game to confirm either.

"My God, my God, why have you forsaken me?" cried Jesus from the cross. Of course, we now know he was reciting a psalm that actually ends on a far different note, one of trust and praise. But at that moment, as I stormed out of the stadium, these words were running through my mind, in loop mode, with the small and shrinking rational part of my brain fighting as hard as ever to keep me from falling head over heels into the blasphemy of comparing my frustration to the gravity of Christ's abandonment and crucifixion.

Football hadn't made me cry since Portugal failed to qualify for USA '94, when I was 13 years old. I honestly thought I was past that phase now. But after walking a few hundred metres it was all too much for me and I sat down with my back to a post, buried my head in my hands and wept like a child.

I remember clearly that at one point somebody crouched down beside me and put their arms around my shoulders, to console me. I didn't look up and, to this day, I have no idea who it was, or whether they knew me.

Finally, my wife called. I considered not answering, but I did, and she heard the state I was in — I could barely talk. She tried to soothe me, but would later confess that I had her worried sick. She'd never heard me like that before.

The trip back to Lisbon was like an endless nightmare. A drive to Brussels, then a flight to some godforsaken airport in Spain, then another hours-long drive back home. Plenty of time to discuss our seventh consecutive loss in a European final, to which an eighth would be added the following year.

There were only two games left in the season. We managed to beat Moreirense, in a gloomy stadium, as FC Porto overcame Paços de Ferreira away, as expected, and happily mocked us in their chants.

That left only the Taça de Portugal final, to be played the following week.

ACT III: REVERSE

The Foja estate is an idyllic farm in central Portugal. An old monastery dating from the 12th century, it was bought by a wealthy businessman in the 19th century, and he left it to his four Godchildren, one of which was my great-grandmother, apparently in the hope that they would marry each other, leaving the estate in the hands of two families. The best laid plans of mice and men … of course, the youngsters did nothing of the sort.

So currently Foja is divided into four extended families, which means that my branch gets two weeks there a year. It's the perfect place to catch up with relatives, eat and drink and relax, with no other worries.

Which makes it all the more incomprehensible that on Sunday May 26, I was heading back down to Lisbon to the Portuguese cup final in Jamor against Vitória, from Guimarães. To this day, I still don't know what possessed my wife to make the trip with me. Perhaps she just felt sorry for me and didn't want me to go alone.

The cup final in the National Stadium in Jamor is a unique experience, which I deal with in greater detail in my book *One Thousand Miles to Jamor*. But on this day, there was not much that could cheer up the legion of Benfica fans who went to the game. We were just going through the motions, and we knew it. Not even a win could dispel the idea that this season had turned into a disaster.

Our opponents were Vitória Sport Clube, generally referred to simply as Guimarães, perhaps the only club in Portugal besides the big three that has strong local support. Oblivious to our suffering, they were having the time of their lives, hoping to win their first ever proper trophy.

I would later hear an anecdote that sums up the day. Both team buses arrived at the same time, Guimarães ahead of Benfica. And as they were maneuvering to get into the parking lot the first bus made the corner in one go, but Benfica's had to reverse. Apparently, in the sub-world of professional footballer superstitions, this is a huge no-no, and as the Benfica driver moved the bus backwards to be able to turn the corner, captain Luisão could be seen placing his hands on his head in anger.

You could cut through the atmosphere in the stands with a knife. At one point, a scuffle broke out a short distance from where we were positioned and when I looked to see what was going on I realised that my wife's cousin, grand-daughter of a former Benfica chairman, had started it when she turned to berate another fan who had not stopped chiding the team since the game began.

The players seemed to be feeling it too, dragging themselves across the pitch as if they were wading through mud. Nonetheless, Gaitán gave us the lead in the 30th minute. So that was something. If the first half had been slow and uninspiring, the second was worse. Benfica were starting to make mistake after mistake, and goalkeeper Artur eventually kicked a ball directly to the feet of a Guimarães player who passed it perfectly to a forward. The referee didn't see the offside and the ball was in the back of the net.

Benfica fell apart. There was no wishful thinking that we couldn't go through the same nightmare again — it was as if this time we were sure, instead, that this was our destiny. Guimarães must have thought the same because only two minutes later, Ricardo Pereira took a shot from outside of the box that was so slow and close to the ground that nobody in their right mind would have considered it a threat. Sure enough, it deflected off Luisão and bounced past a hapless Artur into the goal right in front of our stand.

As the final whistle blew, our players added insult to injury, refusing to form an honour guard for the Vitória players to walk through. Oscar Cardozo, in utter despair at the way the season had turned out, decided to take it out on Jorge Jesus which, to be honest, is what we all felt like doing as well. The two actually pushed and shoved each other before being separated by colleagues. It was all an utter disgrace.

As we headed to the car for our two-hour drive back to Foja, in absolute silence, I had ample time to ponder whether or not this was how I wanted to continue living my life. Was this season God's way of telling me that enough was enough? Did these thoughts not cross the minds of the Apostles after they saw the ministry of this man they had devoted their lives to for three years crash and burn in defeat and misery? For them it was enough to run and hide, and God knows that at that moment I would have happily signed off on never going to see Benfica play again.

And then we arrived at the large country house. Several of my Sporting Lisbon-supporting cousins, and the two Porto-supporting husbands that somehow got through, teased and provoked me over the loss, which was what I had expected. They were baiting me for a reaction, but I didn't have it in me. Surprisingly, it was my wife who came to the rescue and snapped something or other at them to shut them up. As I had many times before, I gave thanks that I had married a Benfica supporter.

And that was enough to bring the spark back to life. We'd have a welcome football-free summer, then it would all start up again in August, because that is what happens. Life follows death, hope follows despair and, as Christians, if we don't believe in that then everything else is in vain.

My long Good Friday had come to its painful and dismal end, but like St. John at the foot of the Cross, I could take some pride in saying that even though it had hurt, I'd been faithful to the end. What I didn't know at the time was that Easter was about to begin.

EPILOGUE

One of the beauties of Easter in the Christian calendar is that it isn't just one day. So important is this date that the Church has decided it should be celebrated not only with a whole week — an Octave in Liturgical terms — but with a week of weeks. That's 49 days during which we recall the Resurrection, His eventual Ascension into Heaven and then, on Pentecost, 50 days after Easter, the Holy Spirit's descent on the Church, which gave the Apostles the energy and courage they needed to go out, preach and make disciples of all nations.

If the 2012-13 season ended with Benfica's Good Friday, then 2014 ended with Easter. Literally. Benfica were crowned champions of Portugal on Easter Sunday, April 20. Given the manager's name, references to Jesus' resurrection were plentiful. That season also saw us win the League Cup, the Cup and qualify for our tenth European final, which we lost to Sevilla, thanks to Guttman, obviously. But it wasn't over yet.

The next season, 2015, we won the Championship once more, this time on Ascension Sunday and then, in 2016, following a shock move by Jorge Jesus to arch-rivals Sporting, a third consecutive title on Pentecost Sunday.

And just as I thought that was that, since there were no more Easter dates available and a Christmas title seemed a little too much to hope for, the Pope announced a visit to Portugal for May 13, 2017, the 100th anniversary of the Apparitions of the Virgin Mary in Fátima. And lo and behold, on that very same day Benfica won their fourth title in a row, something the club had never managed before.

This past Easter I explained to my six-year-old son that Jesus died nailed to a cross. He grimaced and asked me not to talk about that sort of thing. I told him it's OK, because that is not the end of the story, three days later Christ rose from the dead, and that is what really matters. Still, he replied, he didn't want to hear about nails being driven through Jesus' hands and feet.

I was taken aback at first. But then again, I have never been able to bring myself to watch Kelvin's 92nd-minute winner.

LIVERPOOL 2013-14
NEIL ATKINSON

THE FIRST BEGINNING

After Liverpool beat West Ham United 2-1 at Upton Park on April 6 2014, I recorded a show at the top of the tower, St Johns Beacon, which looks out across the whole city. Liverpool had absolutely clawed their way to the sort of 2-1 victory that history has tried to pretend was beyond this side. Sam Allardyce had lashed Andy Carroll up top and hit the big man repeatedly, but Liverpool repelled them time and again. Two penalties. Steven Gerrard tucked away both and Liverpool saw it out.

Liverpool top of the pops. Two clear of Chelsea; four clear of Manchester City, though they had two games in hand. Manchester City up next at Anfield. It was the first time since 2009 that Liverpool had been top in April (then with a Manchester club being two points behind with two games in hand). That, in turn, was the first time since 2002. Liverpool two clear of Arsenal. Who had two games in hand.

While recording the show, I was getting texts about where the drink was happening. The Saddle on Dale Street. I couldn't believe it. With Steve Graves, I walked across town. "I mean, it's not a good pub this, Steve. There must be some mistake. Maybe it is a holding position boozer."

When we opened the door, it hit us. The heat. The sweat. The effervescent glow of smiles on faces. The joy making the light shimmer. And the noise. The wall of noise. Adam Melia and his brother Daniel glorifying *This Is How We Do It* by Montell Jordan on the karaoke and an entire room chanting back at them. The room being as eclectic as it can be. The Saddle receiving the overspill of Liverpool's gay district, its karaoke led by Candi; Liverpool supporters and lesbians and lesbian Liverpool supporters chanting the chorus back at them. South Central does it like nobody does. People on tables, roaring, laughing, dancing, carousing.

This was the happiest I've ever been in my whole life.

You can't tell the story of 2014 without telling the story of all the other bits, the places where the ley lines meet. I'd argue you can't tell the story of 2020 without telling the story of 2014 as well. There's never a neat start to these things. In this book, the better football writers than me will find beginnings. But I don't write about football. Not really. I write about what things felt like ...

THE SECOND BEGINNING

I was in a boozer in London when they sacked Rafa Benítez. Me and Daniel Fitzsimmons were attending some meetings about some film work. Dan's phone buzzed. My phone buzzed. His buzzed again. The people we were meeting said: "Don't you want to check your phones?" No mate. But Dan did. He looked at me. He nodded.

We wrapped the meeting up and went elsewhere and stared off into space. Both upset. Both, frankly, exhausted. What Benítez had shown ...

THE THIRD BEGINNING

When Liverpool made Brendan Rodgers manager, I didn't really know what to think. Let's see, I thought. Let's just see. And, I thought, it will also be nice to have a manager I don't wake up in the night anxious about, you know, like the bloke who nearly died or the bloke who fought for the soul of the club or the bloke who, closer than anyone else alive, personified the soul of the club. I thought maybe this will help. A bloke coming in from outside who no one knows much about. Someone not infected with our nonsense. Maybe he'll get us playing a bit. And if he doesn't, well, we just get rid of him. Whichever way it goes, it'll be nice to get a full night's sleep ...

THE FOURTH BEGINNING

On October 3 2010, Liverpool faced Blackpool at Anfield. Roy Hodgson was in charge. The club was owned by Hicks and Gillett. I didn't go in. I went to the ground but when push came to shove, I just couldn't face it.

They came back into the upstairs of the boozer I was in around the ground in their dribs and drabs. The first was someone called Kev Walsh. He arrived back on about 30. We watched the game and we talked.

Three days later, Liverpool were sold to FSG (then NESV). Not long after that, the court case decided it. Then Roy Hodgson took us to Everton. We got beat 2-0 and he said to win there would have been utopia. Lad, we win there when down to ten men.

Before Christmas, I met Kev in Pogues and we watched a Chelsea game. We agreed that Chelsea were our big team now. We go to the football, we watch Liverpool, but it's nice to see Chelsea do well and win things. We'll watch the cup final if they are involved. We were joking of course but it showed how far Liverpool had fallen and ...

THE FIFTH BEGINNING

You're at the Melbourne Cricket Ground, it is July 2013 and Liverpool are playing. This is obviously weird but an early example of something you call Mad Job Syndrome and go with it. Last night, oddly, you were on stage in front of 1,000 Liverpool supporters at a hotel doing jokes and bits. Dr Karl Kennedy of Neighbours fame and Craig Johnston were both there. Mad Job Syndrome.

There are 100,000 present in Melbourne to watch your football team from your wonderful but frankly weird city in the north-west of England play against Melbourne Roar. They put the lyrics to *You'll Never Walk Alone* on the big screen and in the section put aside for 'active' supporters, you drink your white wine for which Australians have mocked you and you've smiled politely because their beer is frankly awful and no one needs telling that. You think to yourself: "This all has to mean something. You can't be this big and just trundle. This has to have some sense of purpose to it. This cannot just become a nostalgic roadshow."

There has to be something more. There has to be another adventure. Something has to start. You think "fuck nostalgia" and you never stop thinking it because, say what you want, the whole decade of the 10s supports that conclusion. You think it has to be a joy to be alive in the now and if anything is worth working towards, if any story is worth telling, it is that one. Please let the story be that one, you plead ...

THE SIXTH BEGINNING

August 17 2013. Simon Mignolet saves a penalty in the last minute against Stoke City after Daniel Sturridge had given Liverpool a 1-0 lead. Kolo Touré had turned up in the summer and said this was a squad that could win the league. He'd been downright adamant about it, but there was a vague feeling somewhere that this didn't seem quite as strange as it should — Manchester United had lost Alex Ferguson and replaced him with David Moyes, and we knew all about David Moyes and we knew what old footballers looked like. We'd been there.

The end of the 2012-13 season had seen Liverpool score a lot of goals and look very lively. What transpired to be the key positive transfer window of Rodgers' time had just happened. Liverpool had signed Phillipe Coutinho and Daniel Sturridge. The latter, especially, inspired an upturn in form and by the time the campaign had finished, Liverpool had been able to look genuinely dangerous and had gone just shy of two points per game for the second half of the season, which made them much of a muchness with Arsenal, Chelsea, Manchester City and Tottenham.

When Mignolet saved the penalty on his Liverpool debut, the ground exploded. A point against Stoke City on the first day of the season would have killed us. Gerrard grabbed him by the throat after. It is possible Simon never entirely recovered. Steve Graves says out loud: "We can win this league, you know." He makes his case. It is almost as good as Kolo's.

It's a punch in the face, the realisation that, yes, we could win this league, you know. A punch in the face I'm glad I got early. A punch in the face that every Liverpool supporter would get between August 2013 and April 2014. For the first time since April 2009, it is valid to say: "We can win this league, you know," and that is the only sentence ever worth saying.

Sturridge 0-1 vs Villa followed and then Manchester United and David Moyes rocked up. Sturridge 1-0. United looked devoid of ideas. Liverpool played three, won three. Kolo Touré incredible in all three games.

Let's do it. Let's win this league. These are our lads. You know who my favourite players are? The 11 who wear red.

The beginnings. What makes them hard is you know how this ends. You are sentient and you know when this book is published too. You know what has just happened. Liverpool have just won their first league title for 30 years. There are things that have to be said. Liverpool didn't not win the league for 30 years in terms of what it felt like. For me they hadn't won it since 2002, since Emile Heskey went to Leeds and destroyed them, since Vladi Šmicer scored last minute against Chelsea and I was convinced only to be crushed. That was my first time not winning the league. That was my year zero.

For others, they maybe hadn't won it since Istanbul. For some it may be 2009 and others it may actually be this season we're looking at here; 2013-14.

But also, frankly, it is insulting to the vast majority of football supporters to act as though it was 30 years of disappointment. I've mostly had a lovely time and Liverpool won everything else in those

30 years. It did gnaw though. It did gnaw at you. It did grate. Just one. Just give me one of these things those old bastards had 18 of. Just give me the one. I'm begging you. It grew obsessive.

You know when I didn't have a lovely time? From about 2007 to about 2010. Supporting Liverpool, going to the game, talking about the game had been to have an argument, a perpetual argument. Over ownership, leveraged buyouts, protests, net spend, Benítez, our place in the world and our direction of travel. Supporting Liverpool had been supporting a thoroughbred racehorse laden with baggage. Those who can't get beyond having seen behind the curtain, can't get beyond the back room and the gossip, can't get beyond what has gone before. Football minds melded beyond what happens on the green thing to obsess only over what happens everywhere else. I know this. It's hard to get your innocence back. I recognise that. Because that is 2008-09.

Liverpool's title charge in 2008-09 mostly wasn't an enjoyable experience. It was fraught. It was stressful. It was about sticking it to people. Not about the adventure and not even really about sticking it to people who didn't support Liverpool. It was about sticking it to people internally, sticking it to fellow Liverpool supporters. It's an amazing thoroughbred, Benitez's 08-09, because it was carrying all sorts. Mostly weaponry either stuck in it or thrusting weaponry back. It was laden. It was fettered.

I'd never go back to 08-09. Not for a second. Not for a moment. Not even for 1-4 at Old Trafford. It was thoroughly unpleasant, waking at 3am wondering if tomorrow is the day Benítez ridiculously gets sacked, arguing in the ground every other week. But I'd do 13-14 again, knowing what I know now, even living through the glory of 2018 to 2020. I'd live that nine months over and over and over again if I could. Groundhog season. No one was looking to stick anything to anyone. Not when you could give them a cuddle instead. I'd go back in an instant. Back to waking at 3am excited that it is Saturday, Saturday, Saturday and still being up at 3am on Sunday, Sunday, Sunday. I'd go back in the blink of an eye. I'd do it mostly so I could see my friends that happy again, faces moist with sweat, improbability and delight.

2013-14 continued. Luis Suárez got back from his bite and his attempt to move to Arsenal. Not quite sure which of those two things were more irrational.

And then Suárez happened and just kept happening. Transfer requests easily forgotten, biting people easily forgotten, racism issue all too easily, shamefully too easily forgotten. What makes it easier to block the negatives from your mind is that Luis Suárez from October '13 to March '14 happened more than any top-flight footballer in England ever has. It's like playing with 12 men. Possibly 13. He is both a nine and a false nine and he does bits out wide as well. He scores a header from 18 yards and every brilliant performance he puts in, Daniel Sturridge strives to match. The day Suárez heads home from a mile out as part of a hat-trick, Sturridge somehow lobs a keeper who isn't off his line. Suárez gets two at Stoke, Sturridge makes it five by doing keepy-ups on the goal line.

Luis Suárez scores four against Norwich City at Anfield. Let me tell you about the weakest goal — it is reminiscent of Peter Beardsley's volley against Everton at Anfield in 1987. The third best is a 25-yard free-kick. That night, Everton win at Old Trafford. Manchester United are none of our business. This is the first time since 1990 that it is due to their shortcomings rather than ours.

Two weeks after Norwich at home, they go to Tottenham Hotspur at 4pm on the telly. No Steven Gerrard, he's in the studio. They batter them 5-0. Suárez a pleasure but Jordan Henderson and Raheem Sterling are incredible. It's quite possibly Liverpool's best away performance of the decade. After the game, Gerrard remarks he is worried he won't get back into this team. Everyone laughs because they don't understand Gerrard. He is worried he won't get back into this team.

Over Christmas, they lose twice. Once at Manchester City, once at Chelsea and, in the long run, there's an argument that these results are what cost us the title. There is harsh officiating in both matches — Raheem Sterling opens the scoring at the Etihad only for it to be given offside. It wasn't. Samuel Eto'o throws a shocking tackle in early at Chelsea but you can do what you want first five, can't you?

Suárez has a late equaliser chalked off. But Liverpool had gone ahead in the game so what can you say.

Liverpool end the calendar year six points behind Arsenal.

In mid-January, Aston Villa come to Anfield and Liverpool play Steven Gerrard at the base of the midfield and it is difficult to put into words how hard he finds the game. It finishes 2-2 and my God does Gerrard struggle. We host a resurgent Everton the following week, Ross Barkley is in fine form and everyone hopes Rodgers doesn't pick Gerrard there. If Everton win, they go above us.

Rodgers picks Gerrard there. He scores the opener, the sort of header that thunders home. Then Sturridge gets a quick-fire brace, the second a lob in front of the Blues, which is just unreasonable. Suárez makes it four immediately after half-time and then we get a penalty. Gerrard puts his only foot wrong all night. He hands Sturridge the ball. Sturridge misses. Had we made it five, we may have made it 10. We were that good. Steven resplendent. Steven the king of all he surveys.

Steven is suddenly *that* good. Steven is incredible in interviews. Steven is Liverpool captain like he never has been before. Steven says: "If you want to play two on two against these two, all the best."

All the best.

Liverpool drop points at West Brom. Kolo Touré makes a mistake and the side is punished. Then they have Arsenal at Anfield. Arsenal are top of the pile, eight ahead of Liverpool. It's February 8. It's Saturday 12:45 and I have powered into the ground. This is it. It is now or never.

It is now.

It will never, ever be more now.

Liverpool go 4-0 ahead on the 20-minute mark and my God is that flattering to Arsenal. It genuinely should be six. You have never seen the like, not before nor since. Liverpool win the ball back through Henderson and Coutinho and turn Arsenal around so quickly. They can't keep track of Suárez, Sturridge or Sterling. Everywhere there is a runner. Liverpool cut them to absolute ribbons. It's thrilling, visceral stuff. It's also funny. After the fourth goes in there's a sound

I've never heard in the football ground before or since and it is that of thousands of people just laughing in disbelief. After the game, Steven says this:

"I'm trying to think of a performance I can remember in the last 15 years. Maybe one or two in the Champions League got close but that was as explosive as it gets. That is right up there. That's definitely in the top three performances I have been involved in. You are talking about a side that is top of the league with world-class players, ones who are worth £42m. Jack Wilshere, one of the country's big hopes. (Santi) Cazorla, a World Cup winner. We have absolutely demolished a top team from start to finish."

Steven understates it. The first half is the greatest half of football any Liverpool side has played since 1990. It could be the greatest ever. Liverpool punching everyone in the face.

We were out after, out all day, hanging out for *Match of the Day*, staying out for a massive dance. By February of 2009, I felt like an old man. I had seen too much, lived too much. I was strung out. Roll on five years and Liverpool 5, Arsenal 1 makes me feel like a teenager even just thinking of it now. It makes me want to drink in the park. It makes me want to neck. It makes me *want*.

Suddenly, everywhere you went in the city, everyone you spoke to, everything that happened had a buzz. Everyone was talking football, talking The Reds. It helped that Everton were playing well too. The whole city was alive with the sound of togger.

Suddenly, Liverpool was having a pint. Even more of a pint than normal. The Saddle tableau wasn't unique. All over the city, parties were being had every weekend. Boss were putting on Boss Nights which were boss. The whole city bounced to the weekend's rhythm, boozers packed for almost every game that had any sort of an impact at the top, boozers spilling over before, during and after when The Reds played. This wasn't limited just to the city of Liverpool. The worldwide diaspora were going out and watching it together. Suddenly, it was football that made you want to be with your mates, football that made you want to make new mates. Because these Reds.

Suddenly it was a joy to be alive. Suddenly everyone has been punched in the face. We can win this league you know.

They go to Fulham. Kolo Touré makes a mistake but Steven plays the greatest through ball to Daniel Sturridge you have seen in your whole life for the equaliser. Regardless though it is 2-2 last minute and Liverpool get a penalty.

Steven steps up and scores and he wheels away and takes his top off. Look at him there, just look at him roaring at the away end, top whirring, Jordan Henderson in relief behind him. Look into his eyes. This puts Liverpool fourth, but Steven has seen Liverpool fourth. Steven knows fourth. Steven doesn't take his top off for fourth. Steven has been punched in the face.

This is here and this is now. Steven's carried this burden, Atlas-like. The broadest shoulders in Liverpool. Steven's been this man who looked around and lacked players who could make it happen with him. Not now.

All the best.

They didn't stop. Four against Swansea, three at Southampton, three when they dominated David Moyes' Manchester United, Steven drawing Fellaini's actual blood, Liverpool making United metaphorically bleed. Liverpool swanked around Old Trafford that day in a way they hadn't for at least 30 years before or have since. Steven missed a penalty for his hat-trick. It didn't matter.

Six at Cardiff. Four against Tottenham — Liverpool's season aggregate against Spurs being 9-0. Then came Manchester City at Anfield and Liverpool battered them for half an hour. It was only 2-0 and it should have been more. It needed to be more. Anfield was a bear pit. I can't tell you. It was the most vociferous it had been for a league game in years. Manchester City walked into absolute fucking hell, the like of which they walked into again in November 2019. It was no way to play football. It wasn't fair.

And then they were ace. Let me tell you about Manchester City for the 20 minutes after half-time — it was amongst the greatest performances by an away side at Anfield. They penned us not in our own half but our own penalty area. It was terrifying and every single one of those Manchester City players stood up in a way that left you deeply impressed. They had us living on our nerves and they got the two goals back.

The game settled and then Philippe Coutinho scored one of his few goals of the season and Rodgers dipped his knees on the pitch after an arcing drive into the corner and it was bedlam and I couldn't stop crying and the last 10 minutes were as unbearable as I have ever seen in a football ground and Martin Škrtel appeared to handball it 16 times and I mean it when I say I couldn't stop crying and while it would be fair to say we'd all had a drink it would also be fair to say people could barely watch and Jordan Henderson got sent off and finally the final whistle went and then Steven got them all in and got them in a big circle in front of The Kop and Steven told them they were on the verge because they were and then Steven told them that this doesn't slip now and I couldn't stop crying and the ground didn't stop roaring while Steven told them that this does not slip now.

We went out. The 'we' there is practically everyone in Liverpool. It was a Sunday afternoon, Liverpool is a big city, a big drinking city and every pub was bursting at the seams. It was unbridled. It was unfettered. It was freeing.

They went to Norwich on Easter Sunday. Won 2-3, Sterling magnificent. But they missed Henderson you know. They missed him massively.

I have a lot of thoughts about Chelsea at Anfield and Crystal Palace at Selhurst Park. A lot of thoughts:

- Liverpool weren't trying to go hell for leather against Chelsea when Steven slips. If anything, they were too patient, Steven too deep, Liverpool too settled for half-time.

- They did though suffer through not getting the early goal and anxiety setting in.

- Luis Suárez had gone off the boil by that game at Anfield. In part because of tiredness, in part because footballers do.

- In the second half, Liverpool completely lose their heads and this is where Chelsea's frustration tactics work. Steven has about 100 shots, all of them never going in.

- One of the greatest nights of the season is when Liverpool go to Selhurst Park and try to score 10.

- Liverpool had an attempt every three minutes the ball was in play and a load of them were good efforts, unlike Steven's from the weekend before.

- The greatest moment of that season is when Suárez gets the ball out of the goal when it goes 0-3. Nothing has ever summed a football team up more. The snides, the greybeards will say that doing that and then drawing 3-3 sums the team up better, but those people are wrong and no one wants to dance with them, drink with them or kiss them.

- Honestly, let me tell you about him getting the ball. We celebrated it more than the goal, celebrated it like it was two goals, celebrated it like our lives depended on it, celebrated it as it was the greatest release and relief imaginable, celebrated it because it was unzipped, unfettered, unbridled, celebrated it because what else were we in it for but this?

- I still think about Steven not sleeping nights. I still occasionally don't sleep nights because Steven isn't sleeping nights.

- We got what we came for. In a sense, Suárez, Sturridge, Henderson, Rodgers, Sterling et al did too. But Steven didn't take his shirt off at Fulham for this. There is only one nearly man in this story in the end. It isn't me, I had the best time. It wasn't us. It wasn't them. It was Steven.

It is important not to forget what 13-14 felt like. There is a history of football that is handed down to us through record books and television. It's a history that is predominantly written by the grey-bearded and the distant and by the cynics. Some of these dwell within our own parish, a darkness in their souls uncleansed, consistently unable to forgive Brendan Rodgers for one sin or another, perhaps even for bringing the party but perhaps for not being the bloke who nearly died or the bloke who fought for the soul of the club or the bloke who closer than anyone else alive personified that soul of the club.

For many of these, the hard facts of the matter will always prevail. Hard facts can't dance. Hard facts have no rhythm. No one wants to get off with hard facts. The football history that really matters is about the stories, the collective experience, the days and the nights, the coaches and the buzz. Remember not the hard fact of the 3-3 draw, your side losing a three-goal lead, but instead remember that they were trying to score 10. Remember they were trying to do the impossible. Remember how proud you were of how close they came.

Remember too, loving footballers. We learned to love footballers again in 13-14 under Brendan Rodgers, because at his best, he so clearly does. Footballers doing amazing things, making children of us, is a wonderful thing. We learned that goals are paramount to proceedings and learned that without them, nothing can be achieved. These might seem like straightforward and obvious enough virtues but it had been a dark place for far too long. Rodgers brought Delusion. Delusion turned to Hope and then became Belief.

We hadn't had Belief for what felt like the longest time. Without what we had then, without those reminders of what it was meant to be, how it was meant to feel, the how and why of being happy, of being joyous and loving footballers, Jürgen Klopp would have had a steeper mountain.

Regardless though, that is a fresh story. Today, I can close my eyes and see Suárez hitting the post against Arsenal, Steve Graves on John Gibbons' shoulders that night, Henderson forcing it in against Swansea. I can see Škrtel rising against Arsenal, Ben Johnson and Adam Melia singing *I'm On My Way* by The Proclaimers, Jon Flanagan rattling into Roberto Soldado.

Gerrard with his top off against Fulham. Gerrard with his top off against Fulham. Steven with his top off against Fulham.

We nearly had it all. What we had was everything. We nearly found the promised land. We found one another. We nearly won the league. And now you are going to believe us.

.